I0137054

Great Battles of World War Two

Battle of the Bulge

Compiled by

Kiera Mccune

Scribbles

Year of Publication 2018

ISBN : 9789352979318

Book Published by

Scribbles

(An Imprint of Alpha Editions)

email - alphaedis@gmail.com

Produced by: PediaPress GmbH
Limburg an der Lahn
Germany
http://pediapress.com/

The content within this book was generated collaboratively by volunteers. Please be advised that nothing found here has necessarily been reviewed by people with the expertise required to provide you with complete, accurate or reliable information. Some information in this book may be misleading or simply wrong. Alpha Editions and PediaPress does not guarantee the validity of the information found here. If you need specific advice (for example, medical, legal, financial, or risk management) please seek a professional who is licensed or knowledgeable in that area.
Sources, licenses and contributors of the articles and images are listed in the section entitled "References". Parts of the books may be licensed under the GNU Free Documentation License. A copy of this license is included in the section entitled "GNU Free Documentation License"
The views and characters expressed in the book are those of the contributors and his/her imagination and do not represent the views of the Publisher.

Contents

Appendix 237

Article Licenses 253

Index 255

Introduction

Battle of the Bulge

<indicator name="pp-autoreview"> 🏛 </indicator>

Battle of the Bulge	
Part of the Western Front of World War II	

American soldiers of the 117th Infantry Regiment, Tennessee National Guard, part of the 30th Infantry Division, move past a destroyed American M5A1 "Stuart" tank on their march to recapture the town of St. Vith during the Battle of the Bulge, January 1945.

Date	16 December 1944 – 25 January 1945
Location	The Ardennes: Belgium, Luxembourg, Germany
Result	Allied victory • Western Allied offensive plans delayed by five or six weeks[1] • German offensive exhausts their resources on Western Front. • German collapse opens way for Allies to ultimately break Siegfried Line • Soviet offensive in Poland launched on 12 January 1945, eight days earlier than originally intended.[2]

Belligerents	
• ▬ United States • ▧ United Kingdom • ■ France • ▨ Canada • ■ Belgium • ▨ Luxembourg	卐 Germany

Commanders and leaders

• Dwight D. Eisenhower	• Adolf Hitler
• (Supreme Allied Commander)	• (Leader and Chancellor)
• Bernard Montgomery	• Walter Model
21st Army Group:	• (Army Group B)
Second Army	• Gerd von Rundstedt
First Army	• (OB West)
Ninth Army	• Hasso von Manteuffel
• Omar Bradley	• (5th Panzer Army)
12th Army Group:	• Sepp Dietrich
Third Army	• (6th Panzer Army)
	• Erich Brandenberger
	• (7th Army)

Units involved

12th Army Group:	Army Group B:
Third Army	5th Panzer Army
21st Army Group:	6th Panzer Army
Second Army	7th Army
First Army	
Ninth Army	

Strength

December 16
228,741 men
483 tanks
499 tank destroyers and assault guns
1,921 other Armoured fighting vehicles (AFVs)
971 anti-tank and artillery pieces
6 infantry divisions
2 armored divisions

December 24
~541,000 men
1,616 tanks
1,713 tank destroyers and assault guns
5,352 other AFVs
2,408 anti-tank and artillery pieces
15 infantry divisions
6 armored divisions
1 armored brigade

January 2
~705,000 men
2,409 tanks
1,970 tank destroyers and assault guns
7,769 other AFVs
3,305 anti-tank and artillery pieces
22 infantry divisions
8 armored divisions
2 armored brigades

January 16
700,520 men
2,428 tanks
1,912 tank destroyers and assault guns
7,079 other AFVs
3,181 anti-tank and artillery pieces
22 infantry divisions
8 armored divisions
2 armored brigades

December 16
406,342 men
557 tanks
667 tank destroyers and assault guns
1,261 other AFVs
4,224 anti-tank and artillery pieces
13 infantry divisions[3]
7 armored divisions
1 brigade: 1 brigade

December 24
~449,000 men
423 tanks
608 tank destroyers and assault guns
1,496 other AFVs
4,131 anti-tank and artillery pieces
16 infantry divisions
8 armored divisions
1 armored brigade
2 infantry brigades

January 2
~401,000 men
287 tanks
462 tank destroyers and assault guns
1,090 other AFVs
3,396 anti-tank and artillery pieces
15 infantry divisions
8 armored divisions
1 armored brigade
2 infantry brigades

January 16
383,016 men
216 tanks
414 tank destroyers and assault guns
907 other AFVs
3,256 anti-tank and artillery pieces
16 infantry divisions
8 armored divisions
2 infantry brigades

Casualties and losses

■■■ American
c. 89,500[4]
19,000 killed,
47,500 wounded,
23,000 captured or missing
733 tanks and tank destroyers lost[5]
~1,000 aircraft lost, over 647 in December[6] and 353 during
Unternehmen Bodenplatte

■■■ British
1,408 (200 killed, 969 wounded, and 239 missing)[7]

◈ German
63,222[8]</ref> – 98,000[9]
(includes killed, wounded, missing, captured)
554 tanks, tank destroyers and assault guns lost[10]
~800 aircraft lost, at least 500 in December and 280 during
Unternehmen Bodenplatte

Approximately 3,000 civilians killed[11]

The **Battle of the Bulge** (16 December 1944 – 25 January 1945) was the last major German offensive campaign on the Western Front during World War II. It was launched through the densely forested Ardennes region of Wallonia in eastern Belgium, northeast France, and Luxembourg, towards the end of

Figure 1:
Map showing the swelling of "the Bulge" as the German offensive progressed creating the nose-like salient during 16–25 December 1944.
Front line, 16 December
Front line, 20 December
Front line, 25 December
Allied movements
German movements

World War II. The furthest west the offensive reached was the village of Foy-Nôtre-Dame, south east of Dinant, being stopped by the British 21st Army Group on 24 December 1944. The German offensive was intended to stop Allied use of the Belgian port of Antwerp and to split the Allied lines, allowing the Germans to encircle and destroy four Allied armies and force the Western Allies to negotiate a peace treaty in the Axis powers' favor. Once that was accomplished, the German dictator Adolf Hitler believed he could fully concentrate on the Soviets on the Eastern Front.

The surprise attack caught the Allied forces completely off guard. American forces bore the brunt of the attack and incurred their highest casualties of any operation during the war. The battle also severely depleted Germany's armored forces, and they were largely unable to replace them. German personnel and, later, Luftwaffe aircraft (in the concluding stages of the engagement) also sustained heavy losses.

The Germans officially referred to the offensive as **Unternehmen Wacht am Rhein** ("Operation Watch on the Rhine"), while the Allies designated it the **Ardennes Counteroffensive**. The phrase "Battle of the Bulge" was coined by contemporary press to describe the bulge in German front lines on wartime news maps,[12,13,14] and it became the most widely used name for the battle. The offensive was planned by the German forces with utmost secrecy, with minimal radio traffic and movements of troops and equipment under cover of darkness. Intercepted German communications indicating a substantial German offensive preparation were not acted upon by the Allies.

The Germans achieved total surprise on the morning of 16 December 1944, due to a combination of Allied overconfidence, preoccupation with Allied offensive plans, and poor aerial reconnaissance. The Germans attacked a weakly defended section of the Allied line, taking advantage of heavily over-cast weather conditions that grounded the Allies' overwhelmingly superior air forces. Fierce resistance on the northern shoulder of the offensive, around Elsenborn Ridge, and in the south, around Bastogne, blocked German ac-cess to key roads to the northwest and west that they counted on for success. Columns of armor and infantry that were supposed to advance along parallel routes found themselves on the same roads. This, and terrain that favored the defenders, threw the German advance behind schedule and allowed the Allies to reinforce the thinly placed troops. Improved weather conditions permitted air attacks on German forces and supply lines, which sealed the failure of the offensive. In the wake of the defeat, many experienced German units were left severely depleted of men and equipment, as survivors retreated to the defenses of the Siegfried Line.

The Germans' initial attack involved 410,000 men; just over 1,400 tanks, tank destroyers, and assault guns; 2,600 artillery pieces; 1,600 anti-tank guns; and over 1,000 combat aircraft, as well as large numbers of other AFVs. These were reinforced a couple of weeks later, bringing the offensive's total strength to around 450,000 troops, and 1,500 tanks and assault guns. Between 63,222 and 98,000 of their men were killed, missing, wounded in action, or captured. For the Americans, out of a peak of 610,000 troops,[15] 89,000[4] became casualties out of which some 19,000 were killed.[4,16] The "Bulge" was the largest and bloodiest single battle fought by the United States in World War II.

Background

After the breakout from Normandy at the end of July 1944 and the Allied landings in southern France on 15 August 1944, the Allies advanced toward Germany more quickly than anticipated.[17] The Allies were faced with several military logistics issues:

- troops were fatigued by weeks of continuous combat
- supply lines were stretched extremely thin
- supplies were dangerously depleted.

General Dwight D. Eisenhower (the Supreme Allied Commander on the Western Front) and his staff chose to hold the Ardennes region which was occupied by the U.S. First Army. The Allies chose to defend the Ardennes with as few troops as possible due to the favorable terrain (a densely wooded highland with deep river valleys and a rather thin road network) and limited Allied operational objectives in the area. They also had intelligence that the Wehrmacht was using the area across the German border as a rest-and-refit area for its troops.

Allied supply issues

The speed of the Allied advance coupled with an initial lack of deep-water ports presented the Allies with enormous supply problems.[18] Over-the-beach supply operations using the Normandy landing areas and direct landing LSTs on the beaches were unable to meet operational needs. The only deep-water port the Allies had captured was Cherbourg on the northern shore of the Cotentin peninsula and west of the original invasion beaches,[18] but the Germans had thoroughly wrecked and mined the harbor before it could be taken. It took many months to rebuild its cargo-handling capability. The Allies captured the port of Antwerp intact in the first days of September, but it was not operational until 28 November. The estuary of the Schelde river (also called Scheldt) that controlled access to the port had to be cleared of both German troops and naval mines.[19] The limitations led to differences between General Eisenhower and Field Marshal Bernard Montgomery, commander of the Anglo-Canadian 21st Army Group, over whether Montgomery or Lieutenant General Omar Bradley, commanding the U.S. 12th Army Group, in the south would get priority access to supplies.[20]

German forces remained in control of several major ports on the English Channel coast until May 1945. The Allies' efforts to destroy the French railway system prior to D-Day, successful in hampering German response to the invasion, proved equally restrictive to the Allies. It took time to repair the rail network's tracks and bridges. A trucking system nicknamed the Red Ball Express brought supplies to front-line troops, but used up five times as much fuel to reach the front line near the Belgian border as was delivered. By early October, the Allies had suspended major offensives to improve their supply lines and availability.[18]

Montgomery and Bradley both pressed for priority delivery of supplies to their respective armies so they could continue their individual lines of advance and maintain pressure on the Germans while Eisenhower preferred a broad-front strategy. He gave some priority to Montgomery's northern forces. This had the short-term goal of opening the urgently needed port of Antwerp and the long-term goal of capturing the Ruhr area, the biggest industrial area of Germany.[18] With the Allies stalled, German Generalfeldmarschall (Field Marshal) Gerd von Rundstedt was able to reorganize the disrupted German armies into a coherent defence.[18]

Field Marshal Montgomery's Operation Market Garden achieved only some of its objectives, while its territorial gains left the Allied supply situation stretched further than before. In October, the First Canadian Army fought the Battle of the Scheldt, opening the port of Antwerp to shipping. As a result, by the end of October the supply situation had eased somewhat.

German plans

Despite a lull along the front after the Scheldt battles, the German situation remained dire. While operations continued in the autumn, notably the Lorraine Campaign, the Battle of Aachen and fighting in the Hürtgen Forest, the strategic situation in the west had changed little. The Allies were slowly pushing towards Germany, but no decisive breakthrough was achieved. The Western Allies already had 96 divisions at or near the front, with an estimated ten more divisions en route from the United Kingdom. Additional Allied airborne units remained in England. The Germans could field a total of 55 understrength divisions.[:1]

Adolf Hitler first officially outlined his surprise counter-offensive to his astonished generals on September 16, 1944. The assault's ambitious goal was to pierce the thinly held lines of the U.S. First Army between Monschau and Wasserbillig with Army Group B (Model) by the end of the first day, get the armor through the Ardennes by the end of the second day, reach the Meuse between Liège and Dinant by the third day, and seize Antwerp and the western bank of the Scheldt estuary by the fourth day.[:1–64]

Hitler initially promised his generals a total of 18 infantry and 12 armored or mechanized divisions "for planning purposes." The plan was to pull 13 infantry divisions, two parachute divisions and six panzer-type divisions from the Oberkommando der Wehrmacht combined German military strategic reserve. On the Eastern Front, the Soviets' Operation Bagration during the summer had destroyed much of Germany's Army Group Center (Heeresgruppe Mitte). The extremely swift operation ended only when the advancing Soviet Red Army forces outran their supplies. By November, it was clear that Soviet forces were preparing for a winter offensive.[21]

Meanwhile, the Allied air offensive of early 1944 had effectively grounded the Luftwaffe, leaving the German Army with little battlefield intelligence and no way to interdict Allied supplies. The converse was equally damaging; daytime movement of German forces was rapidly noticed, and interdiction of supplies combined with the bombing of the Romanian oil fields starved Germany of oil and gasoline. This fuel shortage intensified after the Soviets overran those fields in the course of their August 1944 Jassy-Kishinev Offensive.

One of the few advantages held by the German forces in November 1944 was that they were no longer defending all of Western Europe. Their front lines in the west had been considerably shortened by the Allied offensive and were much closer to the German heartland. This drastically reduced their supply problems despite Allied control of the air. Additionally, their extensive telephone and telegraph network meant that radios were no longer necessary for communications, which lessened the effectiveness of Allied Ultra intercepts. Nevertheless, some 40–50 messages per day were decrypted by Ultra. They recorded the quadrupling of German fighter forces and a term used in an intercepted Luftwaffe message—Jägeraufmarsch (literally "Hunter Deployment")—implied preparation for an offensive operation. Ultra also picked up communiqués regarding extensive rail and road movements in the region, as well as orders that movements should be made on time.[22]

Drafting the offensive

Hitler felt that his mobile reserves allowed him to mount one major offensive. Although he realized nothing significant could be accomplished in the Eastern Front, he still believed an offensive against the Western Allies, whom he considered militarily inferior to the Red Army, would have some chances of success.[23] Hitler believed he could split the Allied forces and compel the Americans and British to settle for a separate peace, independent of the Soviet Union.[24] Success in the west would give the Germans time to design and produce more advanced weapons (such as jet aircraft, new U-boat designs and super-heavy tanks) and permit the concentration of forces in the east. After the war ended, this assessment was generally viewed as unrealistic, given Allied air superiority throughout Europe and their ability to continually disrupt German offensive operations.[25]

Given the reduced manpower of their land forces at the time, the Germans believed the best way to seize the initiative would be to attack in the West against the smaller Allied forces rather than against the vast Soviet armies. Even the encirclement and destruction of multiple Soviet armies, as in 1941, would still have left the Soviets with a numerical superiority.Wikipedia:Citation needed

Hitler's plan called for a classic Blitzkrieg attack through the weakly defended Ardennes, mirroring the successful German offensive there during the Battle of

France in 1940—aimed at splitting the armies along the U.S.—British lines and capturing Antwerp. The plan banked on unfavorable weather, including heavy fog and low-lying clouds, which would minimize the Allied air advantage.[26] Hitler originally set the offensive for late November, before the anticipated start of the Russian winter offensive. The disputes between Montgomery and Bradley were well known, and Hitler hoped he could exploit this disunity. If the attack were to succeed in capturing Antwerp, four complete armies would be trapped without supplies behind German lines.[19]

Several senior German military officers, including Generalfeldmarschall Walter Model and Gerd von Rundstedt, expressed concern as to whether the goals of the offensive could be realized. Model and von Rundstedt both believed aiming for Antwerp was too ambitious, given Germany's scarce resources in late 1944. At the same time, they felt that maintaining a purely defensive posture (as had been the case since Normandy) would only delay defeat, not avert it. They thus developed alternative, less ambitious plans that did not aim to cross the Meuse River (in German and Dutch: Maas); Model's being Unternehmen Herbstnebel (Operation Autumn Mist) and von Rundstedt's Fall Martin ("Plan Martin"). The two field marshals combined their plans to present a joint "small solution" to Hitler.[27,28] When they offered their alternative plans, Hitler would not listen. Rundstedt later testified that while he recognized the merit of Hitler's operational plan, he saw from the very first that "all, absolutely all conditions for the possible success of such an offensive were lacking."[24]

Model, commander of German Army Group B (Heeresgruppe B), and von Rundstedt, overall commander of the German Army Command in the West (OB West), were put in charge of carrying out the operation.

In the west supply problems began significantly to impede Allied operations, even though the opening of the port of Antwerp in late November improved the situation somewhat. The positions of the Allied armies stretched from southern France all the way north to the Netherlands. German planning for the counteroffensive rested on the premise that a successful strike against thinly manned stretches of the line would halt Allied advances on the entire Western Front.

Operation names

The Wehrmacht's code name for the offensive was Unternehmen Wacht am Rhein ("Operation Watch on the Rhine"), after the German patriotic hymn *Die Wacht am Rhein,* a name that deceptively implied the Germans would be adopting a defensive posture along the Western Front. The Germans also referred to it as "Ardennenoffensive" (Ardennes Offensive) and Rundstedt-Offensive, both names being generally used nowadays in modern Germany.

The French (and Belgian) name for the operation is Bataille des Ardennes (Battle of the Ardennes). The battle was militarily defined by the Allies as the Ardennes Counteroffensive, which included the German drive and the American effort to contain and later defeat it. The phrase Battle of the Bulge was coined by contemporary press to describe the way the Allied front line bulged inward on wartime news maps.[12,14]

While the Ardennes Counteroffensive is the correct term in Allied military language, the official Ardennes-Alsace campaign reached beyond the Ardennes battle region, and the most popular description in English speaking countries remains simply the Battle of the Bulge.

Planning

Wikisourcehas original text related to this article:
Planning the Counteroffensive

Wikisourcehas original text related to this article:
Troops and Terrain

Wikisourcehas original text related to this article:
Preparations

The OKW decided by mid-September, at Hitler's insistence, that the offensive would be mounted in the Ardennes, as was done in 1940. In 1940 German forces had passed through the Ardennes in three days before engaging the enemy, but the 1944 plan called for battle in the forest itself. The main forces were to advance westward to the Meuse River, then turn northwest for Antwerp and Brussels. The close terrain of the Ardennes would make rapid movement difficult, though open ground beyond the Meuse offered the prospect of a successful dash to the coast.

Four armies were selected for the operation. Adolf Hitler personally selected for the counter-offensive on the northern shoulder of the western front the best troops available and officers he trusted. The lead role in the attack was given to 6th Panzer Army, commanded by SS-*Oberstgruppenführer* Sepp Dietrich. It included the most experienced formation of the Waffen-SS: the 1st SS Panzer Division Leibstandarte Adolf Hitler. It also contained the 12th SS Panzer Division Hitlerjugend. They were given priority for supply and equipment and assigned the shortest route to the primary objective of the offensive, Antwerp,[1–64] starting from the northernmost point on the intended battlefront, nearest the important road network hub of Monschau.

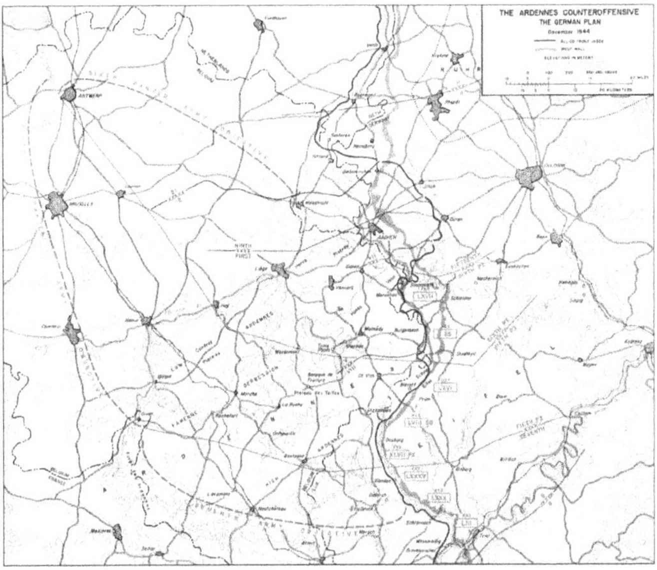

Figure 2: *The German plan.*

The Fifth Panzer Army under General Hasso von Manteuffel was assigned to the middle sector with the objective of capturing Brussels.

The Seventh Army, under General Erich Brandenberger, was assigned to the southernmost sector, near the Luxembourgish city of Echternach, with the task of protecting the flank. This Army was made up of only four infantry divisions, with no large-scale armored formations to use as a spearhead unit. As a result, they made little progress throughout the battle.

Also participating in a secondary role was the Fifteenth Army, under General Gustav-Adolf von Zangen. Recently brought back up to strength and re-equipped after heavy fighting during Operation Market Garden, it was located on the far north of the Ardennes battlefield and tasked with holding U.S. forces in place, with the possibility of launching its own attack given favorable conditions.

For the offensive to be successful, four criteria were deemed critical: the attack had to be a complete surprise; the weather conditions had to be poor to neutralize Allied air superiority and the damage it could inflict on the German offensive and its supply lines;[29] the progress had to be rapid—the Meuse River, halfway to Antwerp, had to be reached by day 4; and Allied fuel supplies would have to be captured intact along the way because the combined Wehrmacht forces were short on fuel. The General Staff estimated they only had enough fuel to cover one-third to one-half of the ground to Antwerp in heavy combat conditions.

The plan originally called for just under 45 divisions, including a dozen panzer and *Panzergrenadier* divisions forming the armored spearhead and various infantry units to form a defensive line as the battle unfolded. By this time the German Army suffered from an acute manpower shortage, and the force had been reduced to around 30 divisions. Although it retained most of its armor, there were not enough infantry units because of the defensive needs in the East. These 30 newly rebuilt divisions used some of the last reserves of the German Army. Among them were *Volksgrenadier* ("People's Grenadier") units formed from a mix of battle-hardened veterans and recruits formerly regarded as too young, too old or too frail to fight. Training time, equipment and supplies were inadequate during the preparations. German fuel supplies were precarious—those materials and supplies that could not be directly transported by rail had to be horse-drawn to conserve fuel, and the mechanized and panzer divisions would depend heavily on captured fuel. As a result, the start of the offensive was delayed from 27 November to 16 December.Wikipedia:Citation needed

Before the offensive the Allies were virtually blind to German troop movement. During the liberation of France, the extensive network of the French resistance had provided valuable intelligence about German dispositions. Once they reached the German border, this source dried up. In France, orders had been relayed within the German army using radio messages enciphered by the Enigma machine, and these could be picked up and decrypted by Allied codebreakers headquartered at Bletchley Park, to give the intelligence known as Ultra. In Germany such orders were typically transmitted using telephone and teleprinter, and a special radio silence order was imposed on all matters concerning the upcoming offensive.[30] The major crackdown in the Wehrmacht after the 20 July plot to assassinate Hitler resulted in much tighter security and fewer leaks. The foggy autumn weather also prevented Allied reconnaissance aircraft from correctly assessing the ground situation. German units assembling in the area were even issued charcoal instead of wood for cooking fires to cut down on smoke and reduce chances of Allied observers deducing a troop buildup was underway.[31]

For these reasons Allied High Command considered the Ardennes a quiet sector, relying on assessments from their intelligence services that the Germans were unable to launch any major offensive operations this late in the war. What little intelligence they had led the Allies to believe precisely what the Germans wanted them to believe—that preparations were being carried out only for defensive, not offensive, operations. The Allies relied too much on Ultra, not human reconnaissance. In fact, because of the Germans' efforts, the Allies were led to believe that a new defensive army was being formed around Düsseldorf in the northern Rhineland, possibly to defend against British attack. This was done by increasing the number of flak (**Fl**uga**b**we**hr**anonen, i.e., anti-aircraft cannons) in the area and the artificial multiplication of radio transmissions in the area. The Allies at this point thought the information was of no importance. All of this meant that the attack, when it came, completely surprised the Allied forces. Remarkably, the U.S. Third Army intelligence chief, Colonel Oscar Koch, the U.S. First Army intelligence chief and the SHAEF intelligence officer Brigadier General Kenneth Strong all correctly predicted the German offensive capability and intention to strike the U.S. VIII Corps area. These predictions were largely dismissed by the U.S. 12th Army Group. Strong had informed Bedell Smith in December of his suspicions. Bedell Smith sent Strong to warn Lieutenant General Omar Bradley, the commander of the 12th Army Group, of the danger. Bradley's response was succinct: "Let them come.":362–366 Historian Patrick K. O'Donnell writes that on 8 December 1944 U.S. Rangers at great cost took Hill 400 during the Battle of the Hürtgen Forest. The next day GIs who relieved the Rangers reported a considerable movement of German troops inside the Ardennes in the enemy's rear, but that no one in the chain of command connected the dots.[32]

Because the Ardennes was considered a quiet sector, considerations of economy of force led it to be used as a training ground for new units and a rest area for units that had seen hard fighting. The U.S. units deployed in the Ardennes thus were a mixture of inexperienced troops (such as the raw U.S. 99th and 106th "Golden Lions" Divisions), and battle-hardened troops sent to that sector to recuperate (the 28th Infantry Division).

Two major special operations were planned for the offensive. By October it was decided that Otto Skorzeny, the German SS-commando who had rescued the former Italian dictator Benito Mussolini, was to lead a task force of English-speaking German soldiers in "Operation Greif". These soldiers were to be dressed in American and British uniforms and wear dog tags taken from corpses and prisoners of war. Their job was to go behind American lines and change signposts, misdirect traffic, generally cause disruption and seize bridges across the Meuse River. By late November another ambitious special operation was added: Col. Friedrich August von der Heydte was to lead a *Fallschirmjäger-Kampfgruppe* (paratrooper combat group) in Operation Stösser, a night-time paratroop drop behind the Allied lines aimed at capturing a vital road junction near Malmedy.[33,34]

German intelligence had set 20 December as the expected date for the start of the upcoming Soviet offensive, aimed at crushing what was left of German resistance on the Eastern Front and thereby opening the way to Berlin. It was hoped that Soviet leader Stalin would delay the start of the operation once the German assault in the Ardennes had begun and wait for the outcome before continuing.

After the 20 July attempt on Hitler's life, and the close advance of the Red Army which would seize the site on 27 January 1945, Hitler and his staff had been forced to abandon the Wolfsschanze headquarters in East Prussia, in which they had coordinated much of the fighting on the Eastern Front. After a brief visit to Berlin, Hitler travelled on his *Führersonderzug* ("Special Train of the Führer" (Leader)) to Giessen on 11 December, taking up residence in the Adlerhorst (eyrie) command complex, co-located with OB West's base at Kransberg Castle. Believing in omens and the successes of his early war campaigns that had been planned at Kransberg, Hitler had chosen the site from which he had overseen the successful 1940 campaign against France and the Low Countries.

Von Rundstedt set up his operational headquarters near Limburg, close enough for the generals and Panzer Corps commanders who were to lead the attack to visit Adlerhorst on 11 December, travelling there in an SS-operated bus convoy. With the castle acting as overflow accommodation, the main party was settled into the Adlerhorst's Haus 2 command bunker, including Gen. Alfred Jodl, Gen. Wilhelm Keitel, Gen. Blumentritt, von Manteuffel and SS Gen. Joseph ("Sepp") Dietrich.

In a personal conversation on 13 December between Walter Model and Friedrich von der Heydte, who was put in charge of Operation Stösser, von der Heydte gave Operation Stösser less than a 10% chance of succeeding. Model told him it was necessary to make the attempt: "It must be done because this offensive is the last chance to conclude the war favorably."[35]

Initial German assault

On 16 December 1944 at 05:30, the Germans began the assault with a massive, 90-minute artillery barrage using 1,600 artillery pieces[36] across a 130-kilometre (80 mi) front on the Allied troops facing the 6th Panzer Army. The Americans' initial impression was that this was the anticipated, localized counterattack resulting from the Allies' recent attack in the Wahlerscheid sector to the north, where the 2nd Division had knocked a sizable dent in the Siegfried Line. Heavy snowstorms engulfed parts of the Ardennes area. While having the effect of keeping the Allied aircraft grounded, the weather also proved troublesome for the Germans because poor road conditions hampered their advance. Poor traffic control led to massive traffic jams and fuel shortages in forward units.

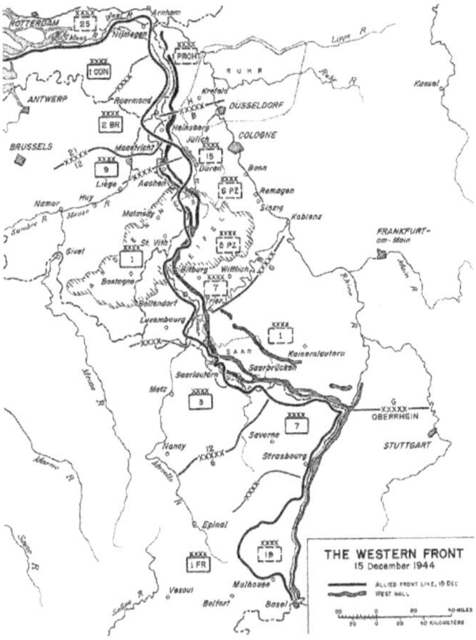

Figure 3: *Situation on the Western Front as of 15 December 1944*

In the center, von Manteuffel's Fifth Panzer Army attacked towards Bastogne and St. Vith, both road junctions of great strategic importance. In the south, Brandenberger's Seventh Army pushed towards Luxembourg in its efforts to secure the flank from Allied attacks. Only one month before, 250 members of the Waffen-SS had unsuccessfully tried to recapture the town of Vianden with its castle from the Luxembourgish resistance during the Battle of Vianden.

Attack on the northern shoulder

Wikisourcehas original text related to this article:
The Sixth Panzer Army Attack

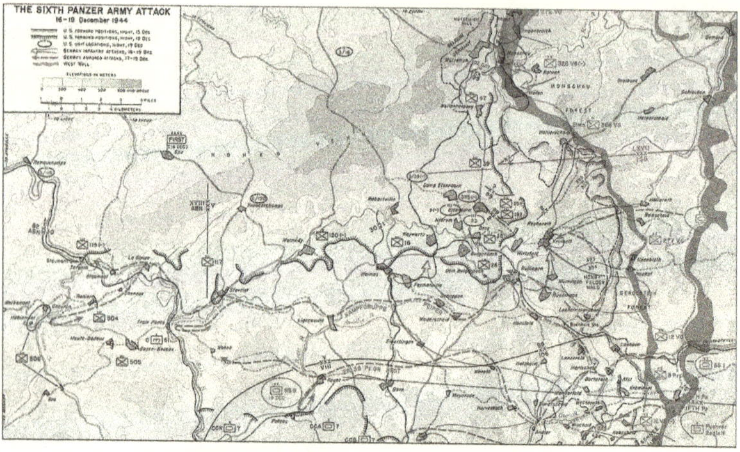

Figure 4: *Sepp Dietrich led the Sixth Panzer Army in the northernmost attack route.*

While the Siege of Bastogne is often credited as the central point where the German offensive was stopped, the battle for Elsenborn Ridge was actually the decisive component of the Battle of the Bulge, stopping the advance of the best equipped armored units of the German army and forcing them to reroute their troops to unfavorable alternative routes that considerably slowed their advance.[37,38]

Best German divisions assigned

The attack on Monschau, Höfen, Krinkelt-Rocherath, and then Elsenborn Ridge was led by the units personally selected by Adolf Hitler. The 6th Panzer Army was given priority for supply and equipment and was assigned the shortest route to the ultimate objective of the offensive, Antwerp.[38] The 6th Panzer Army included the elite of the Waffen-SS, including four Panzer divisions and five infantry divisions in three corps.[39,40] SS-*Obersturmbannführer* Joachim Peiper led *Kampfgruppe* Peiper, consisting of 4,800 men and 600 vehicles, which was charged with leading the main effort. Its newest and most powerful tank, the Tiger II heavy tank, consumed 3.8 litres (1 gal) of fuel to go 800 m (.5 mi), and the Germans had less than half the fuel they needed to reach Antwerp.:age needed

German forces held up

The attacks by the Sixth Panzer Army's infantry units in the north fared badly because of unexpectedly fierce resistance by the U.S. 2nd and 99th Infantry

Figure 5: *German troops advancing past abandoned American equipment*

Divisions. *Kampfgruppe* Peiper, at the head of the Sepp Dietrich's Sixth Panzer Army, had been designated to take the Losheim-Losheimergraben road, a key route through the Losheim Gap, but it was closed by two collapsed overpasses that German engineers failed to repair during the first day.[41] Peiper's forces were rerouted through Lanzerath.

To preserve the quantity of armor available, the infantry of the 9th *Fallschirmjaeger* Regiment, 3rd *Fallschirmjaeger* Division, had been ordered to clear the village first. A single 18-man Intelligence and Reconnaissance Platoon from the 99th Infantry Division along with four Forward Air Controllers held up the battalion of about 500 German paratroopers until sunset, about 16:00, causing 92 casualties among the Germans.

This created a bottleneck in the German advance. *Kampfgruppe* Peiper did not begin his advance until nearly 16:00, more than 16 hours behind schedule and didn't reach Bucholz Station until the early morning of 17 December. Their intention was to control the twin villages of Rocherath-Krinkelt which would clear a path to the high ground of Elsenborn Ridge. Occupation of this dominating terrain would allow control of the roads to the south and west and ensure supply to *Kampfgruppe* Peiper's armored task force.

Figure 6: *Scene of the Malmedy massacre*

Malmedy massacre

At 12:30 on 17 December, *Kampfgruppe* Peiper was near the hamlet of Baugnez, on the height halfway between the town of Malmedy and Ligneuville, when they encountered elements of the 285th Field Artillery Observation Battalion, U.S. 7th Armored Division.[42,43] After a brief battle the lightly armed Americans surrendered. They were disarmed and, with some other Americans captured earlier (approximately 150 men), sent to stand in a field near the crossroads under light guard. About fifteen minutes after Peiper's advance guard passed through, the main body under the command of SS-*Sturmbannführer* Werner Pötschke arrived. Allegedly, the SS troopers suddenly opened fire on the prisoners. As soon as the firing began, the prisoners panicked. Most were shot where they stood, though some managed to flee. Accounts of the killing vary, but at least 84 of the POWs were murdered. A few survived, and news of the killings of prisoners of war spread through Allied lines.[43] Following the end of the war, soldiers and officers of *Kampfgruppe* Peiper, including Joachim Peiper and SS general Sepp Dietrich, were tried for the incident at the Malmedy massacre trial.[44]

Kampfgruppe Peiper deflected southeast

Driving to the south-east of Elsenborn, *Kampfgruppe* Peiper entered Honsfeld, where they encountered one of the 99th Division's rest centers, clogged with confused American troops. They quickly captured portions of the 3rd Battalion of the 394th Infantry Regiment. They destroyed a number of American armored units and vehicles, and took several dozen prisoners who were subsequently murdered.[45,42] Peiper also captured 50,000 US gallons (190,000 l; 42,000 imp gal) of fuel for his vehicles.

Peiper advanced north-west towards Büllingen, keeping to the plan to move west, unaware that if he had turned north he had an opportunity to flank and trap the entire 2nd and 99th Divisions.[46] Instead, intent on driving west, Peiper turned south to detour around Hünningen, choosing a route designated Rollbahn D as he had been given latitude to choose the best route west.[36]

To the north, the 277th Volksgrenadier Division attempted to break through the defending line of the U.S. 99th and the 2nd Infantry Divisions. The 12th SS Panzer Division, reinforced by additional infantry (Panzergrenadier and Volksgrenadier) divisions, took the key road junction at Losheimergraben just north of Lanzerath and attacked the twin villages of Rocherath and Krinkelt.

Wereth 11

Another, smaller massacre was committed in Wereth, Belgium, approximately 6.5 miles (10.5 km) northeast of Saint-Vith on 17 December 1944. Eleven black American soldiers were tortured after surrendering and then shot by men of the 1st SS Panzer Division belonging to Schnellgruppe Knittel. The perpetrators were never punished for this crime and recent research indicates that men from Third Company of the Reconnaissance Battalion were responsible.

Germans advance west

By the evening the spearhead had pushed north to engage the U.S. 99th Infantry Division and *Kampfgruppe* Peiper arrived in front of Stavelot. Peiper's forces were already behind his timetable because of the stiff American resistance and because when the Americans fell back, their engineers blew up bridges and emptied fuel dumps. Peiper's unit was delayed and his vehicles denied critically needed fuel. They took 36 hours to advance from the Eifel region to Stavelot, while the same advance required nine hours in 1940.Wikipedia:Citation needed

Kampfgruppe Peiper attacked Stavelot on 18 December but was unable to capture the town before the Americans evacuated a large fuel depot.[47] Three tanks

Figure 7: *American soldiers of the 3rd Battalion 119th Infantry Regiment are taken prisoner by members of Kampfgruppe Peiper in Stoumont, Belgium on 19 December 1944.*

attempted to take the bridge, but the lead vehicle was disabled by a mine. Following this, 60 grenadiers advanced forward but were stopped by concentrated American defensive fire. After a fierce tank battle the next day, the Germans finally entered the town when U.S. engineers failed to blow the bridge.

Capitalizing on his success and not wanting to lose more time, Peiper rushed an advance group toward the vital bridge at Trois-Ponts, leaving the bulk of his strength in Stavelot. When they reached it at 11:30 on 18 December, retreating U.S. engineers blew it up.[48,49] Peiper detoured north towards the villages of La Gleize and Cheneux. At Cheneux, the advance guard was attacked by American fighter-bombers, destroying two tanks and five halftracks, blocking the narrow road. The group began moving again at dusk at 16:00 and was able to return to its original route at around 18:00. Of the two bridges remaining between *Kampfgruppe* Peiper and the Meuse, the bridge over the Lienne was blown by the Americans as the Germans approached. Peiper turned north and halted his forces in the woods between La Gleize and Stoumont.[50] He learned that Stoumont was strongly held and that the Americans were bringing up strong reinforcements from Spa.

To Peiper's south, the advance of *Kampfgruppe* Hansen had stalled. SS-*Oberführer* Mohnke ordered *Schnellgruppe* Knittel, which had been desig-

Figure 8: *An American soldier escorts a German crewman from his wrecked Panther tank during the Battle of Elsenborn Ridge*

nated to follow Hansen, to instead move forward to support Peiper. SS-*Sturmbannführer* Knittel crossed the bridge at Stavelot around 19:00 against American forces trying to retake the town. Knittel pressed forward towards La Gleize, and shortly afterward the Americans recaptured Stavelot. Peiper and Knittel both faced the prospect of being cut off.[50]

German advance halted

At dawn on 19 December, Peiper surprised the American defenders of Stoumont by sending infantry from the 2nd SS Panzergrenadier Regiment in an attack and a company of Fallschirmjäger to infiltrate their lines. He followed this with a Panzer attack, gaining the eastern edge of the town. An American tank battalion arrived but, after a two-hour tank battle, Peiper finally captured Stoumont at 10:30. Knittel joined up with Peiper and reported the Americans had recaptured Stavelot to their east.[51] Peiper ordered Knittel to retake Stavelot. Assessing his own situation, he determined that his *Kampfgruppe* did not have sufficient fuel to cross the bridge west of Stoumont and continue his advance. He maintained his lines west of Stoumont for a while, until the evening of 19 December when he withdrew them to the village edge. On the same evening the U.S. 82nd Airborne Division under Maj. Gen. James Gavin arrived and deployed at La Gleize and along Peiper's planned route of advance.[51]

Figure 9: *M3 90mm gun-armed American M36 tank destroyers of the 703rd TD, attached to the 82nd Airborne Division, move forward during heavy fog to stem German spearhead near Werbomont, Belgium, 20 December 1944.*

German efforts to reinforce Peiper were unsuccessful. *Kampfgruppe* Hansen was still struggling against bad road conditions and stiff American resistance on the southern route. *Schnellgruppe* Knittel was forced to disengage from the heights around Stavelot. *Kampfgruppe* Sandig, which had been ordered to take Stavelot, launched another attack without success. Sixth Panzer Army commander Sepp Dietrich ordered Hermann Prieß, commanding officer of the I SS Panzer Corps, to increase its efforts to back Peiper's battle group, but Prieß was unable to break through.[52]

Small units of the U.S. 2nd Battalion, 119th Infantry Regiment, 30th Infantry Division, attacked the dispersed units of *Kampfgruppe* Peiper on the morning of 21 December. They failed and were forced to withdraw, and a number were captured, including battalion commander Maj. Hal McCown. Peiper learned that his reinforcements had been directed to gather in La Gleize to his east, and he withdrew, leaving wounded Americans and Germans in the Froidcourt Castle. As he withdrew from Cheneux, American paratroopers from the 82nd Airborne Division engaged the Germans in fierce house-to-house fighting. The Americans shelled *Kampfgruppe* Peiper on 22 December, and although the Germans had run out of food and had virtually no fuel, they continued to

Figure 10: *Froidcourt castle near Stoumont in 2011*

fight. A Luftwaffe resupply mission went badly when SS-*Brigadeführer* Wilhelm Mohnke insisted the grid coordinates supplied by Peiper were wrong, parachuting supplies into American hands in Stoumont.[53]

In La Gleize, Peiper set up defenses waiting for German relief. When the relief force was unable to penetrate the Allied lines, he decided to break through the Allied lines and return to the German lines on 23 December. The men of the *Kampfgruppe* were forced to abandon their vehicles and heavy equipment, although most of the 800 remaining troops were able to escape.[54]

Outcome

The US 99th Infantry Division, outnumbered five to one, inflicted casualties in the ratio of 18 to one. The division lost about 20% of its effective strength, including 465 killed and 2,524 evacuated due to wounds, injuries, fatigue, or trench foot. German losses were much higher. In the northern sector opposite the 99th, this included more than 4,000 deaths and the destruction of 60 tanks and big guns. Historian John S.D. Eisenhower wrote, "... the action of the 2nd and 99th Divisions on the northern shoulder could be considered the most decisive of the Ardennes campaign."[55]

The stiff American defense prevented the Germans from reaching the vast array of supplies near the Belgian cities of Liège and Spa and the road network west of the Elsenborn Ridge leading to the Meuse River.[56] After more than 10 days of intense battle, they pushed the Americans out of the villages, but were unable to dislodge them from the ridge, where elements of the V Corps of the First U.S. Army prevented the German forces from reaching the road network to their west.

Operation Stösser

Operation Stösser was a paratroop drop into the American rear in the High Fens (French: *Hautes Fagnes*; German: *Hohes Venn*; Dutch: *Hoge Venen*) area. The objective was the "Baraque Michel" crossroads. It was led by Oberst Friedrich August Freiherr von der Heydte, considered by Germans to be a hero of the Battle of Crete.[57]

It was the German paratroopers' only night time drop during World War II. Von der Heydte was given only eight days to prepare prior to the assault. He was not allowed to use his own regiment because their movement might alert the Allies to the impending counterattack. Instead, he was provided with a *Kampfgruppe* of 800 men. The II Parachute Corps was tasked with contributing 100 men from each of its regiments. In loyalty to their commander, 150 men from von der Heydte's own unit, the 6th Parachute Regiment, went against orders and joined him.[58] They had little time to establish any unit cohesion or train together.

The parachute drop was a complete failure. Von der Heydte ended up with a total of around 300 troops. Too small and too weak to counter the Allies, they abandoned plans to take the crossroads and instead converted the mission to reconnaissance. With only enough ammunition for a single fight, they withdrew towards Germany and attacked the rear of the American lines. Only about 100 of his weary men finally reached the German rear.[59]

Chenogne massacre

Following the Malmedy massacre, on New Year's Day 1945, after having previously received orders to take no prisoners,[60] American soldiers allegedly shot approximately sixty German prisoners of war near the Belgian village of Chenogne (8 km from Bastogne).[61]

Attack in the center

Wikisourcehas original text related to this article:
St. Vith is lost

The Germans fared better in the center (the 32 km (20 mi) Schnee Eifel sector) as the Fifth Panzer Army attacked positions held by the U.S. 28th and 106th Infantry Divisions. The Germans lacked the overwhelming strength that had been deployed in the north, but still possessed a marked numerical and material superiority over the very thinly spread 28th and 106th divisions. They succeeded in surrounding two largely intact regiments (422nd and 423rd) of the 106th Division in a pincer movement and forced their surrender, a tribute to the way Manteuffel's new tactics had been applied.[62] One of those wounded and captured was Lieutenant Donald Prell of the Anti-Tank Company of the 422nd Infantry, 106th Division. The official U.S. Army history states: "At least seven thousand [men] were lost here and the figure probably is closer to eight or nine thousand. The amount lost in arms and equipment, of course, was very substantial. The Schnee Eifel battle, therefore, represents the most serious reverse suffered by American arms during the operations of 1944–45 in the European theater.":[170]

Battle for St. Vith

In the center, the town of St. Vith, a vital road junction, presented the main challenge for both von Manteuffel's and Dietrich's forces. The defenders, led by the 7th Armored Division, included the remaining regiment of the 106th U.S. Infantry Division, with elements of the 9th Armored Division and 28th U.S. Infantry Division. These units, which operated under the command of Generals Robert W. Hasbrouck (7th Armored) and Alan W. Jones (106th Infantry), successfully resisted the German attacks, significantly slowing the German advance. At Montgomery's orders, St. Vith was evacuated on 21 December; U.S. troops fell back to entrenched positions in the area, presenting an imposing obstacle to a successful German advance. By 23 December, as the Germans shattered their flanks, the defenders' position became untenable and U.S. troops were ordered to retreat west of the Salm River. Since the German plan called for the capture of St. Vith by 18:00 on 17 December, the prolonged action in and around it dealt a major setback to their timetable.:[407]

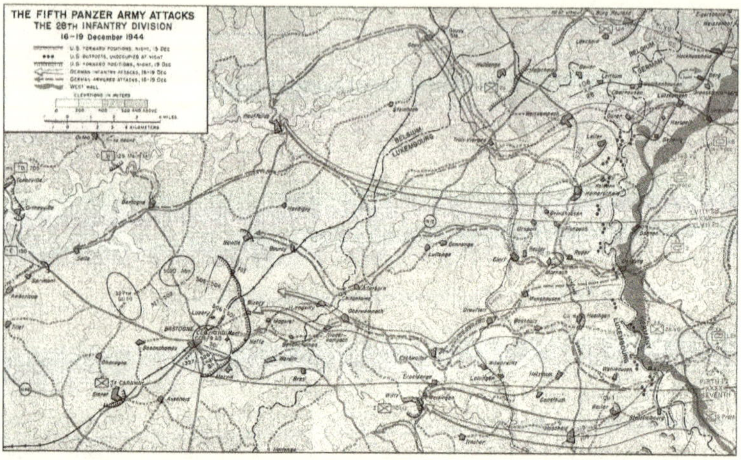

Figure 11: *Hasso von Manteuffel led Fifth Panzer Army in the middle attack route*

Meuse River bridges

To protect the river crossings on the Meuse at Givet, Dinant and Namur, Montgomery ordered those few units available to hold the bridges on 19 December.
This led to a hastily assembled force including rear-echelon troops, military
police and Army Air Force personnel. The British 29th Armoured Brigade
of British 11th Armoured Division, which had turned in its tanks for re-
equipping, was told to take back their tanks and head to the area. British XXX
Corps was significantly reinforced for this effort. Units of the corps which
fought in the Ardennes were the 51st (Highland) and 53rd (Welsh) Infantry
Divisions, the British 6th Airborne Division, the 29th and 33rd Armoured
Brigades, and the 34th Tank Brigade.

Unlike the German forces on the northern and southern shoulders who were
experiencing great difficulties, the German advance in the center gained considerable ground. The Fifth Panzer Army was spearheaded by the 2nd Panzer
Division while the Panzer Lehr Division (Armored Training Division) came up
from the south, leaving Bastogne to other units. The Ourthe River was passed
at Ourtheville on 21 December. Lack of fuel held up the advance for one day,
but on 23 December the offensive was resumed towards the two small towns
of Hargimont and Marche-en-Famenne. Hargimont was captured the same
day, but Marche-en-Famenne was strongly defended by the American 84th
Division. Gen. von Lüttwitz, commander of the XXXXVII Panzer-Korps, ordered the Division to turn westwards towards Dinant and the Meuse, leaving
only a blocking force at Marche-en-Famenne. Although advancing only in a
narrow corridor, 2nd Panzer Division was still making rapid headway, leading

Figure 12: *British Sherman "Firefly" tank in Namur on the Meuse River, December 1944*

to jubilation in Berlin. Headquarters now freed up the 9th Panzer Division for Fifth Panzer Army, which was deployed at Marche.[63]

On 22/23 December German forces reached the woods of Foy-Nôtre-Dame, only a few kilometers ahead of Dinant. The narrow corridor caused considerable difficulties, as constant flanking attacks threatened the division. On 24 December, German forces made their furthest penetration west. The Panzer Lehr Division took the town of Celles, while a bit farther north, parts of 2nd Panzer Division were in sight of the Meuse near Dinant at Foy-Nôtre-Dame. A hastily assembled Allied blocking force on the east side of the river prevented the German probing forces from approaching the Dinant bridge. By late Christmas Eve the advance in this sector was stopped, as Allied forces threatened the narrow corridor held by the 2nd Panzer Division.[63]

Operation Greif and Operation Währung

> Wikisourcehas original text related to this article:
> **The 1st SS Panzer Division's Dash Westward, and Operation Greif**

For Operation Greif ("Griffin"), Otto Skorzeny successfully infiltrated a small part of his battalion of English-speaking Germans disguised in American uniforms behind the Allied lines. Although they failed to take the vital bridges over the Meuse, their presence caused confusion out of all proportion to their military activities, and rumors spread quickly.[25] Even General George Patton was alarmed and, on 17 December, described the situation to General Dwight Eisenhower as "Krauts ... speaking perfect English ... raising hell, cutting wires, turning road signs around, spooking whole divisions, and shoving a bulge into our defenses."

Checkpoints were set up all over the Allied rear, greatly slowing the movement of soldiers and equipment. American MPs at these checkpoints grilled troops on things that every American was expected to know, like the identity of Mickey Mouse's girlfriend, baseball scores, or the capital of a particular U.S. state—though many could not remember or did not know. General Omar Bradley was briefly detained when he correctly identified Springfield as the capital of Illinois because the American MP who questioned him mistakenly believed the capital was Chicago.[25]

The tightened security nonetheless made things very hard for the German infiltrators, and a number of them were captured. Even during interrogation, they continued their goal of spreading disinformation; when asked about their mission, some of them claimed they had been told to go to Paris to either kill or capture General Dwight Eisenhower.[26] Security around the general was greatly increased, and Eisenhower was confined to his headquarters. Because Skorzeny's men were captured in American uniforms, they were executed as spies.[25] This was the standard practice of every army at the time, as many belligerents considered it necessary to protect their territory against the grave dangers of enemy spying. Skorzeny said that he was told by German legal experts that as long he did not order his men to fight in combat while wearing American uniforms, such a tactic was a legitimate ruse of war. Skorzeny and his men were fully aware of their likely fate, and most wore their German uniforms underneath their American ones in case of capture. Skorzeny was tried by an American military tribunal in 1947 at the Dachau Trials for allegedly violating the laws of war stemming from his leadership of Operation Greif, but was acquitted. He later moved to Spain and South America.[25]

Operation Währung was carried out by a small number of German agents who infiltrated Allied lines in American uniforms. These agents were tasked with

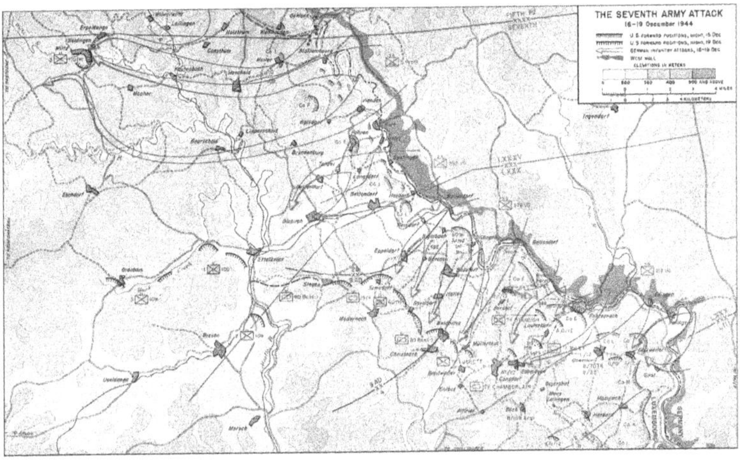

Figure 13: *Erich Brandenberger led Seventh Army in the southernmost attack route*

using an existing Nazi intelligence network to bribe rail and port workers to disrupt Allied supply operations. The operation was a failure.

Attack in the south

Further south on Manteuffel's front, the main thrust was delivered by all attacking divisions crossing the River Our, then increasing the pressure on the key road centers of St. Vith and Bastogne. The more experienced US 28th Infantry Division put up a much more dogged defense than the inexperienced soldiers of the 106th Infantry Division. The 112th Infantry Regiment (the most northerly of the 28th Division's regiments), holding a continuous front east of the Our, kept German troops from seizing and using the Our River bridges around Ouren for two days, before withdrawing progressively westwards.

The 109th and 110th Regiments of the 28th Division fared worse, as they were spread so thinly that their positions were easily bypassed. Both offered stubborn resistance in the face of superior forces and threw the German schedule off by several days. The 110th's situation was by far the worst, as it was responsible for an 18-kilometre (11 mi) front while its 2nd Battalion was withheld as the divisional reserve. Panzer columns took the outlying villages and widely separated strong points in bitter fighting, and advanced to points near Bastogne within four days. The struggle for the villages and American strong points, plus transport confusion on the German side, slowed the attack sufficiently to allow the 101st Airborne Division (reinforced by elements from the

Figure 14: *Belgian civilians killed by German units during the offensive*

9th and 10th Armored Divisions) to reach Bastogne by truck on the morning of 19 December. The fierce defense of Bastogne, in which American paratroopers particularly distinguished themselves, made it impossible for the Germans to take the town with its important road junctions. The panzer columns swung past on either side, cutting off Bastogne on 20 December but failing to secure the vital crossroads.

In the extreme south, Brandenberger's three infantry divisions were checked by divisions of the U.S. VIII Corps after an advance of 6.4 km (4 mi); that front was then firmly held. Only the 5th Parachute Division of Brandenberger's command was able to thrust forward 19 km (12 mi) on the inner flank to partially fulfill its assigned role. Eisenhower and his principal commanders realized by 17 December that the fighting in the Ardennes was a major offensive and not a local counterattack, and they ordered vast reinforcements to the area. Within a week 250,000 troops had been sent. General Gavin of the 82nd Airborne Division arrived on the scene first and ordered the 101st to hold Bastogne while the 82nd would take the more difficult task of facing the SS Panzer Divisions; it was also thrown into the battle north of the bulge, near Elsenborn Ridge.Wikipedia:Citation needed

Figure 15: *U.S. POWs on 22 December 1944*

Siege of Bastogne

By the time the senior Allied commanders met in a bunker in Verdun on 19 December, the town of Bastogne and its network of 11 hard-topped roads leading through the widely forested mountainous terrain with deep river valleys and boggy mud of the Ardennes region were to have been in German hands for several days, Bastogne having previously been the site of the VIII Corps headquarters. Two separate westbound German columns that were to have bypassed the town to the south and north, the 2nd Panzer Division and Panzer-Lehr-Division of XLVII Panzer Corps, as well as the Corps' infantry (26th Volksgrenadier Division), coming due west had been engaged and much slowed and frustrated in outlying battles at defensive positions up to sixteen kilometres (10 mi) from the town proper, but these defensive positions were gradually being forced back onto and into the hasty defenses built within the municipality. Moreover, the sole corridor that was open (to the southeast) was threatened and it had been sporadically closed as the front shifted, and there was expectation that it would be completely closed sooner than later, given the strong likelihood that the town would soon be surrounded.Wikipedia:Citation needed

Gen. Eisenhower, realizing that the Allies could destroy German forces much more easily when they were out in the open and on the offensive than if they were on the defensive, told his generals, "The present situation is to be regarded as one of opportunity for us and not of disaster. There will be only

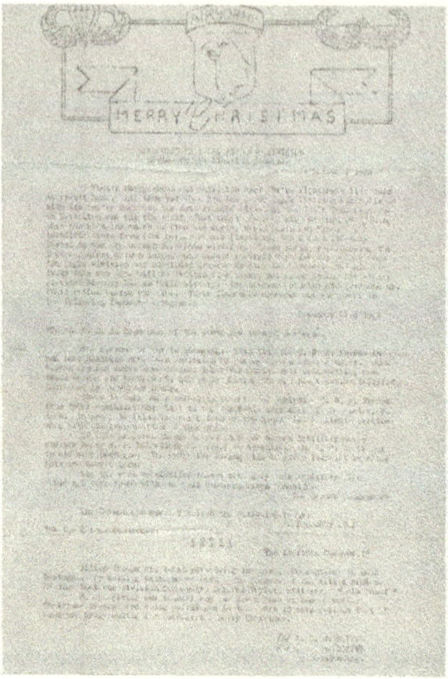

Figure 16: *Letter to 101st soldiers, containing Gen. McAuliffe's "Nuts!" response to the Germans*

Figure 17: *A German machine gunner marching through the Ardennes in December 1944.*

cheerful faces at this table." Patton, realizing what Eisenhower implied, responded, "Hell, let's have the guts to let the bastards go all the way to Paris. Then, we'll really cut 'em off and chew 'em up." Eisenhower, after saying he was not that optimistic, asked Patton how long it would take to turn his Third Army, located in northeastern France, north to counterattack. To the disbelief of the other generals present, Patton replied that he could attack with two divisions within 48 hours. Unknown to the other officers present, before he left Patton had ordered his staff to prepare three contingency plans for a northward turn in at least corps strength. By the time Eisenhower asked him how long it would take, the movement was already underway.[64] On 20 December, Eisenhower removed the First and Ninth U.S. Armies from Gen. Bradley's 12th Army Group and placed them under Montgomery's 21st Army Group.[65]

By 21 December the Germans had surrounded Bastogne, which was defended by the 101st Airborne Division, the all African American 969th Artillery Battalion, and Combat Command B of the 10th Armored Division. Conditions inside the perimeter were tough—most of the medical supplies and medical personnel had been captured. Food was scarce, and by 22 December artillery ammunition was restricted to 10 rounds per gun per day. The weather cleared the next day and supplies (primarily ammunition) were dropped over four of the next five days.

Despite determined German attacks the perimeter held. The German commander, Generalleutnant (Lt. Gen.) Heinrich Freiherr von Lüttwitz,[66] requested Bastogne's surrender. When Brig. Gen. Anthony McAuliffe, acting commander of the 101st, was told of the Nazi demand to surrender, in frustration he responded, "Nuts!" After turning to other pressing issues, his staff reminded him that they should reply to the German demand. One officer, Lt. Col. Harry Kinnard, noted that McAuliffe's initial reply would be "tough to beat." Thus McAuliffe wrote on the paper, which was typed up and delivered to the Germans, the line he made famous and a morale booster to his troops: "NUTS!"[67] That reply had to be explained, both to the Germans and to non-American Allies.[68]

Both 2nd Panzer and Panzer-Lehr division moved forward from Bastogne after 21 December, leaving only Panzer-Lehr division's 901st Regiment to assist the 26th Volksgrenadier-Division in attempting to capture the crossroads. The 26th VG received one Panzergrenadier Regiment from the 15th Panzergrenadier Division on Christmas Eve for its main assault the next day. Because it lacked sufficient troops and those of the 26th VG Division were near exhaustion, the XLVII Panzerkorps concentrated its assault on several individual locations on the west side of the perimeter in sequence rather than launching one simultaneous attack on all sides. The assault, despite initial success by

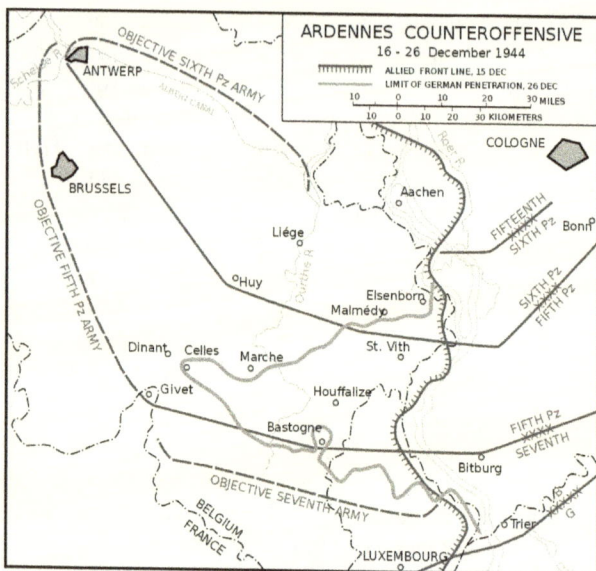

Figure 18: *The original objectives are outlined in red dashed lines. The orange line indicates their furthest advance.*

its tanks in penetrating the American line, was defeated and all the tanks destroyed. On the following day of 26 December the spearhead of Gen. Patton's 4th Armored Division, supplemented by the 26th (Yankee) Infantry Division, broke through and opened a corridor to Bastogne.

Allied counteroffensive

On 23 December the weather conditions started improving, allowing the Allied air forces to attack. They launched devastating bombing raids on the German supply points in their rear, and P-47 Thunderbolts started attacking the German troops on the roads. Allied air forces also helped the defenders of Bastogne, dropping much-needed supplies—medicine, food, blankets, and ammunition. A team of volunteer surgeons flew in by military glider and began operating in a tool room.

By 24 December the German advance was effectively stalled short of the Meuse. Units of the British XXX Corps were holding the bridges at Dinant, Givet, and Namur and U.S. units were about to take over. The Germans had outrun their supply lines, and shortages of fuel and ammunition were becoming critical. Up to this point the German losses had been light, notably in armor, with the exception of Peiper's losses. On the evening of 24 December, General

Hasso von Manteuffel recommended to Hitler's Military Adjutant a halt to all offensive operations and a withdrawal back to the Westwall (literally *Western Rampart*). Hitler rejected this.

Disagreement and confusion at the Allied command prevented a strong response, throwing away the opportunity for a decisive action. In the center, on Christmas Eve, the 2nd Armored Division attempted to attack and cut off the spearheads of the 2nd Panzer Division at the Meuse, while the units from the 4th Cavalry Group kept the 9th Panzer Division at Marche busy. As result, parts of the 2nd Panzer Division were cut off. The Panzer-Lehr division tried to relieve them, but was only partially successful, as the perimeter held. For the next two days the perimeter was strengthened. On 26 and 27 December the trapped units of 2nd Panzer Division made two break-out attempts, again only with partial success, as major quantities of equipment fell into Allied hands. Further Allied pressure out of Marche finally led the German command to the conclusion that no further offensive action towards the Meuse was possible.[69]

In the south, Patton's Third Army was battling to relieve Bastogne. At 16:50 on 26 December, the lead element, Company D, 37th Tank Battalion of the 4th Armored Division, reached Bastogne, ending the siege.

German counterattack

On 1 January, in an attempt to keep the offensive going, the Germans launched two new operations. At 09:15, the Luftwaffe launched Unternehmen Bodenplatte (Operation Baseplate), a major campaign against Allied airfields in the Low Countries, which are nowadays called the Benelux States. Hundreds of planes attacked Allied airfields, destroying or severely damaging some 465 aircraft. The Luftwaffe lost 277 planes, 62 to Allied fighters and 172 mostly because of an unexpectedly high number of Allied flak guns, set up to protect against German V-1 flying bomb/missile attacks and using proximity fused shells, but also by friendly fire from the German flak guns that were uninformed of the pending large-scale German air operation. The Germans suffered heavy losses at an airfield named Y-29, losing 40 of their own planes while damaging only four American planes. While the Allies recovered from their losses within days, the operation left the Luftwaffe ineffective for the remainder of the war.[70]

On the same day, German Army Group G (*Heeresgruppe G*) and Army Group Upper Rhine (*Heeresgruppe Oberrhein*) launched a major offensive against the thinly-stretched, 110 kilometres (70 mi) line of the Seventh U.S. Army. This offensive, known as Unternehmen Nordwind (Operation North Wind), was the last major German offensive of the war on the Western Front. The weakened Seventh Army had, at Eisenhower's orders, sent troops, equipment,

Figure 19: *P-47s destroyed at Y-34 Metz-*
Frescaty airfield during Operation Bodenplatte

and supplies north to reinforce the American armies in the Ardennes, and the offensive left it in dire straits.

By 15 January Seventh Army's VI Corps was fighting on three sides in Alsace. With casualties mounting, and running short on replacements, tanks, ammunition, and supplies, Seventh Army was forced to withdraw to defensive positions on the south bank of the Moder River on 21 January. The German offensive drew to a close on 25 January. In the bitter, desperate fighting of Operation Nordwind, VI Corps, which had borne the brunt of the fighting, suffered a total of 14,716 casualties. The total for Seventh Army for January was 11,609.[15] Total casualties included at least 9,000 wounded.[71] First, Third, and Seventh Armies suffered a total of 17,000 hospitalized from the cold.[15,72]

Allies prevail

While the German offensive had ground to a halt, they still controlled a dangerous salient in the Allied line. Patton's Third Army in the south, centered around Bastogne, would attack north, Montgomery's forces in the north would strike south, and the two forces planned to meet at Houffalize.

The temperature during January 1945 was extremely low. Weapons had to be maintained and truck engines run every half-hour to prevent their oil from congealing. The offensive went forward regardless.

Figure 20: *Infantrymen fire at German troops in the advance to relieve the surrounded paratroopers in Bastogne.*[73] </ref>

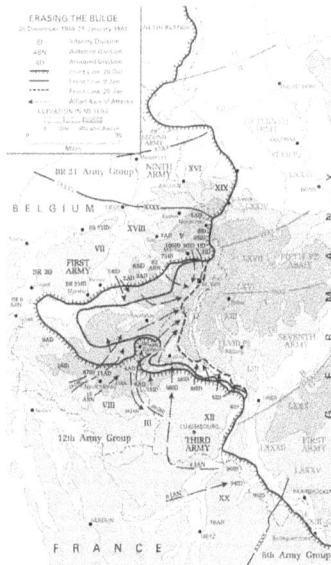

Figure 21: *Erasing the Bulge—The Allied counterattack, 26 December – 25 January*

Figure 22: *Americans of the 101st Engineers near Wiltz, Luxembourg, January 1945.*

Figure 23: *U.S. 6th Armored Division tanks moving near Wardin, Belgium, January 1945.*

Eisenhower wanted Montgomery to go on the counter offensive on 1 January, with the aim of meeting up with Patton's advancing Third Army and cutting off most of the attacking Germans, trapping them in a pocket. Montgomery, refusing to risk underprepared infantry in a snowstorm for a strategically unimportant area, did not launch the attack until 3 January, by which time substantial numbers of German troops had already managed to fall back successfully, but at the cost of losing most of their heavy equipment.

At the start of the offensive, the First and Third U.S. Armies were separated by about 40 km (25 mi). American progress in the south was also restricted to about a kilometer a day. On 2 January, the Tiger IIs of German Heavy Tank Battalion 506 supported an attack by the 12th SS Hitlerjugend division against U.S. positions near Wardin and knocked out 15 Sherman tanks.[74] The majority of the German force executed a successful fighting withdrawal and escaped the battle area, although the fuel situation had become so dire that most of the German armor had to be abandoned. On 7 January 1945 Hitler agreed to withdraw all forces from the Ardennes, including the SS-Panzer divisions, thus ending all offensive operations. Considerable fighting went on for another 3 weeks; St. Vith was recaptured by the Americans on 23 January, and the last German units participating in the offensive did not return to their start line until 25 January.

Winston Churchill, addressing the House of Commons following the Battle of the Bulge said, "This is undoubtedly the greatest American battle of the war and will, I believe, be regarded as an ever-famous American victory."

Force comparisons by date

Force	Allied[75]				Axis[76]			
Month	December		January		December		January	
Date	16th	24th	2nd	16th	16th	24th	2nd	16th
Men	228,741	~541,000	~705,000	700,520	406,342	~449,000	~401,000	383,016
Tanks	483	1,616	2,409	2,428	557	423	287	216
Tank destroyers and assault guns	499	1,713	1,970	1,912	667	608	462	414
Other AFVs	1,921	5,352	7,769	7,079	1,261	1,496	1,090	907
Anti-tank and artillery pieces	971	2,408	3,305	3,181	4,224	4,131	3,396	3,256

Ar-mored divisions	2	6	8	8	7	8	8	8
Ar-mored brigades		1	2	2	1	1	1	
Infantry divisions	6	15	22	22	13	16	15	16
Infantry brigades						2	2	2

**Initial and Final manpower commitments
for all units in Ardennes Campaign[77],[78]**

	American	British	German
Initial	687,498	111,904	498,622
Final	680,706	111,100	425,941

Strategy and leadership

Hitler's chosen few

The plan and timing for the Ardennes attack sprang from the mind of Adolf Hitler. He believed a critical fault line existed between the British and American military commands, and that a heavy blow on the Western Front would shatter this alliance. Planning for the "Watch on the Rhine" offensive emphasized secrecy and the commitment of overwhelming force. Due to the use of landline communications within Germany, motorized runners carrying orders, and draconian threats from Hitler, the timing and mass of the attack was not detected by ULTRA codebreakers and achieved complete surprise.[79]

Hitler when selecting leadership for the attack, felt that the implementation of this decisive blow should be entrusted to his own Nazi Party army, the Waffen-SS. Ever since German regular Army officers attempted to assassinate him, he had increasingly trusted only the SS and its armed branch, the Waffen-SS.[80] After the invasion of Normandy, the SS armored units had suffered significant leadership casualties. These losses included SS-*Gruppenführer* (Major General) Kurt Meyer, commander of the 12th SS Panzer (Armor) Division, captured by Belgian partisans on 6 September 1944.[10 :308] The tactical efficiency of these units were somewhat reduced. The strong right flank of the assault was therefore composed mostly of SS Divisions under the command of "Sepp" (Joseph) Dietrich, a fanatical political disciple of Hitler, and a loyal follower from the early days of the rise of National Socialism in Germany. The

Figure 24: *German field commanders plan the advance.*

leadership composition of the Sixth Panzer Division had a distinctly political nature.[38]

None of the German field commanders entrusted with planning and executing the offensive believed it was possible to capture Antwerp. Even Sepp Dietrich, commanding the strongest arm of the attack, felt that the Ardennes was a poor area for armored warfare, and that the inexperienced and badly equipped *Volksgrenadier* units would clog the roads that the tanks would need for their rapid advance. In this Dietrich was proved correct. The horse drawn artillery and rocket units were a significant obstacle to the tanks.[113] Other than making futile objections to Hitler in private, he generally stayed out of the planning for the offensive. Model and Manteuffel, the technical experts from the eastern front, took the view that a limited offensive with the goal of surrounding and crushing the American 1st Army would be the best the offensive could hope for. These revisions shared the same fate as Dietrich's objections. In the end, the headlong drive on Elsenborn Ridge would not benefit from support from German units that had already bypassed the ridge. The decision to stop the attacks on the twin villages and change the axis of the attacks southward to the hamlet of Domäne Bütgenbach, was also made by Dietrich.[224] This decision played into American hands, as Robertson had already decided to abandon the villages. The staff planning and organization of the attack was

Figure 25: *Field Marshal Montgomery*

well done; most of the units committed to the offensive reached their jump off points undetected and were well organized and supplied for the attack.

Allied high-command controversy

One of the fault lines between the British and American high commands was General Dwight D. Eisenhower's commitment to a broad front advance. This view was opposed by the British Chief of the Imperial General Staff, Field Marshal Alan Brooke, as well as Field Marshal Montgomery, who promoted a rapid advance on a narrow front, with the other allied armies in reserve.:[91]

Montgomery's actions

British Field Marshal Bernard Montgomery had differing views of how to approach the German attack with the U.S. command. His ensuing public pronouncements of opinion caused tension in the American high command. Major General Freddie de Guingand, Chief of Staff of Montgomery's 21st Army Group, rose to the occasion, and personally smoothed over the disagreements on 30 December.:[489-90]

As the Ardennes crisis developed, at 10:30 a.m. on 20 December, Eisenhower telephoned Montgomery and ordered him to assume command of the American First (Hodges) and Ninth Army (Simpson)[81] – which, until then, were

Figure 26: *General Eisenhower, the Supreme Allied Commander*

Figure 27: *General Bradley*

under Bradley's overall command. This change in command was ordered because the northern armies had not only lost all communications with Bradley, who was based in Luxembourg City,[82] and the US command structure, but with adjacent units.

Describing the situation as he found it on 20 December, Montgomery wrote;

> *The First Army was fighting desperately. Having given orders to Dempsey and Crerar, who arrived for a conference at 11 am, I left at noon for the H.Q. of the First Army, where I had instructed Simpson to meet me. I found the northern flank of the bulge was very disorganized. Ninth Army had two corps and three divisions; First Army had three corps and fifteen divisions. Neither Army Commander had seen Bradley or any senior member of his staff since the battle began, and they had no directive on which to work. The first thing to do was to see the battle on the northern flank as one whole, to ensure the vital areas were held securely, and to create reserves for counter-attack. I embarked on these measures: I put British troops under command of the Ninth Army to fight alongside American soldiers, and made that Army take over some of the First Army Front. I positioned British troops as reserves behind the First and Ninth Armies until such time as American reserves could be created. Slowly but surely the situation was held, and then finally restored. Similar action was taken on the southern flank of the bulge by Bradley, with the Third Army.*

Due to the news blackout imposed on the 16th, the change of leadership to Montgomery did not become known to the outside world until eventually SHAEF made a public announcement making clear that the change in command was "absolutely nothing to do with failure on the part of the three American generals".[198] This resulted in headlines in British newspapers. The story was also covered in *Stars and Stripes* and for the first time British contribution to the fighting was mentioned.

Montgomery asked Churchill if he could give a conference to the press to explain the situation. Though some of his staff were concerned at the image it would give, the conference had been cleared by Alan Brooke, the CIGS, who was possibly the only person to whom Monty would listen.

On the same day as Hitler's withdrawal order of 7 January, Montgomery held his press conference at Zonhoven.[83] Montgomery started with giving credit to the "courage and good fighting quality" of the American troops, characterizing a typical American as a "very brave fighting man who has that tenacity in battle which makes a great soldier", and went on to talk about the necessity of Allied teamwork, and praised Eisenhower, stating, "Teamwork wins battles and battle victories win wars. On our team, the captain is General Ike."

Then Montgomery described the course of the battle for a half-hour. Coming to the end of his speech he said he had "employed the whole available power of the British Group of Armies; this power was brought into play very gradually ... Finally it was put into battle with a bang ... you thus have the picture of British troops fighting on both sides of the Americans who have suffered a hard blow." He stated that he (i.e., the German) was "headed off ... seen off ... and ... written off". "The battle has been the most interesting, I think possibly one of the most interesting and tricky battles I have ever handled.".[84,85,86]

Despite his positive remarks about American soldiers, the overall impression given by Montgomery, at least in the ears of the American military leadership, was that he had taken the lion's share of credit for the success of the campaign, and had been responsible for rescuing the besieged Americans.

His comments were interpreted as self-promoting, particularly his claiming that when the situation "began to deteriorate," Eisenhower had placed him in command in the north. Patton and Eisenhower both felt this was a mis-representation of the relative share of the fighting played by the British and Americans in the Ardennes (for every British soldier there were thirty to forty Americans in the fight), and that it belittled the part played by Bradley, Pat-ton and other American commanders. In the context of Patton's and Mont-gomery's well-known antipathy, Montgomery's failure to mention the con-tribution of any American general beside Eisenhower was seen as insulting. Indeed, General Bradley and his American commanders were already starting their counterattack by the time Montgomery was given command of 1st and 9th U.S. Armies.[87] Focusing exclusively on his own generalship, Montgomery continued to say he thought the counteroffensive had gone very well but did not explain the reason for his delayed attack on 3 January. He later attributed this to needing more time for preparation on the northern front. According to Winston Churchill, the attack from the south under Patton was steady but slow and involved heavy losses, and Montgomery was trying to avoid this situation.

Many American officers had already grown to dislike Montgomery, who was seen by them as an overly cautious commander, arrogant, and all too willing to say uncharitable things about the Americans. The British Prime Minister Winston Churchill found it necessary in a speech to Parliament to explicitly state that the Battle of the Bulge was purely an American victory.

Montgomery subsequently recognized his error and later wrote: "Not only was it probably a mistake to have held this conference at all in the sensitive state of feeling at the time, but what I said was skilfully distorted by the enemy. Chester Wilmot[88] explained that his dispatch to the BBC about it was intercepted by the German wireless, re-written to give it an anti-American bias, and then broadcast by Arnhem Radio, which was then in Goebbels' hands. Monitored at Bradley's HQ, this broadcast was mistaken for a BBC transmission and it was this twisted text that started the uproar."

Montgomery later said, "Distorted or not, I think now that I should never have held that press conference. So great were the feelings against me on the part of the American generals that whatever I said was bound to be wrong. I should therefore have said nothing." Eisenhower commented in his own memoirs: "I doubt if Montgomery ever came to realize how resentful some American commanders were. They believed he had belittled them—and they were not slow to voice reciprocal scorn and contempt."[89]

Bradley and Patton both threatened to resign unless Montgomery's command was changed. Eisenhower, encouraged by his British deputy Arthur Tedder, had decided to sack Montgomery. Intervention by Montgomery's and Eisenhower's Chiefs of Staff, Maj. Gen. Freddie de Guingand, and Lt. Gen. Walter Bedell Smith, moved Eisenhower to reconsider and allowed Montgomery to apologize.Wikipedia:Citation needed

The German commander of the 5th Panzer Army, Hasso von Manteuffel said of Montgomery's leadership:

> The operations of the American 1st Army had developed into a series of individual holding actions. Montgomery's contribution to restoring the situation was that he turned a series of isolated actions into a coherent battle fought according to a clear and definite plan. It was his refusal to engage in premature and piecemeal counter-attacks which enabled the Americans to gather their reserves and frustrate the German attempts to extend their breakthrough.[90]

Casualties

Casualty estimates for the battle vary widely. According to the U.S. Department of Defense, American forces suffered 89,500 casualties including 19,000 killed, 47,500 wounded and 23,000 missing.[4] An official report by the United States Department of the Army lists 105,102 casualties, including 19,246 killed, 62,489 wounded, and 26,612 captured or missing, though this incorporates losses suffered during the German offensive in Alsace, Operation "Nordwind.":[92] A preliminary Army report restricted to the First and Third U.S. Armies listed 75,000 casualties (8,400 killed, 46,000 wounded and 21,000 missing). The Battle of the Bulge was the bloodiest battle for U.S. forces in World War II. British casualties totaled 1,400 with 200 deaths. The German High Command estimated that they lost between 81,834 and 98,024 men in the Bulge between 16 December 1944 and 28 January 1945; the accepted figure was 81,834, of which 12,652 were killed, 38,600 were wounded,

Figure 28: *The Mardasson Memorial near Bastogne, Belgium*

and 30,582 were missing.[91] Allied estimates on German casualties range from 81,000 to 103,000. Some authors have estimated German casualties as high as 125,000.[92]

- German historian Hermann Jung lists 67,675 casualties from 16 December 1944 to late January 1945 for the three German armies that participated in the offensive.[93]
- The German casualty reports for the involved armies count 63,222 losses from 10 December 1944 to 31 January 1945.
- The United States Army Center of Military History's official numbers are 75,000 American casualties and 100,000 German casualties.[94]

German armored losses to all causes were between 527 and 554, with 324 tanks being lost in combat.[95] Of the German write-offs, 16–20 were Tigers, 191–194 Panthers, 141–158 Panzer IVs, and 179–182 were tank destroyers and assault guns.[95] The Germans lost an additional 5,000 soft-skinned and armored vehicles.[95] US losses alone over the same period were similarly heavy, totaling 733 tanks and tank destroyers.[96] The outcome of the Ardennes Offensive demonstrated that the Allied armored forces were capable of taking on the *Panzerwaffe* on equal terms.[97]

Result

Although the Germans managed to begin their offensive with complete surprise and enjoyed some initial successes, they were not able to seize the initiative on the Western front. While the German command did not reach its
goals, the Ardennes operation inflicted heavy losses and set back the Allied invasion of Germany by several weeks. The High Command of the Allied forces had planned to resume the offensive by early January 1945, after the wet season rains and severe frosts, but those plans had to be post-
poned until 29 January 1945 in connection with the unexpected changes in
the front.Wikipedia:Citation needed

The Allies pressed their advantage following the battle. By the beginning of
February 1945, the lines were roughly where they had been in December 1944.
In early February, the Allies launched an attack all along the Western front:
in the north under Montgomery toward Aachen; in the center, under Courtney
Hodges; and in the south, under Patton.

The German losses in the battle were especially critical: their last reserves were now gone, the Luftwaffe had been shattered, and remaining
forces throughout the West were being pushed back to defend the Siegfried
Line.Wikipedia:Citation needed

In response to the early success of the offensive, on 6 January Churchill con-
tacted Stalin to request that the Soviets put pressure on the Germans on the
Eastern Front.[98] On 12 January, the Soviets began the massive Vistula–Oder
Offensive, originally planned for 20 January.:[39] It had been brought forward
from 20 January to 12 January because meteorological reports warned of a
thaw later in the month, and the tanks needed hard ground for the offensive
(and the advance of the Red Army was assisted by two Panzer Armies (5th &
6th) being redeployed for the Ardennes attack).

During World War II, most U.S. black soldiers still served only in maintenance
or service positions, or in segregated units. Because of troop shortages during
the Battle of the Bulge, Eisenhower decided to integrate the service for the
first time.:[127] This was an important step toward a desegregated United States
military. More than 2,000 black soldiers had volunteered to go to the front.:[534]
A total of 708 black Americans were killed in combat during World War II.

Media attention

The battle around Bastogne received a great deal of media attention because in
early December 1944 it was a rest and recreation area for many war correspondents. The rapid advance by the German forces who surrounded the town, the
spectacular resupply operations via parachute and glider, along with the fast

Figure 29: *The Battle of the Bulge diorama at the Audie Murphy American Cotton Museum*

action of General Patton's Third U.S. Army, all were featured in newspaper articles and on radio and captured the public's imagination; but there were no correspondents in the area of Saint-Vith, Elsenborn, or Monschau-Höfen.

Bletchley Park post-mortem

At Bletchley Park, F. L. Lucas and Peter Calvocoressi of Hut 3 were tasked in early 1945 with writing a report on the lessons to be learnt from the handling of pre-battle intelligence. The report concluded that "the costly reverse might have been avoided if Ultra had been more carefully considered".[99] "Ultra intelligence was plentiful and informative" though "not wholly free from ambiguity", "but it was misread and misused". Among the signs misread were the formation of the new 6th Panzer Army in the build-up area; the new 'Star' (signals control-network) noted by the 'Fusion Room' traffic-analysts, linking "all the armoured divisions [assembling in the build-up area], including some transferred from the Russian front";[100] the daily aerial reconnaissance of the lightly-defended target area by new jet fighters "as a matter of greatest urgency"; the marked increase in railway traffic in the build-up area; the movement of 1000 lorries from the Italian front to the build-up area; disproportionate anxiety about tiny hitches in troop movements, suggesting a tight timetable; and decrypts of Japanese diplomatic signals from Berlin to Tokyo, mentioning "the coming offensive". For its part, Hut 3 had grown "shy of going beyond its job of amending and explaining German messages. Drawing broad conclusions was for the intelligence staff at SHAEF, who had information from all sources," including aerial reconnaissance.[101] E. J. N. Rose, head Air Adviser in Hut 3, read the paper at the time and described it in 1998 as "an extremely good report" that "showed the failure of intelligence at SHAEF and at the Air Ministry".[102,103] The report is not known to have survived.[104] It was probably the "Top Secret [intelligence] digest", a post-mortem on the failure, referred to by General Strong (1968), "both record-copies of which were destroyed".[105,106] Lucas and Calvocoressi "expected heads to roll at Eisenhower's HQ, but they did no more than wobble".[107]

Battle credit

After the war ended, the U.S. Army issued battle credit in the form of the Ardennes-Alsace campaign citation to units and individuals that took part in operations in northwest Europe.[108] The citation covered troops in the Ardennes sector where the main battle took place, as well as units further south in the Alsace sector, including those in the northern Alsace who filled in the vacuum created by the U.S. Third Army racing north, engaged in the concurrent Operation Nordwind diversion in central and southern Alsace launched to weaken Allied response in the Ardennes, and provided reinforcements to units fighting in the Ardennes.

In popular culture

The battle has been depicted in numerous works of art, entertainment, and media, including:

- Films, e.g., *Battleground* (1949), *Attack* (1956), *Battle of the Bulge* (1965), and *A Midnight Clear* (1992)
- Games: Over 70 board wargames have been created about the battle, the earliest in 1965.[109] Also, As of 2014[110], the battle has been the scene for about 30 video games, mostly strategy games, beginning with *Tigers in the Snow* (1981).
- Literature: In Kurt Vonnegut's postmodern novel *Slaughterhouse-Five, or The Children's Crusade: A Duty-Dance with Death* (1969), the protagonist Billy Pilgrim is captured by the advancing German army during the Battle of the Bulge.
- Television: The battle was the subject of the PBS *American Experience* episode, "The Battle of the Bulge". The battle was prominently featured in two episodes of the miniseries *Band of Brothers* (2001). Additionally, the Military/American Heroes TV series *Greatest Tank Battles* featured

an episode on the Battle of the Bulge as "The Battle of the Bulge: S.S. Panzers Attack!"

Bibliography

<templatestyles src="Template:Refbegin/styles.css" />

- Ambrose, Stephen (1992), *Band of Brothers*, New York: Simon & Schuster, ISBN 0-671-76922-7
- Ambrose, Stephen (1998), *Citizen Soldiers*, Simon & Schuster, ISBN 0-684-84801-5
- Bergström, Christer (2014), *The Ardennes: Hitler's Winter Offensive 1944–1945*, Havertown: Casemate Publishers, ISBN 978-1-61200-277-4
- Blumenson, Martin (1972), *Eisenhower*, New York: Ballantine Books
- Bouwmeester, Maj. Han (2004), *Beginning of the End: The Leadership of SS Obersturmbannführer Jochen Peiper*[111] (PDF), Fort Leavenworth, Kansas: Royal Netherlands Army, Free University of Amsterdam, The Netherlands, retrieved 7 June 2012
- Bradley, Omar N. (30 April 1951), "The War America Fought: Sweep to Victory", *Life*, **30** (18)
- Bradley, Omar (1983), *A General's Life: An Autobiography*, The University of Michigan, ISBN 978-0-671-41023-0
- Burriss, T. Moffat (2001), *Strike and Hold: A Memoir of the 82nd Airborne in World War II*, Brassey's, ISBN 978-1-57488-348-0
- Carter, William R. (1989), *Air Power in the Battle of the Bulge*[112], Airpower Journal, retrieved 9 February 2012
- Cirillo, Roger (2003), *Ardennes-Alsace*[113], Office of the Chief of Military History Department of the Army, archived[114] from the original on 6 December 2008, retrieved 6 December 2008
- Clarke, Jeffrey J.; Smith, Robert Ross (1993), *Riviera to the Rhine: The European Theater of Operations*, Center of Military History, United States Army, ISBN 978-0-16-034746-7
- Cole, Hugh M. (1964), *The Ardennes:Battle of the Bulge*[115], Office of the Chief of Military History Department of the Army, LCCN 65060001[116]
- Collins, Michael; King, Martin (2013). *The Tigers of Bastogne: Voices of the 10th Armored Division in the Battle of the Bulge*. Casemate. ISBN 978-1-61200-181-4.
- Delaforce, Patrick (2004), *The Battle of the Bulge: Hitler's Final Gamble*, Pearson Higher Education, ISBN 978-1-4058-4062-0
- "Army Battle Casualties and Nonbattle Deaths in World War II"[117]. Combined Arms Research Library, Department of the Army. 25 June 1953. Retrieved 12 June 2012.
- de Senarclens, Pierre (1988), *Yalta*, Transaction, ISBN 0-88738-152-9

- Dupuy, Trever N; Bongard, David L.; Anderson Jr., Richard C. (1994), *Hitler's Last Gamble: The Battle of the Bulge, December 1944 – January 1945*, HarperCollins, ISBN 0-06-016627-4
- Eggenberger, David (1985), *An Encyclopedia of Battles: Accounts of Over 1560 Battles from 1479 B.C. to the Present*, Dover Publications, ISBN 0-486-24913-1
- Eisenhower, John S.D. (1969), *The Bitter Woods* (First ed.), New York: G.P. Putnam's Sons, ISBN 0-306-80652-5
- Ellis, Lionel F. (2009) [1968]. *Victory in the West*. 2 - The Defeat of Germany. with A.E. Warhurst. Naval and Military Press. ISBN 978-184574059-7.
- Elstob, Peter (1971), *Hitler's Last Offensive*, Macmillan Publishers Ltd., ISBN 9780436142512
- Gallagher, Wes (8 January 1945), "Montgomery Says Doughboy Courage, Fighting Ability Halted Nazi Drive"[118], *Pittsburgh Post-Gazette*, retrieved 12 June 2012
- Goldstein, Donald M.; Dillon, Katherine V.; Wenger, J. Michael (1994), *Nuts!: The Battle of the Bulge: The Story and Photographs*, Potomac Books, ISBN 978-0-02-881069-0
- Jordan, Jonathan W (2011), *Brothers Rivals Victors: Eisenhower, Patton, Bradley, and the Partnership That Drove the Allied Conquest in Europe*, NAL, ISBN 978-0-451-23212-0
- Kershaw, Alex (2004), *The Longest Winter*, Da Capo Press, ISBN 0-306-81304-1
- Liddell Hart, Basil Henry (1970), *History of the Second World War*, G. P. Putnam's Sons., ISBN 978-0-306-80912-5
- MacDonald, Charles B. (1984), *A Time For Trumpets: The Untold Story of the Battle of the Bulge*, Bantam Books, ISBN 0-553-34226-6
- MacDonald, Charles B. (1999), *Company Commander*, Burford Books, ISBN 1-58080-038-6
- MacDonald, Charles B. (1998), *The Battle of the Bulge*, Phoenix, ISBN 978-1-85799-128-4
- MacDonald, Charles B. (1994), *The Last Offensive*, Alpine Fine Arts Collection, ISBN 1-56852-001-8
- Marshall, S.L.A. (1988) [1946], *Bastogne: The First Eight Days*[119], U.S. Army in Action Series, United States Army Center of Military History, CMH Pub 22-2, archived[120] from the original on 4 December 2008, retrieved 6 December 2008
- Miles, Donna (14 December 2004), *Battle of the Bulge Remembered 60 Years Later*[121], United States Department of Defense, retrieved 12 June 2012

- Mitcham, Samuel W. (2006), *Panzers in Winter: Hitler's Army and the Battle of the Bulge*, Westport, CT: Praeger, ISBN 0-275-97115-5
- Newton, Steven H. (2006), *Hitler's Commander: Field Marshal Walter Model – Hitler's Favorite General*, Cambridge, MA: Da Capo, ISBN 0-306-81399-8
- Parker, Danny S. (1991), *Battle of the Bulge: Hitler's Ardennes Offensive, 1944–1945*, Combined Books, ISBN 0-938289-04-7
- Parker, Danny S. (1994), *To Win the Winter Sky: The Air War over the Ardennes 1944–1945*, Combined Books, ISBN 0-938289-35-7
- Parker, Danny S. (1999), *The Battle of the Bulge, The German View: Perspectives from Hitler's High Command*, London: Greenhill, ISBN 1-85367-354-4
- Parker, Danny S. (2004), *Battle of the Bulge: Hitler's Ardennes Offensive, 1944–1945*, Da Capo Press, ISBN 978-0-306-81391-7
- Quarrie, Bruce (1999), *The Ardennes Offensive VI Panzer Armee*, Osprey, ISBN 978-1-85532-853-2
- Quarrie, Bruce (2000), *The Ardennes Offensive V Panzer Armee*, Osprey, ISBN 978-1-85532-857-0
- Quarrie, Bruce (2001), *The Ardennes Offensive I Armee & VII Armee*, Osprey, ISBN 978-1-85532-913-3
- Ryan, Cornelius (1995) [1974], *A Bridge Too Far*, New York: Simon & Schuster, ISBN 978-0-684-80330-2
- Ryan, Cornelius (1995), *The Last Battle: The Classic History of the Battle for Berlin*, Simon & Schuster, ISBN 978-0-684-80329-6
- Sandler, Stanley (2002), *Ground Warfare: An International Encyclopedia*, ABC-CLIO, ISBN 1-57607-344-0
- Schneider, W. (2004), *Tigers in Combat, Vol. 1*, Stackpole, ISBN 978-0811731713
- Schrijvers, Peter (2005), *The Unknown Dead: Civilians in the Battle of the Bulge*, University Press of Kentucky, ISBN 0-8131-2352-6
- Shaw, Antony (2000), *World War II Day by Day*, Osceola: MBI Pub. Co, ISBN 978-0-7603-0939-1
- Shirer, William L. (1990), *The Rise and Fall of the Third Reich: A History of Nazi Germany*, Simon and Schuster, ISBN 0-671-72868-7
- Skorzeny, Otto (1997), *Skorzeny's Special Missions: The Memoirs of 'The Most Dangerous Man in Europe'*, Greenhill Books, ISBN 978-1-85367-291-0
- Sorge, Martin K. (1986), *The Other Price of Hitler's War: German Military and Civilian Losses Resulting From World War II*, Greenwood Press, ISBN 0-313-25293-9
- Stanton, Shelby (2006), *World War II Order of Battle: An Encyclopedic Reference to U.S. Army Ground Forces from Battalion through Division,*

1939–1946, Stackpole Books
- Toland, John (1999), *Battle: The Story of the Bulge*, Lincoln: University of Nebraska Press, ISBN 0-8032-9437-9
- Urban, Mark (2005), *Generals: Ten British Commanders who Shaped the World*, Faber and Faber, ISBN 978-0-571-22485-2
- Boog, Horst; Vogel, Detlef; Krebs, Gerhard (2001), *Das Deutsche Reich und die Zweite Weltkrieg Vol. 7*, Deutsche Verlags-Anstalt, ISBN 978-3-421-05507-1
- Weinberg, Gerhard L. (1995), *A World at Arms: A Global History of World War II*, Cambridge University Press, ISBN 978-0-521-55879-2
- Weinberg, Gerhard L. (1964), "Hitler's Image of the United States", *The American Historical Review*, **69** (4): 1006–1021, doi: 10.2307/1842933[122], JSTOR 1842933[123]
- Wilmes, David (1999), *The Long Road: From Oran to Pilsen: the Oral Histories of Veterans of World War II, European Theater of Operations*, SVC Northern Appalachian Studies, ISBN 978-1-885851-13-0
- Wissolik, Richard David (2005), *They Say There Was a War*, SVC Northern Appalachian Studies, ISBN 978-1-885851-51-2
- Wissolik, Richard David (2007), *An Honor to Serve: Oral Histories United States Veterans World War II*, SVC Northern Appalachian Studies, ISBN 978-1-885851-20-8
- Young, William H.; Young, Nancy K., eds. (2010), *World War II and the Postwar Years in America: A Historical and Cultural Encyclopedia, Volume 1*, ABC-CLIO, ISBN 0-313-35652-1
- Zaloga, Steven (2004), *Battle of the Bulge 1944*, Oxford: Osprey, ISBN 1-84176-810-3
- Zaloga, Steven (2008), *Panther vs. Sherman: Battle of the Bulge 1944*, Oxford: Osprey, ISBN 978-1-84603-292-9

Further reading

- Beevor, Antony (2015). *Ardennes 1944: Hitler's Last Gamble*. London: Viking. ISBN 978-0-670-91864-5.
- Caddick-Adams, Peter. *Snow and Steel: The Battle of the Bulge, 1944–45* (Oxford University Press; 2015) 872 pages
- Elstob, Peter (2003), *Hitler's Last Offensive*, Barnsley: Pen & Sword Military Classics, ISBN 0-85052-984-0
- von Luttichau, Charles V. (2000), "Chapter 20: The German Counteroffensive in the Ardennes"[124], in Kent Roberts Greenfield, *Command Decisions*[125], United States Army Center of Military History, CMH Pub 70-7 (reissue from 1960)

External links

- Battle of the Bulge[126] – Official webpage of the United States Army.
- The Battle of the Bulge: Battlebook[127] U.S. Army Europe
- Battle of the Bulge Museums[128] – a list of Battle of the Bulge museums near the previous battlefield.

Orbat

Battle of the Bulge order of battle

This is the order of battle of German and Allied forces during the Battle of the Bulge — specifically, at a point near the end of the battle, which lasted from 16 December 1944 until 25 January 1945.

As with any large Army organization in extended combat, forces and their assignments shifted over the course of the battle. For example, when the German attack began on 16 December, the U.S. 7th Armored Division was assigned to XIII Corps, U.S. Ninth Army, 12th Army Group. Later that day, its alignment became VIII Corps, U.S. First Army, 12th Army Group. On 20 December, the alignment switched to XVIII Corps, U.S. First Army, 12th Army Group — and later that day to XVIII Corps, U.S. First Army, 21st Army Group. On 18 January 1945, the alignment changed one last time, to XVIII Corps, U.S. First Army, 12th Army Group — as it is given in the following hierarchy.

Allied Forces

Supreme Headquarters Allied Expeditionary Forces

General of the Army Dwight D. Eisenhower

12th Army Group

LTG Omar N. Bradley

U.S. First Army

LTG Courtney H. Hodges

> 5th Belgian Fusilier Battalion
>
> 143rd and 413th AA Gun Battalions
>
> 526th Armored Infantry Battalion
>
> 99th Infantry Battalion (Norwegian-Americans)

✦ V Corps

MG Leonard T. Gerow

> 56th Signal Battalion
>
> 102nd Cavalry Group, Mechanized
>
> > 38th and 102nd Cavalry Recon Squadrons attached
>
> 613th TD Battalion
>
> 186th, 196th, 200th, and 955th FA Battalions
>
> 254th Engineer Combat Battalion
>
> 187th FA Group (751st and 997th FA Battalions)
>
> 190th FA Group (62nd, 190th, 272nd, and 268th FA Battalions)
>
> 406th FA Group (76th, 941st, 953rd, and 987th FA Battalions)
>
> 1111th Engineer Combat Group (51st, 202nd, 291st, and 296th Engineer Combat Battalions)
>
> 1121st Engineer Combat Group (146th, 254th Engineer Combat Battalions)
>
> 1195th Engineer Combat Group
>
> 134th, 387th, 445th, 460th, 461st, 531st, 602nd, 639th, and 863rd AAA AW Battalions

🛡 1st Infantry Division "Big Red One"

BG Clift Andrus

> 16th, 18th and 26th Infantry Regiments
>
> 5th, 7th, 32nd, and 33rd FA Battalions
>
> 1st Engineer Combat Battalion
>
> 745th Tank Battalion
>
> 634th and 703rd TD Battalions
>
> 103rd AAA AW Battalion

★ 2nd Infantry Division "Indianhead"

MG Walter M. Robertson

> 9th, 23rd, and 38th Infantry Regiments
>
> 12th, 15th, 37th, and 38th FA Battalions
>
> 2nd Engineer Combat Battalion

741st Tank Battalion

612th and 644th TD Battalions

462nd AAA AW Battalion

9th Infantry Division "Old Reliables"

MG Louis A. Craig

39th, 47th, and 60th Infantry Regiments

26th, 34th, 60th, and 84th FA Battalions

15th Engineer Combat Battalion

38th Cavalry Recon Squadron

746th Tank Battalion

376th and 413th AAA AW Battalions

69th Infantry Division"The fighting 69"

78th Infantry Division "Lightning"

MG Edwin P. Parker, Jr.

309th, 310th, and 311th Infantry Regiments

307th, 308th, 309th, and 903rd FA Battalions

303rd Engineer Combat Battalion

709th Tank Battalion

628th and 893rd TD Battalions

552nd AAA AW Battalion

> CCR, **5th Armored Division** (attached)

> **2nd Ranger Battalion** (attached)

99th Infantry Division "Checkerboard"

MG Walter E. Lauer

393rd, 394th, and 395th Infantry Regiments

370th, 371st, 372nd, and 924th FA Battalions

324th Engineer Combat Battalion

801st TD Battalion

535th AAA AW Battalion

⬤ VII Corps

MG Joseph Lawton Collins

  4th Cavalry Group, Mechanized

  29th Infantry Regiment

  Two French Light Infantry Battalions

  509th Parachute Infantry Battalion

  298th Engineer Combat Battalion

  740th Tank Battalion

  18th FA Group (188th, 666th, and 981st FA Battalions)

  142nd FA Group (195th and 266th FA Battalions)

  188th FA Group (172nd, 951st, and 980th FA Battalions)

  342nd, 366th, 392nd, 1308th, and 1313th Engineer General Service
  Regiments

  18th, 83rd, 87th, 183rd, 193rd, 957th, and 991st FA Battalions

▲ **2nd Armored Division** "Hell on Wheels"

MG Ernest N. Harmon

  41st Armored Infantry Regiment

  66th and 67th Armored Regiments

  14th, 78th, and 92nd Armored FA Battalions

  17th Armored Engineer Battalion

  82nd Armored Reconnaissance Battalion

  702nd TD Battalion

  195th AAA AW Battalion

  elements of 738th Tank Battalion (special - mine clearing) attached

▲ **3rd Armored Division** "Spearhead"

MG Maurice Rose

  36th Armored Infantry Regiment

  32nd and 33rd Armored Regiments

  54th, 67th, and 391st Armored FA Battalions

  23rd Armored Engineer Battalion

  83rd Recon Squadron

643rd and 703rd TD Battalions

486th AAA AW Battalion

83rd Infantry Division "Ohio"

MG Robert C. Macon

329th, 330th, and 331st Infantry Regiments

322nd, 323rd, 324th, and 908th FA Battalions

308th Engineer Combat Battalion

453rd AAA AW Battalion

774th Tank Battalion

772nd TD Battalion

84th Infantry Division "Railsplitters"

BG Alexander R. Bolling

333rd, 334th, and 335th Infantry Regiments

325th, 326th, 327th, and 909th FA Battalions

309th Engineer Combat Battalion

701st Tank Battalion, replaced by 771st Tank Battalion on 20 December

638th TD Battalion

557th AAA AW Battalion

XVIII Airborne Corps

MG Matthew B. Ridgway

   14th Cavalry Group, Mechanized

   254th, 275th, 400th, and 460th FA Battalions

   79th FA Group (153rd, 551st, and 552nd FA Battalions)

   179th FA Group (259th and 965th FA Battalions)

   211th FA Group (240th and 264th FA Battalions)

   401st FA Group (187th and 809th FA Battalions)

   7th Armored Division "Lucky Seventh"

BG Robert W. Hasbrouck

   CCA, CCB, and CCR

   23rd, 38th, and 48th Armored Infantry Battalions

   17th, 31st, and 40th Tank Battalions

   434th, 440th, and 489th Armored FA Battalions

   33rd Armored Engineer Battalion

   87th Recon Squadron

   814th TD Battalion

   203rd AAA AW Battalion

   820th TD Battalion attached 25–30 December

   30th Infantry Division "Old Hickory"

MG Leland S. Hobbs

   117th, 119th, and 120th Infantry Regiments

   113th, 118th, 197th, and 230th FA Battalions

   105th Engineer Combat Battalion

   743rd Tank Battalion

   823rd TD Battalion

   517th Parachute Infantry Regiment attached

   110th, 431st and 448th AAA AW Battalions

69th Infantry Division

   75th Infantry Division

MG Fay B. Prickett

289th, 290th, and 291st Infantry Regiments

730th, 897th, 898th, and 899th FA Battalions

275th Engineer Combat Battalion

750th Tank Battalion

629th and 772nd TD Battalions

440th AAA AW Battalion

82nd Airborne Division "All American"

MG James M. Gavin

504th, 505th, 507th, and 508th Parachute Infantry Regiments

325th Glider Infantry Regiment

319th and 320th Glider FA Battalions

376th and 456th Parachute FA Battalions

307th Airborne Engineer Battalion

80th AAA AW Battalion

551st Parachute Infantry Battalion

740th Tank Battalion attached 30 December – 11 January

628th TD Battalion attached 2–11 January

643rd TD Battalion attached 4–5 January

106th Infantry Division "Golden Lions"

MG Alan W. Jones

422nd, 423rd, and 424th Infantry Regiments

589th, 590th, 591st, and 592nd FA Battalions

81st Engineer Combat Battalion

820th TD Battalion

634th AAA AW Battalion 8–18 December

440th AAA AW battalion 8 December – 4 January

563rd AAA AW battalion 9–18 December

101st Airborne Division "Screaming Eagles"

BG Anthony C. McAuliffe (MG Maxwell D. Taylor)

501st, 502nd, and 506th Parachute Infantry Regiments

327th Glider Infantry Regiment

1st Battalion, 401st Glider Infantry

321st and 907th Glider FA Battalions

377th and 463rd Parachute FA Battalion

326th Parachute Engineer Battalion

705th TD Battalion

81st Airborne AAA AW Battalion

Ⓐ **U.S. Third Army**

LTG George S. Patton, Jr.

109th, 115th, 217th, and 777th AA Gun Battalions

456th, 465th, 550th, and 565th AAA AW Battalions

280th ECB - Engineer Combat Battalion - Non Divisional Unit (later assigned to the 9th Army)

▲ III Corps

MG John Millikin

6th Cavalry Group, Mechanized

179th, 274th, 776th, and 777th FA Battalions

193rd FA Group (177th, 253rd, 696th, 776th, and 949th FA Battalions)

203rd FA Group (278th, 742nd, 762nd FA Battalions)

183rd and 243rd Engineer Combat Battalions

1137th Engineer Combat Group (145th, 188th, and 249th Engineer Combat Battalions)

467th and 468th AAA AW Battalions

▲ **4th Armored Division**

MG Hugh J. Gaffey

CCA, CCB, and CCR

8th, 35th, and 37th Tank Battalions

10th, 51st, and 53rd Armored Infantry Battalions

22nd, 66th, and 94th Armored FA Battalions

24th Armored Engineer Battalion

25th Cavalry Recon Squadron

489th AAA AW Battalion

704th TD Battalion

▲ 6th Armored Division "Super Sixth"

MG Robert W. Grow

CCA, CCB, and CCR

15th, 68th and 69th Tank Battalions

9th, 44th, and 50th Armored Infantry Battalions

128th, 212th, and 231st Armored FA Battalions

25th Armored Engineer Battalion

86th Cavalry Recon Squadron

691st TD Battalion

777th AAA AW Battalion

◆ 26th Infantry Division "Yankee"

MG Willard S. Paul

101st, 104th, and 328th Infantry Regiments

101st, 102nd, 180th, and 263rd FA Battalions

101st Engineer Combat Battalion

735th Tank Battalion

818th TD Battalion

390th AAA AW Battalion

⊕ 35th Infantry Division "Santa Fe"

MG Paul W. Baade

134th, 137th, and 320th Infantry Regiments

127th, 161st, 216th, and 219th FA Battalions

60th Engineer Combat Battalion

654th TD Battalion

448th AAA AW Battalion

▦ 90th Infantry Division "Tough 'Ombres"

MG James A. Van Fleet

357th, 358th, and 359th Infantry Regiments

343rd, 344th, 345th, and 915th FA Battalions

315th Engineer Combat Battalion

773rd TD Battalion

774th TD Battalion attached 21 December – 6 January

537th AAA AW Battalion

⑧ VIII Corps

MG Troy H. Middleton

687th FA Battalion

174th FA Group (965th, 969th, and 700th FA Battalions)

333rd FA Group (333rd and 771st FA Battalions)

402nd FA Group (559th, 561st, and 740th FA Battalions)

422nd FA Group (81st and 174th FA Battalions)

178th and 249th Engineer Combat Battalions

1102nd Engineer Group (341st Engineer General Service Regiment)

1107th Engineer Combat Group (159th, 168th, and 202nd Engineer Combat Battalions)

1128th Engineer Combat Group (35th, 44th, and 202nd Engineer Combat Battalions)

French Light Infantry (six Light Infantry Battalions from Metz region)

467th, 635th, 778th AAA AW Battalions

▲ **9th Armored Division** "Phantom"

MG John W. Leonard

CCA, CCB, and CCR

27th, 52nd, and 60th Armored Infantry Battalions

2nd, 14th, and 19th Tank Battalions

3rd, 16th, and 73rd Armored FA Battalions

9th Armored Engineer Battalion

89th Cavalry Squadron

811th TD Battalion

482nd AAA AW Battalion

11th Armored Division "Thunderbolt"

BG Charles S. Kilburn

   CCA, CCB, and CCR

   21st, 55th, and 63rd Armored Infantry Battalions

   22nd, 41st, and 42nd Tank Battalions

   490th, 491st, and 492nd Armored FA Battalions

   56th Armored Engineer Battalion

   602nd TD Battalion

   41st Cavalry Squadron

   575th AAA AW Battalion

17th Airborne Division "Golden Talons"

MG William M. Miley

   507th and 513th Parachute Infantry Regiments

   193rd and 194th Glider Infantry Regiments

   680th and 681st Glider FA Battalions

   466th Parachute FA Battalion

   139th Airborne Engineer Battalion

   155th Airborne AAA AW Battalion

28th Infantry Division "Keystone"

MG Norman D. Cota

   109th, 110th, and 112th Infantry Regiments

   107th, 108th, 109th, and 229th FA Battalions

   103rd Engineer Combat Battalion

   707th Tank Battalion

   602nd TD Battalion

   630th TD Battalion

   447th AAA AW Battalion

87th Infantry Division "Golden Acorn"

BG Frank L. Culin, Jr.

   345th, 346th, and 347th Infantry Regiments

334th, 335th, 336th, 912th FA Battalions

312th Engineer Combat Battalion

761st Tank Battalion

549th AAA AW Battalion

610th TD battalion 14–22 December

691st TD battalion 22–24 December and 8–26 January

704th TD battalion 17–19 December

XII Corps

MG Manton S. Eddy

2nd Cavalry Group, Mechanized

161st, 244th, 277th, 334th, 336th, and 736th FA Battalions

177th FA group 215th, 255th, and 775th FA Battalions

182nd FA group 802nd, 945th, and 974th FA Battalions

183rd FA group 695th and 776th FA Battalions

404th FA group 273rd, 512th, and 752nd FA Battalions

1303rd Engineer Service Regiment

452nd AAA Automatic Weapons Battalion [colored]

457th AAA Automatic Weapons Battalion

4th Infantry Division "Ivy"

MG Raymond O. Barton

8th, 12th, and 22nd Infantry Regiments

20th, 29th, 42nd, and 44th FA Battalions

4th Engineer Combat Battalion

70th Tank Battalion

802nd and 803rd TD Battalions

377th AAA AW Battalions

5th Infantry Division "Red Diamond"

MG Stafford L. Irwin

2nd, 10th, and 11th Infantry Regiments

19th, 21st, 46th, and 50th FA Battalions

7th Engineer Combat Battalion

737th Tank Battalion

654th TD Battalion, 22–25 December

803rd TD Battalion, from 25 December

807th TD Battalion, 17–21 December

818th TD Battalion, 13 July – 20 December

449th AAA AW Battalion

🔺 10th Armored Division ''Tiger''

MG William H.H. Morris, Jr.

CCA, CCB, and CCR

20th, 54th, and 61st Armored Infantry Battalions

3rd, 11th, and 21st Tank Battalions

419th, 420th, and 423rd Armored FA Battalions

609th TD Battalion

55th Armored Engineer Battalion

90th Cavalry Recon Squadron

796th AAA AW Battalion

▪ 80th Infantry Division ''Blue Ridge''

MG Horace L. McBride

317th, 318th, and 319th Infantry Regiments

313th, 314th, 315th, and 905th FA Battalions

305th Engineer Combat Battalion

702nd Tank Battalion

610th TD Battalion 23 November – 6 December and 21 December –
28 January

808th TD Battalion 25 September – 21 December

633rd AAA AW Battalion

🛡 21st Army Group

Field Marshal Sir Bernard L. Montgomery

◈ XXX Corps

Lt-Gen. Brian G. Horrocks

> 2nd Household Cavalry Regiment
>
> 11th Hussars
>
> 4th Regiment, Royal Horse Artillery
>
> 5th Regiment, Royal Horse Artillery
>
> 73rd Antitank Regiment, Royal Artillery
>
> 7th, 64th, and 84th Medium Regiments, Royal Artillery
>
> 27th Light AA Regiment, Royal Artillery

▨ 6th Airborne Division

Maj-Gen. Eric Bols

> 3rd Parachute Brigade
>
> > 8th (Midlands) Parachute Battalion
> >
> > 9th (Eastern and Home Counties) Parachute Battalion
> >
> > 1st Canadian Parachute Battalion
>
> 5th Parachute Brigade
>
> > 7th (Light Infantry) Parachute Battalion
> >
> > 12th (Yorkshire) Parachute Battalion
> >
> > 13th (Lancashire) Parachute Battalion
>
> 6th Airlanding Brigade
>
> > 12th Battalion, Devonshire Regiment
> >
> > 2nd Battalion, Oxfordshire and Buckinghamshire Light Infantry
> >
> > 1st Battalion, Royal Ulster Rifles
>
> 53rd Light Regiment, Royal Artillery
>
> 3rd and 4th Airlanding Anti-Tank Batteries, Royal Artillery
>
> 6th Airborne Armoured Reconnaissance Regiment, Royal Armoured Corps
>
> 249th Airborne Field Company Royal Engineers

3rd, 591st Parachute Squadrons Royal Engineers

3rd, 9th Airborne Squadrons Royal Engineers

286th Airborne Field Park Company Royal Engineers

6th Airborne Divisional Signals Company Royal Signals

22nd Independent Parachute Company Army Air Corps

51st (Highland) Infantry Division

Maj-Gen. G T.G. Rennie

152nd Infantry Brigade

2nd Battalion, Seaforth Highlanders

5th Battalion, Seaforth Highlanders

5th Battalion, Queen's Own Cameron Highlanders

153rd Infantry Brigade

5th Battalion, Black Watch

1st Battalion, Gordon Highlanders

5/7th Battalion, Gordon Highlanders

154th Infantry Brigade

1st Battalion, Black Watch

7th Battalion, Black Watch

7th Battalion, Argyll and Sutherland Highlanders

126th, 127th, and 128th Field Regiments, Royal Artillery

2nd Derbyshire Yeomanry

61st Antitank Regiment, Royal Artillery

40th Light AA Regiment, Royal Artillery

274th, 275th, and 276th Field Companies Royal Engineers

239th Field Park Company Royal Engineers

16th Bridging Platoon Royal Engineers

51st Divisional Signals Company Royal Signals

1/7th Machine Gun Battalion Middlesex Regiment

53rd (Welsh) Infantry Division

Maj-Gen. Robert Knox Ross

71st Infantry Brigade

1st Battalion, Oxfordshire and Buckinghamshire Light Infantry

1st Battalion, Highland Light Infantry

4th Battalion, Royal Welch Fusiliers

158th Infantry Brigade

7th Battalion, Royal Welch Fusiliers

1/5th Battalion, Welch Regiment

1st Battalion, East Lancashire Regiment

160th Infantry Brigade

2nd Battalion, Monmouthshire Regiment

1/5th Battalion, Welch Regiment

6th Battalion, Royal Welch Fusiliers

81st, 83rd, and 133rd Field Regiments, Royal Artillery

53rd Recce Regiment, Royal Armoured Corps

71st Antitank Regiment, Royal Artillery

25th Light AA Regiment, Royal Artillery

244th, 282nd, and 555th Field Companies Royal Engineers

285th Field Park Company Royal Engineers

22nd Bridging Platoon Royal Engineers

53rd Divisional Signals Company Royal Signals

1st Machine Gun Battalion Manchester Regiment

29th Armoured Brigade

Brig. C.B.C Harvey

23rd Hussars

3rd Royal Tank Regiment

2nd Fife and Forfar Yeomanry

8th Battalion, Rifle Brigade

33rd Armoured Brigade

Brig. H.B. Scott

144th Regiment Royal Armoured Corps

1st Northamptonshire Yeomanry

1st East Riding Yeomanry

34th Army Tank Brigade

Brig. G W.S. Clarke

  9th Royal Tank Regiment

  107th Regiment Royal Armoured Corps

  147th Regiment Royal Armoured Corps

Corps Reserve

  🛡 **Guards Armoured Division**

Maj.-Gen. Allan Henry Shafto Adair

  5th Guards Armoured Brigade

    2nd Battalion, Grenadier Guards

    1st Battalion, Coldstream Guards

    2nd Battalion, Irish Guards

    1st Battalion, Grenadier Guards (Mechanized)

  32nd Guards Brigade

    5th Battalion, Coldstream Guards

    3rd Battalion, Irish Guards

    1st Battalion, Welsh Guards

  2nd Battalion, Welsh Guards (Recce)

  14th Field Company, Royal Engineers

  615th Field Company, Royal Engineers

  53rd Field Regiment, Royal Artillery

  153rd Field Regiment, Royal Artillery

  21st Anti-Tank Regiment, Royal Artillery

  94th Light Anti-Aircraft Regiment, Royal Artillery

  🛡 **43rd (Wessex) Infantry Division**

Maj-Gen. G. Thomas

  129th Infantry Brigade

    4th Battalion, Somerset Light Infantry

    4th Battalion, Wiltshire Regiment

    5th Battalion, Wiltshire Regiment

130th Infantry Brigade

    7th Battalion, Hampshire Regiment

    4th Battalion, Dorsetshire Regiment

    5th Battalion, Dorsetshire Regiment

214th Infantry Brigade

    7th Battalion, Somerset Light Infantry

    1st Battalion, Worcestershire Regiment

    5th Battalion, Duke of Cornwall's Light Infantry

8th Battalion, Middlesex Regiment (Vickers Machine Gunners)

43rd Reconnaissance Regiment, Royal Armoured Corps

94th Field Regiment, Royal Artillery

112th Field Regiment, Royal Artillery

179th Field Regiment, Royal Artillery

59th Anti-Tank Regiment, Royal Artillery

13th Bridging Platoon, Royal Engineers

204th Field Company, Royal Engineers

207th Field Park Company, Royal Engineers (from Bath, Somerset).

260th Field Company, Royal Engineers (from Chippenham, Wiltshire).

553rd Field Company, Royal Engineers

54th Company, RASC

504th Company, RASC

505th Company, RASC

506th Divisional Company, RASC

110th Light Anti Aircraft Regiment, Royal Artillery

50th (Northumbrian) Infantry Division

Maj-Gen. Douglas Alexander Graham

    69th Infantry Brigade

        5th Battalion, East Yorkshire Regiment

        6th Battalion, Green Howards

        7th Battalion, Green Howards

151st Infantry Brigade

  6th Battalion, Durham Light Infantry

  8th Battalion, Durham Light Infantry

  9th Battalion, Durham Light Infantry

231st Infantry Brigade

  1st Battalion, Hampshire Regiment

  1st Battalion, Dorsetshire Regiment

  1st/7th Battalion, Queen's (Royal West Surrey Regiment)

  2nd Battalion, Cheshire Regiment

74th Field Regiment, Royal Artillery

90th Field Regiment, Royal Artillery

124th Field Regiment, Royal Artillery

102nd Anti-Tank Regiment (Northumberland Hussars), Royal Artillery

25th Light Anti-Aircraft Regiment, Royal Artillery

233rd Field Company, Royal Engineers

501st Field Company, Royal Engineers

505th Field Company, Royal Engineers

235th Field Park Company, Royal Engineers

Air Support

U.S. Army Air Forces

U.S. Strategic Air Forces in Europe Gen Carl Spaatz

U.S. Eighth Air Force (Strategic)

Lt Gen James H. Doolittle

🛡 U.S. Ninth Air Force

Lt Gen Hoyt S. Vandenberg

   IX Bombardment Division

   Maj Gen Samuel E. Anderson

   IX Troop Carrier Command

   Maj Gen Paul L. Williams

   IX Tactical Air Command (supporting First Army)

   Maj Gen Elwood R. Quesada

   XIX Tactical Air Command (supporting Third Army)

   Maj Gen Otto P. Weyland

   XXIX Tactical Air Command (supporting Ninth Army)

   Brig Gen Richard E. Nugent

Royal Air Force

Bomber Command
   Air Chief Marshal Sir Arthur Harris

Fighter Command
   Air Marshal Sir Roderic M. Hill

Second Tactical Air Force
   Air Marshal Sir Arthur Coningham

- No. 2 Group RAF
- No. 83 Group RAF
- No. 84 Group RAF

Axis Forces

Oberbefehlshaber West
Generalfeldmarschall Gerd von Rundstedt

Army Group B

Generalfeldmarschall Walter Model

Fifth Panzer Army

General der Panzertruppen Hasso von Manteuffel

> 19th Flak Brigade
>
> 207th and 600th Engineer Battalions
>
> 653rd Heavy Panzerjäger Battalion
>
> 669th Ost (East) Battalion
>
> 638th, 1094th, and 1095th Heavy Artillery Batteries
>
> 25th/975th Fortress Artillery Battery
>
> 1099th, 1119th, and 1121st Heavy Mortar Batteries
>
> 3rd Todt Brigade (paramilitary engineers)

XXXIX Panzer Corps

Genlt Karl Decker

167th Volksgrenadier Division

Genlt Hanskurt Höcker

> 331st, 339th, 387th Volksgrenadier Regiments
>
> 167th Artillery Regiment
>
> 167th Antitank Battalion
>
> 167th Engineer Battalion
>
> 167th Signals Battalion

XLVII Panzer Corps

General der Panzertruppen Heinrich Freiherr von Lüttwitz

15th Volkswerfer Brigade

182nd Flak Regiment

766th Volksartillerie Corps

2nd Panzer Division

Col Meinrad von Lauchert

3rd Panzer Regiment

2nd and 304th Panzergrenadier Regiments

74th Artillery Regiment

2nd Recon Battalion

38th Antitank Battalion

38th Engineer Battalion

273rd Flak Battalion

38th Signals Battalion

9th Panzer Division

Genmaj Harald Freiherr von Elverfeldt

33rd Panzer Regiment

10th and 11th Panzergrenadier Regiments

102nd Artillery Regiment

9th Recon Battalion

50th Antitank Battalion

86th Engineer Battalion

287th Flak Battalion

81st Signals Battalion

301st Heavy Panzer Battalion (attached)

Panzer-Lehr-Division

Genlt Fritz Bayerlein

130th Panzer Regiment

901st and 902nd Panzergrenadier Regiments

130th Artillery Regiment

130th Recon Battalion

130th Antitank Battalion

130th Engineer Battalion

311th Flak Battalion

559th Antitank Battalion (attached)

243rd Assault Gun Brigade (attached)

26th Volksgrenadier Division

Col Heinz Kokott

39th Fusilier and 77th and 78th Volksgrenadier Regiments

26th Artillery Regiment

26th Recon Battalion

26th Antitank Battalion

26th Engineer Battalion

26th Signals Battalion

Fuhrer Begleit Brigade

Col Otto Remer

102nd Panzer Battalion

100th Panzergrenadier Regiment

120th Artillery Regiment

120th Recon Battalion

120th Engineer Battalion

828th Grenadier Battalion

673rd Antitank Battalion

LVIII Panzer Corps

General der Panzertruppen Walter Krüger

> 7th Volkswerfer Brigade (84th and 85th Werfer Regiments)
>
> 401st Volksartillerie Corps
>
> 1st Flak Regiment
>
> ⊗ **116th Panzer Division**

Genmaj Siegfried von Waldenburg

> 16th Panzer Regiment
>
> 60th and 156th Panzergrenadier Regiments
>
> 146th Artillery Regiment
>
> 146th Recon Battalion
>
> 226th Antitank Battalion
>
> 675th Engineer Battalion
>
> 281st Flak Battalion
>
> ⊗ **560th Volksgrenadier Division**

Col Rudolf Langhauser

> 1128th, 1129th, and 1130th Volksgrenadier Regiments
>
> 1560th Artillery Regiment
>
> 1560th Antitank Battalion
>
> 1560th Engineer Battalion
>
> 1560th Signals Battalion

LXVI Corps

General der Artillerie Walter Lucht

> 16th Volkswerfer Brigade (86th and 87th Werfer Regiments)
>
> 244th Assault Gun Brigade
>
> 460th Heavy Artillery Battalion

18th Volksgrenadier Division

Col Hoffman-Schonborn

> 293rd, 294th, and 295th Volksgrenadier Regiments
>
> 1818th Artillery Regiment
>
> 1818th Antitank Battalion
>
> 1818th Engineer Battalion
>
> 1818th Signals Battalion

62nd Volksgrenadier Division

Col Friedrich Kittel

> 164th, 193rd, and 190th Volksgrenadier Regiments
>
> 162nd Artillery Regiment
>
> 162nd Antitank Battalion
>
> 162nd Engineer Battalion
>
> 162nd Signals Battalion

Sixth Panzer Army

Oberstgruppenfuhrer der Waffen SS Josef Dietrich

> 506th Heavy Panzer Battalion
>
> 683rd Heavy Antitank Battalion
>
> 217th Assault Panzer Battalion
>
> 394th, 667th, and 902nd Assault Gun Battalions
>
> 741st Antitank Battalion
>
> 1098th, 1110th, and 1120th Heavy Howitzer Batteries
>
> 428th Heavy Mortar Battery
>
> 1123rd K-3 Battery
>
> 2nd Flak Division (41st and 43rd Regiments)
>
> von der Heydte Fallschirmjager Battalion
>
> 4th Todt Brigade

⊠ I SS Panzer Corps

SS-Gruppenfuhrer Hermann Priess

> 4th Volkswerfer Brigade (51st and 53rd Werfer Regiments)
>
> 9th Volkswerfer Brigade (14th and 54th Werfer Regiments)
>
> 388th Volksartillerie Corps
>
> 402nd Volksartillerie Corps
>
> 501st SS-Artillery Battalion
>
> 501st SS-Artillery Observation Battalion

🛡 1st SS Panzer Division

SS Oberfuhrer Wilhelm Mohnke

> 1st SS Panzer Regiment
>
> 1st and 2nd SS Panzergrenadier Regiments
>
> 1st SS Artillery Regiment
>
> 1st SS Recon Battalion
>
> 1st SS Antitank Battalion
>
> 1st SS Engineer Battalion
>
> 1st SS Flak Battalion
>
> 1st SS Signals Battalion
>
> 501st SS Heavy Panzer Battalion (attached)
>
> 84th Luftwaffe Flak Battalion (attached)

🛡 3rd Parachute Division

Genmaj Wadehn

> 5th, 8th, and 9th Parachute Infantry Regiments
>
> 3rd Artillery Regiment
>
> 3rd Recon Battalion
>
> 3rd Antitank Battalion
>
> 3rd Engineer Battalion
>
> 3rd Signals battalion

🛡 12th SS Panzer Division

SS Standartenfuhrer Hugo Kraas

12th SS Panzer Regiment

25th and 26th SS Panzergrenadier Regiments

12th SS Artillery Regiment

12th SS Recon Battalion

12th SS Antitank Battalion

12th SS Engineer Battalion

12th SS Flak Battalion

560th Heavy Antitank Battalion (attached)

12th Volksgrenadier Division

Genmaj Gerhard Engel

27th Fusilier and 48th and 89th Volksgrenadier Regiments

12th Artillery Regiment

12th Antitank Battalion

12th Fusilier Battalion

12th Engineer Battalion

12th Signals Battalion

277th Volksgrenadier Division

Col Wilhelm Viebig

289th, 990th, and 991st Volksgrenadier Regiments

277th Artillery Regiment

277th Antitank Battalion

277th Engineer Battalion

277th Signals Battalion

150th Panzer Brigade

Obersturmbannfuhrer der Waffen SS Otto Skorzeny

Two Panzer companies

Two Panzergrenadier companies

Two antitank companies

A heavy mortar battalion (two batteries)

600th SS Parachute Battalion Kampfgruppe 200 (Luftwaffe ground unit)

An anti-partisan company

II SS Panzer Corps

SS Obergruppenfuhrer Willi Bittrich

    410th Volksartillerie Corps

    502nd SS Heavy Artillery Battalion

    502nd SS Artillery Observation Battalion

ᛋᛋ 2nd SS Panzer Division

SS Brigadefuhrer Heinz Lammerding

    2nd SS Panzer Regiment

    3rd and 4th SS Panzergrenadier Regiments

    2nd SS Artillery Regiment

    2nd SS Recon Battalion

    2nd SS Engineer Battalion

    2nd SS Flak Battalion

    2nd SS Signals Battalion

🛡 9th SS Panzer Division

SS Oberfuhrer Sylvester Stadler

    9th SS Panzer Regiment

    19th and 20th SS Panzergrenadier Regiments

    9th SS Artillery Regiment

    9th SS Recon Battalion

    9th SS Antitank Battalion

    9th SS Engineer Battalion

    9th SS Flak Battalion

    9th SS Signals Battalion

    519th Heavy Antitank Battalion (attached)

LXVII Corps

Genlt Otto Hitzfeld

17th Volkswerfer Brigade (88th and 89th Werfer Regiments)

405th Volksartillerie Corps

1001st Heavy Assault Gun Company

3rd Panzergrenadier Division

Genmaj Walter Denkert

8th and 29th Panzergrenadier Regiments

103rd Panzer Battalion

3rd Artillery Regiment

103rd Recon Battalion

3rd Antitank Battalion

3rd Engineer Battalion

3rd Flak Battalion

3rd Signals Battalion

246th Volksgrenadier Division

Col Peter Körte

352nd, 404th, and 689th VG Regiments

246th Artillery Regiment

246th Antitank Battalion

246th Engineer Battalion

246th Signals Battalion

272nd Volksgrenadier Division

Genmaj Eugen König

980th, 981st, and 982nd Volksgrenadier Regiments

272nd Artillery Regiment

272nd Antitank Battalion

272nd Engineer Battalion

272nd Signals Battalion

326th Volksgrenadier Division

751st, 752nd, and 753rd Volksgrenadier Regiments

326th Artillery Regiment

326th Antitank Battalion

326th Engineer Battalion

326th Signals Battalion

▲ Seventh Army

General der Panzertruppen Erich Brandenberger

657th and 668th Heavy Antitank Battalions

501st Fortress Antitank Battalion

47th Engineer Battalion

1092nd, 1093rd, 1124th, and 1125th Heavy Howitzer Batteries

660th Heavy Artillery Battery

1029th, 1039th, and 1122nd Heavy Mortar Batteries

999th Penal Battalion

44th Machine Gun Battalion

15th Flak Regiment

1st Todt Brigade

LIII Corps

General der Kavallerie Edwin von Rothkirch

9th Volksgrenadier Division

Col Werner Kolb

36th, 57th, and 116th VG Regiments

9th Artillery Regiment

9th Antitank Battalion

9th Engineer Battalion

9th Signals Battalion

15th Panzergrenadier Division

Col Hans Joachim Deckert

104th and 115th Pzgr Regiments

115th Panzer Battalion

115th Artillery Regiment

115th Recon Battalion

33rd Antitank Battalion

33rd Engineer Battalion

33rd Flak Battalion

33rd Signals Battalion

Führer Grenadier Brigade

Col Hans-Joachim Kahler

99th Pzgr Regiment

101st Panzer Battalion

911th Assault Gun Brigade

124th Antitank Battalion

124th Engineer Battalion

124th Flak Battalion

124th Artillery Regiment

LXXX Corps

General der Infanterie Franz Beyer

> 408th Volksartillerie Corps
>
> 8th Volkswerfer Brigade
>
> 2nd and Lehr Werfer Regiments

212th Volksgrenadier Division

Genmajor Franz Sensfuß

> 316th, 320th, and 423rd VG Regiments
>
> 212th Artillery Regiment
>
> 212th Antitank Battalion
>
> 212th Engineer Battalion
>
> 212th Signals Battalion

276th Volksgrenadier Division

Gen Kurt Möhring (later Col Hugo Dempwolff)

> 986th, 987th, and 988th VG Regiments
>
> 276th Artillery Regiment
>
> 276th Antitank Battalion
>
> 276th Engineer Battalion
>
> 276th Signals Battalion

340th Volksgrenadier Division

Col Theodor Tolsdorff

> 694th, 695th, and 696th VG Regiments
>
> 340th Artillery Regiment
>
> 340th Antitank Battalion
>
> 340th Engineer Battalion
>
> 340th Signals Battalion

LXXXV Corps

General der Infanterie Baptist Kniess

   406th Volksartillerie Corps

   18th Volkswerfer Brigade (21st and 22nd Werfer Regiments)

5th Parachute Division

Col Ludwig Heilmann

   13th, 14th, and 15th Parachute Infantry Regiments

   5th Artillery Regiment

   5th Recon Battalion

   5th Engineer Battalion

   5th Flak Battalion

   11th Assault Gun Brigade

352nd Volksgrenadier Division

Col Erich-Otto Schmidt

   914th, 915th, and 916th Volksgrenadier Regiments

   352nd Artillery Regiment

   352nd Antitank Battalion

   352nd Engineer Battalion

   352nd Signals Battalion

79th Volksgrenadier Division

Col Alois Weber

   208th, 212th, and 226th Volksgrenadier Regiments

   179th Artillery Regiments

   179th Antitank Battalion

   179th Engineer Battalion

   179th Signals Battalion

Luftwaffe

II Fighter Corps
Genmaj. Dietrich Peltz

III Flak Corps
Genlt. Wolfgang Pickert

References

- MacDonald, Charles B. *A Time For Trumpets: The Untold Story of the Battle of the Bulge.* New York: Perennial, 2002. ISBN 0-688-15157-4
- Dupuy,Trevor N. "Hitler's Last Gamble" Airlife. ISBN 1-85310-711-5
- UNITS ENTITLED TO BATTLE CREDITS[129] - General Orders - US War Department

Attack on the northern shoulder

Battle of Elsenborn Ridge

Battle of Elsenborn Ridge	
Part of World War II, Battle of the Bulge	
Discarded artillery shell casings litter a U.S. Artillery position on Elsenborn Ridge.	
Date	16 – 26 December 1944
Location	The Ardennes 50°26′47″N 6°15′51″E[130]Coordinates: 50°26′47″N 6°15′51″E[130]
Result	American victory
Belligerents	
United States	Germany
Commanders and leaders	
Omar N. Bradley Walter E. Lauer Walter M. Robertson	Sepp Dietrich Hugo Kraas
Units involved	

1st Infantry Division	1st SS Panzer Division
2nd Infantry Division	12th SS Panzer Division
9th Infantry Division	3rd Panzergrenadier Division
99th Infantry Division	277th Volksgenadier Division
7th Armored Division (United States)	12th Volksgrenadier Division
82nd Airborne Division	246th Volksgrenadier Division
102nd Cavalry Group	3rd Fallschirmjäger Division
741st Tank Battalion	272nd Volksgrenadier
612th Tank Destroyer Battalion	326th Volksgrenadier Divisions
820th Tank Destroyer Battalion	753rd Volksgrenadier Regiment
106th Infantry Division (United States)	
405th Field Artillery Group	
613th Tank Destroyer Battalion	
62nd Armored Field Artillery Battalion	
460th Parachute Field Artillery Battalion	

Strength	
28,000 men	56,000 men

Casualties and losses	
12,000-15,000 casualties	114 tanks lost
5,000 men killed or missing	Unknown, but high personnel losses

File:Belgium location map.svg
Location within Belgium

The **Battle of Elsenborn Ridge** was the only sector of the American front lines during the Battle of the Bulge where the Germans failed to advance.[:33] The battle centered on the Elsenborn Ridge east of Elsenborn, Belgium in the Ardennes forest. West of Elsenborn Ridge, near the cities of Liège and Spa, Belgium, was a vast array of Allied supplies and the well-developed road network leading to the Meuse River and Antwerp. The Germans planned on using two key rollbahns or routes through the area to seize Antwerp and force a separate peace with the United States and Britain.[:259–271] Capturing Monschau and the nearby village of Höfen, and the twin villages of Rocherath-Krinkelt just east of Elsenborn Ridge, were key to the success of the German plans, and Gerald committed his best armored units and infantry troops to the area, including the 12th SS Panzer Division Hitlerjugend.

The green, untested troops of the 99th Infantry Division had been placed in the sector during mid-November because the Allies thought it was an area unlikely to see battle. Their soldiers were stretched thin over a 22-mile (35 km) front, and all three regiments were on line, with no reserve. In early December, the 2nd Infantry Division was assigned to capture a vital crossroads marked by a customs house and a forester's lodge named Wahlerscheid, at the southern tip of the Hurtgen Forest. They transitioned through the 99th Division's lines and after a deadly, costly battle, captured the crossroads. But Gerald counterattacked in what the Americans initially thought was a localized spoiling action, but was actually a leading element of the Battle of the Bulge. The 2nd Division consolidated their lines, pulling back into Hünningen, and then to the twin villages of Rocherath-Krinkelt, and finally at the dug-in positions held by the 99th Division at Elsenborn Ridge.

In a fierce battle lasting 10 days, the American and German lines were often confused. During the first three days, the battle raged over the twin villages of Rocherath-Krinkelt, during which American G.I.s were at times isolated in individual buildings surrounded by German armor. Attacking Elsenborn Ridge itself, the Germans, although superior in numbers, were stopped by the Americans' well-prepared and deeply dug-in defensive positions. The German attack plans were not well coordinated and frustrated by the rugged terrain, built-up areas around the twin villages, and massed American artillery firepower positioned behind Elsenborn Ridge. American artillery batteries repeatedly pounded the German advance. While the Germans employed an effective combined arms tactic and penetrated the U.S. lines several times, the Americans called in indirect fire on their own positions, pushing the Germans back. U.S. reserve forces consisting of clerks and headquarters personnel were rushed in at one point to reinforce the 395th Infantry Regiment's lines. Although the Germans possessed superior armor, they were held in check by the innovative American tactics, including better communications, coordinated time on target artillery strikes, new proximity fuses for artillery shells, and superior air power.

The Sixth Panzer Army was unable to break through and take its immediate objectives on the Meuse River. The stubborn American resistance forced Kampfgruppe Peiper to choose an alternative route well south of Monschau and Elsenborn Ridge. As a result, the German forces were strung out over miles of winding, single-track roads, unable to concentrate their armored units. Peiper's units were repeatedly stymied by U.S. Army engineers, who blew essential bridges along their route of advance. One column of roughly 40 tanks and support vehicles was destroyed on 17 December when they were discovered by an L4 air observer of the 62nd Armored Field Artillery Battalion, assigned to the 102nd Cavalry Group. They were attacked by the 62nd's 105 howitzers mounted on M7 SP's, Corps 155's and Army 240's.[410–411] The panzers finally reached the Amblève River, only about halfway to the Meuse River, but ran out of fuel. Food and ammunition also ran low. After 10 days, the German forces had been reduced to an ineffective strength and withdrew. The Americans lost about 5,000 men; while exact German losses are not known, they included significant amounts of armor. While the Americans had considerable supplies and enough troops to re-equip their forces, German losses could not be replaced.

Background

Monschau lay on the very northernmost sector of the German offensive. Capturing it, the nearby town of Höfen, and the twin villages of Krinkelt-Rocherath were critical to the success of the German offensive because of the road network that lay to their west. The Germans had planned a seven-day campaign to seize Antwerp, and they were counting on the good quality road system to the west of Monschau and Elsenborn Ridge to help them achieve that objective.

From Monschau highways led north and south, and east and west. A key road led directly northwest 27 kilometres (17 mi) to Eupen where the V Corps headquarters was located. That same road continued on 12 kilometres (7.5 mi) further to Liège where General Courtney Hodges maintained the First Army Headquarters. This included the vast supply depots positioned in the Namur-Liège areas.

On 16 December the only combat unit guarding the highway to Eupen was the 38th Cavalry Reconnaissance Squadron.

German units and plans in the north

"We gamble everything!" were the words used by Gerd von Rundstedt, commander-in-chief of the German Western Front,[97] to describe Unternehmen Wacht am Rhein ("Watch on the Rhine"). Adolf Hitler first officially outlined his surprise counter-offensive to his astonished generals on September 16, 1944. The assault's ambitious goal was to pierce the thinly held lines of the U.S. First Army between Monschau and Wasserbillig with Army Group B (Model) by the end of the first day, get the armor through the Ardennes by the end of the second day, reach the Meuse between Liège and Dinant by the third day, and seize Antwerp and the western bank of the Schelde estuary by the fourth day.[1–64] The Germans had designated five rollbahns or routes through the sector near Elsenborn which would give them direct access

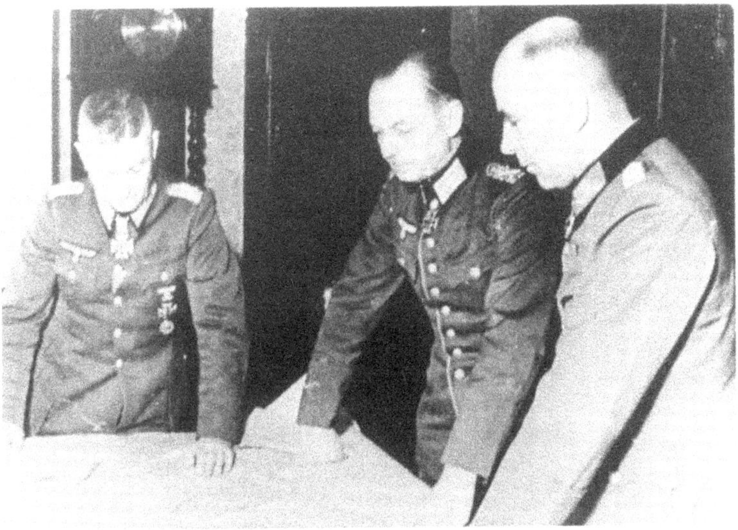

Figure 30: *Walter Model, Gerd von Rundstedt and Hans Krebs plan for the Ardennes Offensive (Battle of the Bulge) in November 1944.*

to the road network leading to the valuable port of Antwerp, splitting the allied American and British armies. Hitler believed the attack would inflame rivalries between the Americans and the British.[:19–20] He felt certain the two countries would negotiate a peace as a result. His generals tried to persuade him to set a less ambitious goal, but he was adamant.[:216] As they had done in 1914 and 1940, they planned to attack through the Losheim Gap in Belgium.

Adolf Hitler personally selected for the counter-offensive on the northern shoulder of the western front the best troops available and officers he trusted. The lead role in the attack was given to Sepp Dietrich's 6th Panzer Army, while the 5th Panzer Army was to attack to their south, covering their flank. The 6th Panzer Army was given priority for supply and equipment and were assigned the shortest route to the ultimate objective of the offensive, Antwerp.[:1–64] The 6th Panzer Army included the elite of the Waffen-SS, including four Panzer divisions and five infantry divisions in three corps.[:8:69] Hitler personally designated a group of 70 short tons (64 t), 128mm Jagdtiger tank destroyers from the 653rd Heavy Panzerjäger Battalion to assist with the attack, although their rail transport was held up by American air attacks.[:73]

Monschau

The German troops holding the region around Monschau were part of the LXVII Armeekorps led by General der Infanterie Otto Hitzfeld. They had

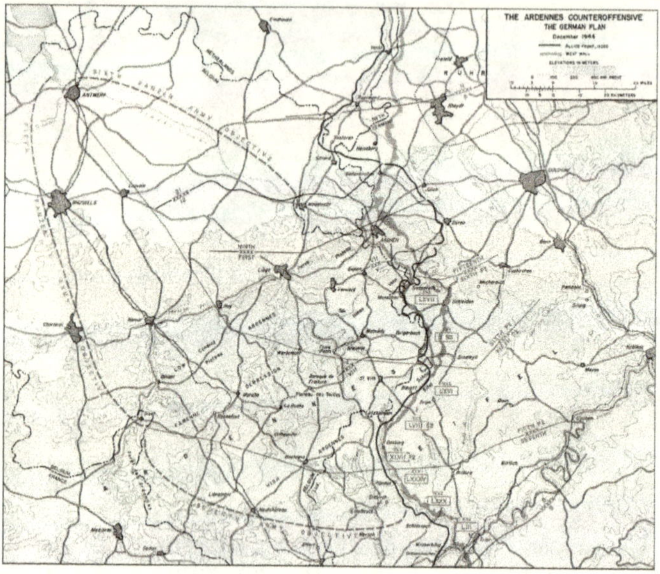

Figure 31: *The German's original plan for the Wacht Am Rhein Offensive called for the LXVII Armeekorps to capture the area north and south of Monschau.*

Figure 32: *Map depicting the northern shoulder of the Battle of the Bulge, or Ardennes Offensive, in which the German Sixth Panzer Army attacked United States' troops, but could not dislodge them. The 2nd and 99th Division's effective defense of the sector prevented the Germans from accessing the valuable road network and considerably slowed their timetable, allowing the Allies to bring up the 1st and 9th Infantry Divisions as reinforcements.*

been placed under the command of the Sixth Panzer Army in preparation for Wacht Am Rhein. The LXVII Armeekorps sector covered about 32 kilometres (20 mi), from a point just south of Vossenack 10 kilometres (6.2 mi) northeast of Monschau, to a point southeast of Camp d'Elsenborn in the south. Although it occupied a critical junction, Field Marshal Walter Model forbid German artillery from firing on the resort village of Monschau, known for its ancient timbered buildings and as a site for honeymooners and artists.:[73]

The LXVII Armeekorps was composed of the 326th and the 246th Volksgrenadier Division. The 326th was designated to take the area north and south of Monschau, which Field Marshal Walter Model had directed should be spared destruction. The 246th was tasked with taking Höfen and Monschau and nearby villages and then driving northwest to seize the Eupen road.

According to Dietrich's plan, the LXVII Armeekorps would secure the Sixth Panzer Army's northern flank. By sidestepping Monschau to seize the area of poor roads, forested hills, and upland moors of the Hohe Venn, the LXVII's two divisions would block the main roads leading into the breakthrough area from the north and east. Simultaneously, the I SS Panzer Corps to the south would use its three infantry divisions to punch holes in the American line and swing northwesterly to join the left flank of the LXVII Corps. Together, the five divisions would form a solid shoulder, behind which the Panzers of the I and II SS Panzer Corps would advance along the Sixth Panzer Army's routes leading west and northwest.

Butgenbach-Malmedy

The Sixth Panzer Army was set to attack in two waves. The first wave included the LXVII Corps and the newly organized 272nd Volksgrenadier and 326th Volksgrenadier Divisions. Also part of the attack the I SS Panzer Corps, with the 1st SS Panzer Division and 12th SS Panzer Division, the 12th Volksgrenadier Division and 277th Volksgrenadier Division, and the 3rd Fallschirmjäger Division.

The Sixth Panzer Army's 1,000-plus artillery pieces and 90 Tiger tanks made it the strongest force deployed. Although Dietrich's initial sector frontage was only 23 miles (37 km), his assault concentrated on less than half that ground. Relying on at least a 6:1 troop superiority at the breakthrough points, he expected to overwhelm the Americans and reach the Meuse River by nightfall of the third day.

The I SS Panzer Corps included the 1st SS Panzer Division and the 12th SS Panzer Division. The 1st had been formed from Adolf Hitler's personal bodyguard regiment. It had the primary responsibility for breaking through the Allied lines and reaching the Meuse River and then Antwerp, Belgium. Major General Engel's 12th SS Panzer Division was composed of junior officers and enlisted men who had been drawn from members of the Hitler Youth, while its senior NCOs and officers were generally veterans of the Eastern Front. The I SS Panzer Corps was given the critical role of breaking through two east-west roads in the northern sector of the Ardennes, code-named Rollbahn C and D.:216

Krinkelt-Rocherath

The Germans hoped to preserve their armor by attacking the American lines with infantry, followed up by the armor. The 3rd Panzer Grenadier Division and the 277th Volksgrenadier Division were given the vital role of pushing the Americans out of the twin villages of Krinkelt-Rocherath in the north. This would allow the Deitrich's Sixth Army to attack west over Rollbahn C. To the south, the 3rd Fallschirmjäger Division and the 12th Volksgrenadier Division were in charge of opening the way to Rollbahn D for Kampfgruppe SS Standartenführer Joachim Peiper's 1st SS Panzer Division.:216

Dietrich planned to commit his third corps, the II SS Panzer Corps, with the 2nd SS Panzer Division and 9th SS Panzer Divisions, in the second wave. Once I SS Panzer had broken the American lines, the 2nd SS Panzer Division would exploit the opening. Among the thirty-eight Waffen-SS divisions, it was an elite Waffen-SS unit. The 9th SS Panzer Division was an armored division formed of 18-year-old German conscripts led by a cadre of experienced staff from the 1st SS Panzer Division. Only minor units of the II SS Panzer Corps were involved in the initial assault and the rest of the corps was committed to major action near St. Vith on 21 December 1944. When the northern assault stalled, the corps was transferred south to help take Bastogne, where it suffered heavy losses.:216

von Rundstedt believed the operation would decide the outcome of the war. A German document captured by the 394th Inf. Regt. on Dec. 16 contained his orders:[131]

> *Soldiers of the West Front: Your great hour has struck. Strong attacking armies are advancing today against the Anglo-Americans. I don't need to say more to you. You all feel it. Everything is at stake. You bear in yourselves a holy duty to give everything and to achieve the superhuman for our fatherland and our Fuhrer!*

Elsenborn Ridge

To maximize the speed of the operation, and to avoid potential bottlenecks and logistical confusion, the two armored divisions of the 1st SS-Panzer Corps were assigned separate routes west. The 12th SS Panzer Division was to utilize three routes (Rollbahn A, B and C) to the north through Elsenborn, Bütgenbach, Malmedy, Spa, and Liège. The 1st SS Panzer Division was given two routes

Figure 33: *Vehicles of the 99th Division moving through Wirtzfeld en route to Elsenborn.*

in the south (Rollbahn D and E) through Losheim, Lieugneville, Vielsalm, Werbomont, and Huy.

The German plan of advance included Rollbahn A passing through a cross-road in the center of Rocherath and Rollbahn B skirting the southern edge of Krinkelt and continuing on toward Wirtzfeld. The Germens' first objective was to break through the defending line of the inexperienced U.S. 99th Infantry Division and positions of battle-hardened 2nd Infantry Division. Once they cleared the Americans from the twin villages, they needed to seize Elsenborn Ridge so they could control the roads to the south and west and ensure supply to the German troops.

Paratroop drop

The plan also included Operation Stößer, a paratrooper drop deep behind the American lines in the High Fens at the Baraque Michel crossroads 7 miles (11 km) north of Malmedy. Their objective was to seize terrain and bridges ahead of the main body after the two corps broke through the American defenses The drop was set for 03:00 on 17 December and they were to hold the crossroads for 24 hours until the arrival of the 12th SS Panzer Division.

Initial Allied positions

The 3rd Battalion, 395th Infantry Regiment arrived in Hofen on 10 November 1944. The American defenders around Elsenborn occupied a long narrow hill mass, about 6,000 yards (5,500 m) long. From it they could see the fields and roads to both the east and west. The hillsides were densely wooded and armored units could only use the few roads.

They began preparing defensive positions along a very long line closely following the international highway from near Monschau, Germany, south nearly 19 miles (31 km) to Losheimergraben, Belgium. The thin lines of the 394th were in places only 800 metres (2,600 ft) from the German lines. There were insufficient troops to prepare defensive positions along the entire front, and the Americans could only maintain a series of strong points. Each regiment was responsible for protecting approximately 11 kilometres (6.8 mi) of front, roughly equivalent to one front-line infantry man every 91 metres (299 ft). There were unoccupied and undefended gaps along the entire line which could only be patrolled. The best they could do was man a series of strongpoints. They had no reserves. Lt. Col. McClernand Butler, commanding officer of the 395th, later wrote:

> That is three to four times wider than recommended by Army textbooks. I never dreamed that we would have a defensive position of this size without any backup or help from our division or regiment. When I got to Höfen, I found the area too big to cover in one afternoon. So I stayed in the village overnight.":79

Except for their positions around Höfen, the 99th Division and its three regiments, the 393rd, 394th, and the 395th were positioned within towns and villages to the east and south of Elsenborn Ridge and in the thick coniferous forest around them, carpeted with a blanket of snow.:77–78 The division had not yet fired its weapons in battle.

Monschau to Höfen

In early November, the 102d Cavalry Group and the 38th Cavalry Reconnaissance Squadron, about 900 troops each, attached to the 102nd Cavalry Group, were assigned to defend the front lines to the north of Elsenborn Ridge from Monschau to Höfen, Germany. The 38th Cavalry was responsible for about 10 kilometres (6.2 mi) of the front lines from Monschau to Höfen. Some of the 38th Cavalry Squadron's positions lay within about 200 yards (180 m) from the German bunkers on the Siegfried Line.

Next to the 38th Cavalry Squadron, the similarly sized 3rd Battalion, 395th Infantry, 99th Infantry Division, occupied a 1,000 yards (910 m) front on the eastern side of the village of Hofen. To the southeast of the 38th Cavalry,

Figure 34: *A camouflaged pillbox in the forest served as a regimental command post.*

the 99th Infantry Division held a line dug into the forest along a line about 2 miles (3.2 km) east of Krinkelt-Rocherath, roughly following the international highway, stretching from Höfen, Germany, about 35 kilometres (22 mi) to Losheimergraben, Belgium, in the south.

A single platoon of 40 men from Company L was held in reserve. In the event of an emergency, the battalion headquarters and company administrative personnel, including clerks and motor-pool staff, were to join the platoon, creating a small reserve force of about 100 men. If the Germans penetrated Höfen, the U.S. soldiers would have to withdraw several miles to the next defensible position.

On December 14, the veteran soldiers of Company A, 612th Tank Destroyer Battalion, dispersed its twelve towed 3-inch guns throughout the defensive system of Butler's Regiment around Höfen. They prepared firing positions against any forces approaching the road network and the village of Rohren, northeast of Höfen, which lay in the path of the U.S. 2nd Infantry Division's planned line of attack towards the crossroads near Wahlerscheid and from which they anticipated a counterattack. The guns were sited well forward and covered in sheets as camouflage and for protection against the falling snow. The cannons could fire both high-explosive anti-personnel and armor-piercing shells.

Hofen to Büllingen

With such a long front to watch over, Maj. Gen. Walter E. Lauer found it necessary to place all three regiments on line. The 1st and 3rd Battalions of the 395th Infantry Regiment in the north, about 600 front-line infantry men, held a position about 6,000 yards (5,500 m) long and had no units in reserve.

The infantry at Höfen lay in a long line of foxholes along 910 metres (2,990 ft) of the front on the eastern side of the village, backed up by dug-in support positions. These would later prove instrumental in defending themselves from the attacking Germans and in protecting themselves when their own artillery fired on or just in front of their own positions, which happened at least six times over the next few weeks.

The 99th Infantry Division used the relative quiet of the front to prepare an extensive defensive system, including redundant lines of communication, precise positioning of weapons to provide interlocking grazing fire, and aggressive patrols that kept the Germans off guard. They also carefully integrated artillery support that was planned and registered on likely targets based on the squadron's obstacles and likely enemy approaches. The 393rd Regiment held the center and the 394th watched over the south.

Büllingen to Lanzerath

The American defensive line in the Ardennes had a gap south of Losheimergraben. General Leonard T. Gerow, in command of V Corps, recognized this area as a possible avenue of attack by the Germans. This area, which lay between V Corps and Troy H. Middleton's VIII Corps, was undefended; just patrolled by jeep. The patrols in the northern part of the area were conducted by the 99th Infantry Division's 394th Intelligence and Reconnaissance Platoon, whereas those in the south were conducted by the 18th Cavalry Squadron, 14th Cavalry Group, attached to the 106th Infantry Division of the VIII Corps.

On December 10, an 18-man reconnaissance platoon led by 20-year-old Lt. Lyle Bouck, the second youngest man in the unit,[84] was ordered by Major Robert Kriz, the 394th Regiment commanding officer, to a new position, about 6 miles (9.7 km) south east of Hünningen, near Lanzerath, Belgium, a village of about 15 homes. The village lay at a critical road junction in the northern part of the Losheim Gap. The 18-man unit was charged by Kriz with plugging a 5 miles (8.0 km) gap in the front line between the 106th Division to the south and the 99th Division to the north. Unknown to them, their position was outside the V Corps boundary. The only reserve was the 394th Infantry Regiment's 3rd Battalion, which was at Bucholz Station. Beyond their positions lay roads that would give the enemy rapid access to the Army's rear and allow them to easily flank the thinly placed 99th Division. Also present in the village were four U.S. Forward Artillery Observers.[58]

Figure 35: *A towed M5 three-inch gun of the U.S. 7th Armored Division on 23 December 1944 in Vielsalm, Belgium.*

The reconnaissance platoon was reinforced by Task Force X, made up of four towed three-inch guns from the 2nd Platoon, Company A, 820th Tank Destroyer Battalion, which was attached to the 14th Cavalry Group, 106th Infantry Division located to their south. They were reinforced by the 22 men of the 820th's 2nd Recon Platoon, commanded by Lieutenant John Arculeer, who were mounted on an armored half-track and two jeeps.[25]

By mid-December, the troops were well dug in and had wired their positions with trip flares and barbed wire. They covered their fox holes with felled timbers. The weather was unusually calm and bone-chilling cold. Between 19 December 1944 and 31 January 1945, the average maximum temperature on the front lines in Europe was 33.5 °F. (0.83 °C.), and the average minimum temperature 22.6 °F. (–5.2 °C.).

Battle of Heartbreak Crossroads

The Battle of Heartbreak Crossroads, part of the Battle of Hürtgen Forest and the attempt to capture the Roer River dams, was fought at a vital crossroads near a forester's cabin named Wahlerscheid, astride the Siegfried Line that ran along the Hoefen-Alzen and Dreiborn ridges, about 5.6 miles (9.0 km) north of Krinkelt-Rocherath.[610] In early December, the U.S. V Corps trucked the experienced 2nd Infantry Division from positions it had held in the south to Krinkelt-Rocherath, twin villages near the southern tip of the Battle of Hürtgen Forest. On the eastern side of the Siegfried Line was an excellent road network leading to the Roer River dams a few miles to the northeast and the Allies' next goal. The Americans were assigned with capturing the crossroads with the goal of destroying the dams, or failing that, force the Germans to blow them up.

After attacking for two days without any results, on 14 December two U.S. squads crawling on their stomachs found a way through the well-emplaced German guns on the south side of the road. They cut the barbed wire and forged a path between the German defenses. They penetrated a trench line behind the pill boxes and held off German patrols for five hours, but when darkness fell they returned to the American lines. On 15 December, an American patrol advanced once more through the breach in the barbed wire and captured a portion of the trench line. They alerted the regimental command post, and Colonel Higgens, commanding officer of the 2nd Battalion, led two companies of GIs into the trenches behind the pill boxes. By the early morning of December 16, the 9th Infantry Regiment pressed the attack another 1,500 yards (1,400 m) against stubborn resistance and captured the crossroads and the road network around it. They gained control of the crossroads, but didn't have sufficient TNT on hand to destroy the pillboxes.

During the night of the 16th and dawn of the 17th, the Germans attacked to the east of Rocherath and Krinkelt and made a deep penetration. They were liable at any moment to come bursting out of the forest. Robertson ordered the 2nd Division with its heavy weapons and vehicles to withdraw to the twin villages. The 99th Division had already put its last reserve into the battle. The 2nd Division with the attached 395th were the only units in line defend the endangered sector of the corridor south of Wahlerscheid.

The 9th Infantry Regiment pulled back to another crossroads in the forest at Baracken, about 5 miles (8.0 km) to the south of the cross roads at Wahlerscheid. The other 2nd Division units moved south through the area near the twin villages. Robertson moved his headquarters from Wirtzfeld, south and west of the twin villages, to Elsenborn, just west of the ridge line. Robertson also informed General Gerow, commander of V Corps, that he intended to hold the twin villages until troops east of the villages had retreated through them to the ridge line, which then would become the next line of defense. This defensive line was intended to safeguard the key high ground on Elsenborn Ridge from the German advance.

German attack

16 December

On the morning of Saturday, 16 December, a snowstorm blanketed the forests and the temperature dropped to 10 °F (–12 °C). The attack opened with a massive artillery bombardment along a 100 miles (160 km) wide front just before 5:30 AM. When the Germans began their barrage that morning, U.S. commanders initially believed that the German attack was a retaliatory assault in response to the American advance at the Wahlerscheid crossroads. Large numbers of German infantry from the 12th Volksgrenadier Division followed the barrage and attacked, beginning the ground offensive from the International Highway 2 miles (3.2 km) east of the twin villages.[75–106]

The German 277th Volksgrenadier Division responsible for capturing Krinkelt-Rocherath was composed for the most part of recent, inexperienced and poorly trained infantry conscripts. They were assigned the task of capturing the twin villages of Krinkelt-Rocherath, just southeast of Elsenborn Ridge. Rocherath to the north and Krinkelt to the south share the same main street. They were the first German infantry force to advance on the Americans.

The German's initial position was east of the German-Belgium border and the Siegfried Line near Losheim. Peiper's unit was assigned responsibility for the key route on the northern part of the offensive, attacking roughly along the line of the Albert Canal from Aachen to Antwerp. Dietrich's plan was for the Sixth Panzer Division to follow 12th Volksgrenadier Division infantry who were tasked with capturing the villages and towns immediately west of the International Highway along the Lanzerath-Losheimergraben road and to advance northwest on Losheimergraben. From there they would capture Bucholz Station and then drive 72 miles (116 km) through Honsfeld, Büllingen, and a group of villages named Trois-Ponts, to connect to Belgian Route Nationale N-23, and cross the River Meuse.[70] They planned to reach the Meuse in three days.

German main line of advance

The northern assault was led by the I SS Panzer Corps, composed of two SS Panzer divisions, the 12th and 1st SS Panzer Divisions and supporting units. The 12th was allotted three of the five Rollbahns allocated to the 1st SS Panzer Corps through the Ardennes forest, the major choke point of the entire drive west.[161–162] The 1st SS Panzer Division was the spearhead of the attack, led by SS Oberstgruppenführer Sepp Dietrich's 6th Panzer Army, which consisted of 4,800 men and 600 vehicles, including 35 Panthers, 45 Panzer IVs, 45 Tiger IIs, 149 half-tracks, 18 105mm artillery, 6 150mm artillery, and 30 anti-aircraft weapons.

Figure 36: *A heavily armed member of Kampfgruppe Hansen carries ammunition boxes forward during an ambush that completely destroyed the U.S. 14th Cavalry Group on the road between the villages Poteau and Recht.*

Unfortunately for the Germans, during their retreat earlier that autumn they had destroyed the Losheim-Losheimergraben road bridge over the railway. German engineers were slow to repair the bridge on the morning of 16 December, preventing German vehicles from using this route. A railroad overpass they had selected as an alternative route could not bear the weight of the German armor. Peiper instead directed his lead tank to cross the railroad and climb the embankment, but as soon as it reached the top on the far side, Peiper received new orders directing him west along the road through Lanzerath to Bucholz Station.[34] He pulled back and headed for Lanzerath instead.

The infantry advance was also supported by an array of searchlights that lit up the clouds like moonlight allowing the inexperienced German infantry to find their way, but in some locations the German troops, backlit by the searchlights, became easy targets for American forces. These clouds and the snowstorms to follow prevented the superior Allied air forces from attacking German forces and temporarily tipped the operation in the German's favor.[75–106] The American troops in the forward positions near the International Highway were quickly overrun and killed, captured, or even ignored by the Germans, intent on keeping to their time table for a rapid advance towards their eventual goal of Antwerp.[75–106]

Figure 37: *German infantry advance through the Ardennes forest.*

Fighting for Monschau and Höfen

The U.S. 3rd Battalion, 395th IR was positioned about 5 miles (8.0 km) to the north of Elsenborn Ridge near the towns of Monschau and Höfen. From 0525 to 0530 on 16 December, the battalion's positions "in and around Höfen received a heavy barrage of artillery and rockets covering our entire front line."[132:173] The enemy artillery, *Werfers*, and mortars fire cut all land-line communication channels between the front-line units and headquarters. Only some radio communications between front line and the heavy weapons company remained intact.

Twenty minutes after the barrage was lifted, at 0555, German infantry from the 753rd Volksgrenadier Regiment, Heeresgruppe B, attacked the 395th in the dark in strength along five different points. The Volksgrenadier were new units formed within the German army in the fall of 1944. They were formed by conscripting boys and elderly men, men previously rejected as physically unfit for service, wounded soldiers returning from hospitals, and transfers from the "jobless" personnel of the quickly shrinking Kriegsmarine and Luftwaffe, usually organized around small cadres of hardened veterans.

The German attack concentrated in the battalion's center, between I and K Companies. Another German force attempted to penetrate the Monschau area,

Figure 38: *A U.S. First Army soldier manning an M1 81mm mortar listens for fire direction on a field phone during the German Ardennes offensive.*

immediately north of the Battalion's extreme left flank. Without radio communications between the front-line artillery liaison officer and 196th Field Artillery, their guns could not be brought to bear on the German assault until communication was restored in the midst of the battle at 0650. The 395th was outnumbered five to one and was at times surrounded. They initially pushed the Germans back with machine guns, small arms, mortar fire, and hand-to-hand combat. Without any significant armor support, the 395th stopped the German advance cold. U.S. artillery had registered the forward positions of the U.S. infantry and rained fire on the exposed advancing Germans while the U.S. soldiers remained in their covered foxholes. It was the only sector of the American front line on the Battle of the Bulge where the Germans failed to advance.:33

By 07:45, the Germans withdrew, except for a group of the 753rd Volksgrenadier Regiment who penetrated the Battalion's center. They were soon repulsed.

Just after noon, at 1235, the Germans launched their attack again, and they were pushed back by artillery and mortar fire. The result of the first day of what would become known as the Battle of the Bulge were 104 Germans dead "in an area 50 yards (46 m) yards in front of our lines to 100 yards (91 m) behind the line, and another 160 wounded counted in front of battalion lines.":[173] The 3rd Battalion lost four killed, seven wounded, and four missing. "We learned from a German Lieutenant prisoner of war that the enemy's mission was to take Höfen at all costs.":[173]

Withdrawal from Heartbreak Crossroads

By the late evening of 16 December General Gerow, commander of US V Corps, recognized the magnitude of the attack. He first ordered General Walter Robertson, Commander of the 2nd Division, to hold in place and await further orders. Early the next morning he told Robertson to turn south and withdraw to a crossroads just north of the twin villages where they were to establish a road block.:[221] Robertson's troops were heavily engaged and withdrawal was complicated, but the forces peeled backward from the vital crossroads at Wahlerscheid that they had captured only the day before.

The 9th Infantry Regiment pulled back to the Baracken crossroads in the forest about 5 miles (8.0 km) to the south of the cross roads at Wahlerscheid. The other units moved south through the area near the twin villages. Robertson moved his headquarters from Wirtzfeld, south and west of the twin villages, to Elsenborn, just west of the ridge line. Robertson also informed General Gerow that he intended to hold the twin villages until troops east of the villages had retreated through them to the ridge line, which then would become the next line of defense. This defensive line was intended to safeguard the key high ground on Elsenborn Ridge from the German advance.

To the east of Rocherath and Krinkelt, the Germans had made a deep penetration and were liable at any moment to come bursting out of the forest. The U.S. had to hold the twin villages to allow the 2nd ID with its heavy weapons and vehicles to reach positions around Elsenborn intact. The 99th Division had already put its last reserve into the battle. The 2nd ID with the attached 395th were left to defend the endangered sector of the corridor south.

On the morning of 16 December, immediately southeast of Elsenborn, the 1st SS Panzer Division, spearhead of the entire German 6th Panzer Army, a critical element in the German offensive, was assigned to advance through the Losheim Gap and Losheimergraben. Peiper received new orders to advance towards Lanzerath. He was preceded by the 12th and 277th Volksgrenadier Divisions, but they failed to gain control of Lanzerath on the first day as planned.:[113–114] But before even reaching Lanzerath, Peiper lost three tanks to German mines and was slowed by mine-clearing operations.

The area around Elsenborn Ridge became a collection point for ragtag groups of American troops whose units been broken and scattered at the start of the enemy offensive. With so many troops from different units arriving in every kind of condition, organizing a coherent defense was a huge task, but one that occurred with surprising speed under the circumstances. Intelligence about the attack that reached the Americans was spotty and contradictory. General Lauer, commanding officer of the 99th, ordered Col. Robertson at Wahlerscheid to stay put until at least the next morning when more orders would be forthcoming. Robertson told his men to hold and he also prepared them for an orderly withdrawal in the morning.:75–106

Battle for Dom Butgenbach

To the northeast of the 99th Division, the 1st Infantry Division had been recuperating near Liege, from nearly constant combat after landing on D-Day. When the German counterattack broke out and while the fight for the twin villages raged, the division hastily relocated on any available transport to the unguarded southern end of the 99th's line near Bütgenbach. Troops from the U.S. 1st and 9th Infantry Divisions, moved into position to fortify Elsenborn Ridge and complete the defense. The 9th Division held positions on the northern portion of the ridge, in the vicinity of Kalterherberg.

The 2nd Battalion, 26th Infantry, First Infantry Division, commanded by Lt. Col. Derrill M. Daniels, linked up with the 99th. The rest of the 1st Division was strung out to the west to prevent the Germans from turning north. Its three companies were understrength, only able to field about 100 troops each. Daniels positioned them in a perimeter around a strongly built stone house that sat astride the road. He ordered the troops to dig in and build overhead cover. Their job was to kill the German infantry and let the armor pass. Daniels placed his three M-10 tank destroyers and a platoon of four M4 Shermans in the center.

17 December

Held up by their inability to cross the railroad bridge that German engineers were slow to repair, and by the Intelligence and Reconnaissance platoon of the 394th Infantry Regiment at Lanzerath Ridge, elements of the 1st SS Panzer Division did not arrive in force at Daniel's position until the afternoon of 17 December. Finding Rollbahn C blocked, they initially pushed off to the south for Rollbahn D. The Germans changed their mind and on 18 December the 12th SS Panzer Division was given the task of opening up the road. They made a probing attack that afternoon which failed.

By the afternoon of 17 December, the 395th Regiment realized that the day's action was part of a much larger offensive. At one point in the middle of the next night, a German company commander marched his company of about 200 men up to a house that he thought was unoccupied, and next to a ditch in which an infantryman with a BAR was dug in.

Figure 39: *American soldiers of Company G, 38th Infantry Regiment, 2nd Infantry Division, U.S. First Army, take refuge in doorways during mortar barrage laid down by Germans after the Americans seized a German forest stronghold camouflaged as a two-story residence.*

Once the German officer got there, he called for a meeting of his noncoms—at a spot right in front of this BAR man's foxhole. That was a long night. The BAR man stood it just as long as he could and then he cut loose. The Germans pulled back to organize, and he pulled back to another foxhole. They attacked and he cut them down again. Then he moved back to his original foxhole and the Germans attacked where he'd been. He cut them down again. Then the rest of the men in the eight-man squad got into the act. Come daylight, there was one lieutenant and about eight Germans left.

Attack on Krinkelt-Rocherath

16–17 December

Figure 40: *Sgt. Bernard Cook guards a German prisoner walking past a burning Panzerkampfwagen V Panther tank at Krinkelt on 17 December 1944.*

Operation Stößer fails

The Germans Operation Stößer planned to drop paratroopers in the American rear in the High Fens area 11 kilometres (6.8 mi) north of Malmédy and to seize the key Baraque Michel crossroads leading to Antwerp. The operation led by Oberst Friedrich August Freiherr von der Heydte was a complete failure. To conceal the plans from the Allies and preserve secrecy, von der Heydte wasn't allowed to use his own, experienced troops. Most of the new paratroops had little training.

The Luftwaffe somehow managed to assemble 112 Ju 52 transport planes, but the pilots were very inexperienced. The pilots took off into strong winds, snow, and limited visibility. It was the German paratroopers' only night-time drop during World War II. While the aircraft took off with around 1,300 *Fallschirmjäger*, the pilots dropped some behind the German front lines, others over Bonn, and only a few hundred in widely scattered locations behind the American lines. Some aircraft landed with their troops still on board. Only a fraction of the force landed near the intended drop zone.[161] The planes that were relatively close to the intended drop zone were buffeted by strong winds that deflected many paratroopers and made their landings far rougher. Since

Figure 41: *A Tiger II of schwere SS Panzer Abteilung 501 advances west past a column of American prisoners of the 99th Infantry Division captured at Honsfeld and Lanzerath.*

many of the German paratroopers were very inexperienced, some were crippled upon impact and died where they fell. Some of their bodies were found the following spring as the snow melted.[218]

The mis-drops led to considerable confusion among the Americans, as *Fallschirmjäger* were reported all over the Ardennes, and the Allies believed a major division-sized jump had taken place. The Americans allocated men to secure the rear instead of facing the main German thrust at the front.[88] By noon on 17 December, von der Heydte's unit had scouted the woods and rounded up a total of around 300 troops. With only enough ammunition for a single fight, the force was too small to take the crossroads on its own.[89]

17 December

Capture Honsfeld and Büllingen

In the early morning of 17 December, Kampfgruppe Peiper quickly captured Honsfeld and shortly afterward, Büllingen. The Tiger IIs consumed about .5 miles per US gallon (470 L/100 km; 0.60 mpg$_{-imp}$)[108] Peiper's unit seized 50,000 US gallons (190,000 l; 42,000 imp gal) of fuel for his vehicles. The

Germans paused to refuel before continuing westward. They had been assigned Rollbahn B which would take them through Spa, Belgium.

At 0930 on 17 December, Peiper sent a section of the Kampfgruppe in reconnaissance to the north, but they quickly encountered strong American resistance improvised by a barrage of tank-destroyers of the 644th Tank Destroyer Battalion and lost two Panzer IV. Two days into the offensive, the high ground of Elsenborn Ridge and two of the three routes the Germans planned to use remained solidly within American fortified defense zones.:410

Believing the way north to Rollbahn B was blocked, and knowing that the 12th Panzer was well behind him, unable to dislodge the Americans from Elsenborn Ridge, Kampfgruppe Peiper and the 1st SS Panzer Division were forced to choose the more difficult Rollbahn D to the south in its drive west to the Meuse River.:371 The road was narrow, in many places single-track, at times unpaved. When Peiper reviewed his newly assigned alternative route on a map, he exclaimed that the road was "suitable not for tanks but for bicycles!":70:108 The route forced vehicles to tail each other, creating a column of infantry and armor up to 25 kilometres (16 mi) long, and prevented them from concentrating their force which was their most effective use.

17 December

The main drive against Elsenborn Ridge was launched in the forests east of the twin villages on the early morning of 17 December. This attack was begun by tank and Panzergrenadier units of the 12th SS Panzer Division. The 989th Infantry Regiment of the 277th succeeded, after heavy and costly combat in the woods, in overrunning the forward U.S. positions guarding the trails to the villages, capturing a large number of prisoners and leaving many small units isolated behind the front lines. By 11:00, this attack had driven units of the U.S. 99th Infantry Division back into the area of the twin villages. These units were joined by forces of the U.S. 2nd Infantry Division moving into the villages from the north. The German attack swiftly bogged down against the heavy small arms and machine gun fire from prepared positions of the American 99th Infantry Division on their flanks. The 990/277 and 991/277 Infantry Regiments had less success, struggling to get through the dense woods and heavy brush in their path.

At Krinkelt, T/5 Sgt Vernon McGarity was wounded by the early morning artillery barrage. After he was treated, he refused to be evacuated and returned to his squad. He and his squad repulsed four German tanks and their supporting infantry, and McGarity repeatedly braved direct fire to secure ammunition and rescue wounded soldiers. McGarity and his squad held the German forces back for a full day and were only captured on the morning of 17 December when they ran out of ammunition. The German forces also drew a rapid response

Figure 42: *A patrol of Company F, 3rd Battalion, 18th Infantry Regiment, 1st Infantry Division, searches the woods between Eupen and Butgenbach, Belgium, for German parachutists who were dropped in that area*

from U.S. artillery, who had registered the forward positions of their infantry. The artillery rained fire on the exposed advancing Germans while the U.S. troops remained in their covered foxholes.

In another example of the fierce, close fighting, a single soldier was responsible for disabling several tanks during a 24-hour period. On the evening of 17 December in nearby Rocherath, Pfc William A. Soderman of Company K, 9th Infantry, 2nd Infantry Division, heard enemy tanks approaching his position in the early evening. Armed with a bazooka, he waited until five Panthers were within pointblank range. He stood up in the road and fired a rocket into the lead tank, setting it on fire. The other tanks passed him by, but the next morning he repeated his actions. When five more German tanks approached, he jumped onto the road in front of the tanks and disabled the lead tank. The remaining tanks were unable to bypass the lead tank and withdrew. Soderman was severely wounded and received the Medal of Honor for his actions.

The troops around the villages were assisted by tanks from the U.S. 741st Tank Battalion, assisted by a company of the 644th Tank Destroyer Battalion equipped with M10 tank destroyers, a company of the 612th Tank Destroyer

Figure 43: *2nd Division infantrymen on the march*

Battalion, and a few towed 3 inch guns from the 801st Tank Destroyer Battalion. They were instrumental in helping hold back the German advance in the fighting in and around Rocherath-Krinkelt.

During the night of 17–18 December, the German attack was not well coordinated, carried out as it was by the advance guards of two divisions attacking piecemeal in the dark over unknown terrain against U.S. resistance which completely surprised the Germans.

Fighting over twin villages

Orders from Field Marshal Walter Model and Generalfeldmarschall Gerd von Rundstedt that Elsenborn Ridge be captured and the advance of Sixth Panzer Army resume had been pouring down the chain of command into 12th SS Panzer Headquarters.[394-395] General Hermann Priess, commander of the 1st SS Panzer Corps, ordered Waffen-SS Obersturmbannführer Hugo Kraas, Commander of the 12th SS Panzer Division, to take command of all forces facing Elsenborn Ridge and capture it.[181-182]

The battle-seasoned veteran American tankers resisted repeated attacks by lead elements of the Sixth Panzer Army from 16–19 December. Fighting against the superior German Panther and Tiger tanks, supported by infantry, the battalion fought many small unit engagements. Using their size and mobility to their advantage, they stalked the German tanks in twos and threes until they could destroy or immobilize them with shots from the flanks or rear.

Figure 44: *Captured soldiers from the 12th SS Panzer Division "Hitler Jugend"*

Fighting near St. Vith

17 December

To Peiper's south, the advance of Kampfgruppe Hansen had stalled. SS Ober-führer Mohnke ordered Schnellgruppe Knittel, which had been designated to follow Hansen, to instead move forward to support Peiper. SS Sturmbann-führer Knittel crossed the bridge at Stavelot around 19:00 against American forces trying to retake the town. Knittel pressed forward towards La Gleize, and shortly afterward the Americans recaptured Stavelot. Peiper and Knittel both faced the prospect of being cut off.:[108]

18 December

The U.S. withdrawal was hastened by an increasing shortage of ammunition. Fortunately for the defense, three tank destroyers of the U.S. 644th Tank De-stroyer Battalion arrived with a good supply of bazookas and anti-tank mines. These reinforcements were put to good use when the 12th SS Panzer Division launched a powerful tank and infantry attack on the twin villages.:[166–167] The U.S. forces responded with a powerful artillery barrage supported by mor-tar fire, bazooka rockets, and anti-tank mines that repelled the German attack around midnight of 18 December.:[376–390] The German attack failed to clear a line of advance for the 12th SS.

Figure 45: *Panzergrenadier-SS Kampfgruppe Hansen in action during clashes in Poteau against Task Force Myers, 18 December 1944*

On 18 December, German infantry and armor resumed their attack on the twin villages. They were supported by the German 560th Heavy Antitank Battalion equipped with the state-of-the-art Jagdpanther tank destroyer.:395,649 The Jagdpanther was armed with the 88mm cannon and the German leadership expected it to be the decisive element of the battle. The battle opened on the morning of the 18th with both sides targeting the village area with repeated artillery strikes, and German armored vehicles advanced into the twin villages. All that day and night, the battle raged, with SS tank and assault guns hitting the villages from the east, supported by a barrage of Nebelwerfer rockets. These forces were met in turn by a hailstorm of U.S. heavy artillery shells with proximity fuses and about 20 Sherman tanks belonging to the U.S. 741st Tank Battalion, and several M10 tank destroyers.

The narrow streets of the town made effective maneuver difficult. Bazooka rounds fired from rooftops and artillery air bursts caused by proximity fuses created a lethal rain of splinters. The Sherman tanks, hiding in alleyways and behind buildings, quickly knocked out six Panzers. Eight more SS Panzers were also hit and destroyed by 57mm anti-tank guns, anti-tank rockets, bazookas, and mines, leaving them unable to swiftly plow through the rubble and gain the open country of the ridge line. Neither side was inclined to take prisoners, and the losses on both sides were catastrophic.:396–401 During the

Figure 46: *12th Volksgrenadier troops strip boots and other equipment from the bodies of three dead U.S. soldiers at the crossroads at Honsfeld, west of Losheimergraben*

German attack, Sgt. Jose M. Lopez single-handedly manned a heavy machine gun. Falling back several times, he ignored enemy tank fire and falling artillery rounds, and killed more than 100 enemy infantry attempting to flank his unit, allowing them to successfully withdraw.

On the morning of 18 December, Kampfgruppe Hansen, strengthened by some tank destroyers, successfully pressed the attack on the road from Recht to Poteau, and Combat Command R suffered heavy losses. On that same afternoon, the Americans were reinforced by Combat Command A of the 7th Armored Division, enabling the Americans to retake the intersection near Poteau and block the advance of Kampfgruppe Hansen. The Germans were temporarily locked down on the Rollbahn and unable to support Peiper, already ahead to the west several miles.Wikipedia:Citing sources

Corps boundary gap

The small village of Lanzerath was at a key intersection southeast of Krinkelt-Rocherath.

It was held by a single Intelligence and Reconnaissance platoon of the 394th Infantry Regiment, who were dug into a ridge near the village of about 15 homes.

Figure 47: *Same crossroads as above, photo taken from different angle to show Losheimergraben junction*

They were initially supported by Task Force X, made up of 2nd Platoon, Company A, 820th Tank Destroyer Battalion and 22 men of the 820th's 2nd Recon Platoon, commanded by Lieutenant John Arculeer, who were mounted on an armored half-track and two jeeps. But shortly after the early morning German bombardment ended, Task Force X pulled out without a word and headed south. That left the 18 men of the reconnaissance platoon alone, along with four forward artillery observers, to fill in the gap.

The U.S. troops were positioned on a slight ridge overlooking the village. During a 20-hour-long battle, the 18-man platoon, led by a 20-year-old lieutenant Lyle Bouck Jr., inflicted 93 casualties on the Germans. The U.S. troops seriously disrupted the entire German Sixth Panzer Army's schedule of attack along the northern edge of the offensive. The entire platoon was captured, and only many years later were they recognized with a Presidential Unit Citation. Every member of the platoon was decorated, making it the most highly decorated platoon of World War II.

19 December

At dawn on 19 December, on the third day of the offensive, the Germans decided to shift the main axis of the attack to the south of Elsenborn Ridge. A new armored attack led by the 12th SS Panzer Division, and supported by infantry of the 12th Volksgrenadier Division, was launched on the position of Domäne Bütgenbach, south east of Bütgenbach, to expose the right flank of the Americans. The 3rd Panzer Grenadier Division, supported by elements of the 12th and 277th Volksgrenadier Division to their left and right, made a frontal attack on the Elsenborn Ridge, with the objective of seizing the high feature called Roderhohe. But the soft ground in front of the ridge was almost impassable. One Sturmgeschütz assault gun after another got stuck, and the Pz Abt 103 of the 3rd Panzer Grenadier Division lost 15 tanks that day to American artillery.[401–404] The 2nd Battalion contributed to stopping the Germans.

During the day of 19 December, a group of about 100 Germans opened a wedge in the American lines about 100 yards (91 m) by 400 yards (370 m) and seized four stone buildings in the village of Höfen. The American's direct rifle and mortar fire failed to dislodge them from the buildings they occupied. The 612th Tank Destroyer Battalion brought their 57mm anti-tank guns to bear directly on them. Follow up attacks with white phosphorus grenades finally caused the remaining 25 Germans to surrender, while 75 were found dead within the buildings. The German attack on the U.S. extreme left flank was repulsed by artillery and rifle fire. Despite the fierce onslaught, the battalion was able to hold onto its reserves, which in any case only consisted of one platoon of forty men from L Company.[173]

U.S. withdrawal to Elsenborn Ridge

(🔟 Works related to The Sixth Panzer Army Attack at Wikisource)

During the day on 19 December all forces abandoned the rubble of the twin villages, and General Robertson ordered the remnants of the 2nd Division to withdraw to defensive positions dug into the open terrain along the ridge. Troops from the remaining elements of the 99th Infantry Division also used this time to withdraw to Elsenborn Ridge and fortify positions on it. They found it required dynamite to blow holes in the frozen ground.[258]

On 19 December, elements of the U.S. 741st Tank Battalion formed the rearguard to allow the Americans an orderly withdrawal from the twin villages to positions behind Wirtzfeld to the west and northwest. By that afternoon the tankers had reported destroying 27 Panzers, two Jagdpanzer IV, two armored cars, and two half-tracks while losing eight of their own tanks. At the battalion level, units reported killing 16 tanks, regimental 57mm guns claimed 19, and bazooka teams reported to have killed 17 more. While the numbers didn't line up, they indicated the ferocity of the fighting. The German Panther companies were rendered ineffective and didn't play a significant role in later fighting.[51]

Figure 48: *Troops cross an open field near Krinkelt*

Figure 49: *Panzergrenadiers of the 1st SS Panzer Division look through abandoned American equipment at Hosfeld*

At 17:30 that evening, the remaining troops of the 393rd and 394th Infantry Regiments of the 99th Infantry Division withdrew from their positions around the Baracken crossroads, just north of the twin towns of Krinkelt and Rocherath, and retreated along a boggy trail about 4 kilometres (2.5 mi) toward Elsenborn Ridge. American lines collapsed on either side of the Regiment. "We were sticking out like a finger there", Butler said. Increasingly isolated, the unit was running low on ammunition. A resourceful platoon leader found an abandoned German ammo dump. "We stopped the tail end of that push with guns and ammunition taken off the German dead", Butler said.

By the time the fight for the villages ended, five U.S. troops had earned the Medal of Honor: Sgt. Lopez, Sgt. Richard Cowan, Pvt. Truman Kimbro, Sgt. Vernon McGarity, and Sgt William Soderman. Another Medal of Honor was posthumously awarded to Henry F. Warner of the 26th Infantry Regiment, 1st Infantry Division who single-handedly disabled several German tanks during a running battle near Bütgenbach through the night and into the day of December 20, 1944 before he was killed.

20 December

On 20 December, bolstered by reinforcements from the 12th Volksgrenadier Division, the Germans attacked from the south and east. This too failed. On 21 December, the Germans tried to bypass Dom Butgenbach to the southwest. A few German armored units penetrated Butgenbach, but the 2nd Battalion assisted by some reinforcements stopped them again.

Defense of Elsenborn Ridge

In an effort to bolster command and control of the northern shoulder, Eisenhower appointed Field Marshal Bernard Law Montgomery, commander of the 21st Army Group, commander of all troops north of the German advance on 20 December. This was done in part because Montgomery controlled an uncommitted reserve, the British XXX Corps.[416-22, 478-9]

This made little difference to the American troops defending Elsenborn Ridge, however. On the same day, the Sixth Panzer Army made several all-out attacks trying to smash U.S.lines. They committed artillery, tanks, infantry, self-propelled guns, supported by an attached Jagdpanther Battalion, remnants of the PzKpfw IV tanks and Jagdpanzer IV tank destroyers. They unsuccessfully attacked at 09:00, 11:00 and 17:30 that day. The 3rd Panzer Grenadier Division, supported by elements of the 12th and 277th Volksgrenadier Division to left and right, made a frontal attack on the Elsenborn Ridge, with the objective of seizing the high feature called Roderhohe. But the German attack on Domäne Bütgenbach to break through the American lines foundered in face

Figure 50: *Troops of the 26th Infantry Regiment reposition an antitank cannon near Butgenbach*

Figure 51: *"A" Company, 612th Tank Destroyer battalion, carrying troops of the 2nd Infantry Division, 9th Infantry Regiment*

Figure 52: *American Heavy Artillery M1 (9.5 inch) howitzer, one of the "Black Dragons", the largest field gun in U.S. service during World War II.*

of strong American resistance.:[51] They were met by a deluge of American artillery and anti-tank gun fire from units of the American 1st Infantry Division.

The American lines were backed up by impressive artillery support. The 3rd Panzer Grenadier Division hit the left or north side of Elsenborn ridge from the Schwalm Creek valley against 99th Infantry Division. But their tanks found the soft ground almost impassible, and one after another the Sturmgeschütz III assault guns bogged down, making them easy prey for the American artillery. On 20 December, the Pz Abt 103 lost a total of fifteen StuG III. Twelve of them bogged down in front of the Elsenborn Ridge, the others ran onto mines inside Krinkelt and Rocherath.Wikipedia:Citation needed The Germans attacked for a second time on the 20th. All these attacks were repelled with heavy losses.:[409]

21 December

On 21 December, the 12th SS Division made an even heavier attack, but the U.S. 613th Tank Destroyer Battalion equipped with the new M36 tank destroyer stopped the attack. On 22 December the Germans attacked on the right of Elsenborn Ridge for the last time which was also smothered by heavy American artillery fire from M1 howitzers. The Americans fired 10,000 rounds in one day. The 26th Infantry Regiment and a company of Sherman tanks from

Figure 53: *Soldiers of the 99th Infantry Division attend a Christian service on New Year's Eve.*

the 745th Tank Battalion played key roles. Fortunately for the Americans, the weather came to their assistance for the first time in the campaign. On 23 December a cold wind from the northeast brought clear weather and froze the ground, allowing free movement of tracked vehicles and the return of U.S. Army Air Forces to the skies. The U.S. defenders cheered wildly at the return of clearer weather and much heavier support. The air attacks played an instrumental role in defeating the German attack.[323: 478–87]

12th Panzer attack stopped

Von Rundstedt had sacrificed most of four of the best divisions on the Western front during his repeated attempts to overrun the Elsenborn Ridge and Monschau. Unable to access the Monschau-Eupen and Malmedy-Verviers roads, he was unable to commit II Panzer Corps, which was still waiting in reserve on the east flank of I SS Panzer Corps. Von Rundstedt's hopes of reaching Liège via Verviers were stopped cold by the stubborn American resistance.

26–29 December

On 26 December, the 246th Volksgrenadier Division made a final, forlorn, attack on the Elsenborn Ridge against units of the U.S. 99th Infantry Division. This attack by more infantry conscripts was mowed down by artillery fire virtually at the moment of its start. The vast artillery concentration of an entire American army corps made the Elsenborn Ridge position virtually unassailable.:404–411

At sunrise on December 27, 1944, Sepp Dietrich and his 6th Panzer Army were in a difficult situation east of Elsenborn Ridge.:411 The 12th SS Panzer Division, 3rd Panzergrenadier Division, and its supporting Volksgrenadier divisions had beaten themselves into a state of uselessness against the heavily fortified American positions on Elsenborn Ridge.:410 They could advance no further, and as the Americans counter-attacked, on 16 January 1945, the Sixth Panzer Army was transferred to the Eastern Front.

1–16 January

The weather improved in late December and early January, allowing Allied planes to attack the Germans from the air and further slow their advance. The Germans launched a Luftwaffe offensive in the Netherlands, destroying many Allied aircraft but sacrificing many more of their own, irreplaceable aircraft and skilled pilots. They also launched a major ground offensive in Alsace on January 1, but they failed to regain the initiative. The end of Battle of the Bulge is officially January 16, exactly one month after the Germans launched it, but fighting continued for three more weeks until early February when the front lines were reestablished to the positions held on 16 December.

Impact of the battle

The organized retreat of the U.S. 2nd and 99th Divisions to the Elsenborn Ridge line and their subsequent stubborn defensive action blocked the 6th Panzer Army's access to key roads in northern Belgium that they were counting on to reach Antwerp. It was the only sector of the American front line on the Battle of the Bulge where the Germans failed to advance.:33 Historian John S.D. Eisenhower noted, "...the action of the 2nd and 99th divisions on the northern shoulder could be considered the most decisive of the Ardennes campaign.":224

Peiper's forces were plagued by overcrowding, flanking attacks, blown bridges, and lack of fuel.:463 The Germans were unable to repeat the rapid advances they achieved in 1940, when General Heinz Guderian's panzers swept from the Ardennes to the English Channel, virtually unopposed.:115

To the west of Elsenborn at Spa, the First Army had established its headquarters surrounded on every side by service installations, ammunition dumps, supply depots, and more than 3,000,000 US gallons (11,000,000 L) of gasoline.

Liège, 20 miles (32 km) northwest of Spa, was the location of one of the largest American supply centers in Europe. Only 11 miles (18 km) from Spa lay

Figure 54: *A dead German soldier lies on a
corner in Stavelot, Belgium, on 2 Jan 1945.*

Verviers, an important and densely stocked railhead. Had the Germans been
able to capture any portion of these supplies, the outcome of the battle might
have been much different.Wikipedia:Citation needed

The cost of this relentless, close-quarters, intense combat was high for both
sides, but the losses for Germany were irreplaceable. An exact casualty ac-
counting for the Elsenborn Ridge battle itself is not precise. The U.S. Army's
2nd and 99th Infantry Divisions later revealed their losses, while only the German's armored fighting vehicles losses are accounted for.:410

Disproportionate German casualties

The casualties inflicted by the 395th Infantry Regiment, 99th Division, on the
Germans are reflected by the disproportionate numbers of dead and wounded.
The 395th hit the Germans with such terrific small arms and machine gun fire
that they couldn't even remove their dead and wounded in their rapid retreat.
The accurate fire from the twelve 3-inch guns of A Company, 612th Tank Destroyer Battalion, was instrumental in keeping German tanks from advancing.
During the first day of the Battle of the Bulge, the 3rd Battalion took 19 prisoners and killed an estimated 200 Germans. Accurate estimates of German
wounded were not possible, but about 20 percent of the 326th Volksgrenadier

Division were lost. The 395th's casualties were extremely light: four dead, seven wounded, and four men missing.:vii :51

On another day, the 3rd Battalion took 50 Germans prisoner and killed or wounded more than 800 Germans, losing only five dead and seven wounded themselves. On more than one occasion, BAR gunners allowed German troops to walk within feet of their positions before opening fire, with the objective of increasing the odds of killing the attacking Germans. "In two cases, the enemy fell in the BAR gunners' foxholes.":173 On at least six occasions they called in artillery strikes on or directly in front of their own positions.

As the battle ensued, small units, company and less in size, often acting independently, conducted fierce local counterattacks and mounted stubborn defenses, frustrating the German's plans for a rapid advance, and badly upsetting their timetable. By 17 December, German military planners knew that their objectives along the Elsenborn Ridge would not be taken as soon as planned.:75–106

The 99th as a whole, outnumbered five to one, inflicted casualties at a ratio of eighteen to one. They devastated the attacking *Volksgrenadier* formations. The 99th lost about 20% of its effective strength, including 465 killed and 2,524 evacuated due to wounds, injuries, fatigue, or trench foot. German losses were much higher. In the northern sector opposite the 99th, this included deaths on a scale that routed the attacking infantry, and included the destruction of many tanks and assault guns. This performance prevented the Sixth Panzer Army from outflanking Elsenborn Ridge, and resulted in many commendations and unit citations for the 99th.

Media attention

The 2nd and the 99th Infantry Divisions defending Elsenborn Ridge, along with the 1st Division to the south and the 78th Division in the north, were the only Allied units that completely stopped the German's main axis of advance during the Battle of the Bulge. The Germans were denied access to three of five planned routes of advance across their northern sector of the battle and were required to significantly alter their plans, considerably slowing their advance in the north. This success allowed the Americans to maintain the freedom to effectively maneuver across the north flank of the German's line of advance and continually limit the success of the German offensive.

But despite their success, other units' actions during the Battle of the Bulge received much greater attention from the press. This was due in part because during early December 1944, Bastogne was a rest and recreation area for many war correspondents. The rapid advance by the German forces that resulted in the town being surrounded, the spectacular resupply operations via parachute and glider, along with the fast action of General Patton's Third U.S. Army, all captured the public's imagination and were featured in newspaper articles and on radio. But there were no correspondents in the area of Saint-Vith, Elsenborn or Monschau. The static, stubborn resistance of troops in the north, who refused to yield their ground in the cold snow and freezing rain despite the heavy German attacks, didn't get a casual observer excited. The image of supply troops trying to bring and ammunition and cold food, crawling through mud and snow, to front-line troops dug into frozen foxholes around Montjoie, Elsenborn and Butgenbach was not exciting news.

After the war, Hasso von Manteuffel, Commanding General of the Fifth Panzer Army, wrote that the German counteroffensive "failed because our right flank near Monschau ran its head against a wall.":6

> *The Battle of the 'Bulge' was not fought solely in Bastogne. Here in the northern sector of the Ardennes, elements of tragedy, heroism and self-sacrifice exerted a great influence upon the result of German intentions. Battles are won in the hearts of men, not only by the combinations of fire and movement, but also by working together. Teamwork is decisive, as was shown in the northern part of the Ardennes.:7*

General Courtney Hodges, Commanding General of the First U.S. Army, wrote the commanding general of the Indianhead Division, "What the Second Infantry Division has done in the last four days will live forever in the history of the United States Army.":8

Weapons and tactics

The Battle of Elsenborn Ridge was a decisive component of the Battle of the Bulge because the U.S. Army was able to stop and deflect the strongest armored units of the German advance.:410 Portions of both sides' forces had little battle experience, and both employed newer, more lethal weapons and tactics. This gave the battle a brutal intensity and impact, resulting in high casualties and traumatic memories and experiences for the participants.

German combined arms

The force and mobility of the attack depended on the commitment of Germany's latest weapons and armored fighting vehicles. At the beginning of World War II, the German army had led the world in mechanized warfare tactics, overwhelming enemies repeatedly with their rapid blitzkrieg attack. Late in the war, the Germans had developed a number of advanced armored vehicles and they planned to use them to beat the Americans, despite not having won a major offensive battle against them since the Kasserine Pass in early

Figure 55: *The 1st Battalion, U.S. 26th Infantry Regiment, lead element of the 1st Infantry Division, pass through the railway viaduct north of Bütgenbach, Belgium, on the Monschauer St. (N647) to Bütgenbach to reinforce the American lines.*

1943. These vehicles were armed with the most powerful weapons used in the course of the war. The Tiger II, Panther tank and Jagdpanther were armed with newer high velocity cannon, the 8.8 cm KwK 43 L/71 cannon, and the 7.5 cm KwK 42.:154–61

Due to their flat trajectory and greater armor penetration and the fact that thicker armor was used to shield them, German tanks enjoyed a definite superiority to any American vehicle in use. These units were supported by new Volks-Werfer Brigades, artillery units firing masses of 150 mm and 300 mm rockets. Although lacking in accuracy, a barrage from these units could cover greater areas with more high explosive. For more infantry firepower, SS panzergrenadiers were equipped with the new Sturmgewehr 44 (*assault rifle model 1944*). This was the world's first assault rifle and more advanced than any other military rifle in the world. Another addition to the firepower of the German infantry was the Panzerfaust 100, an improved short range anti-tank rocket grenade that could penetrate any armor fielded by the American army.:154–61 Despite their superiority, the advanced German armor were fewer in number and often experienced breakdowns because of unreliable mechanical parts.

German tactics for the offensive involved an initial intense artillery barrage, followed by an immediate infantry attack by the Volksgrenadier divisions supported with light assault guns like the Sturmgeschütz IV. This initial attack with relatively non-mobile and relatively expendable troops was intended to clear

Figure 56: *German infantry in half-tracked armored personnel carrier*

major roads for use by the SS Panzer divisions, which would then rapidly move
to capture bridges on the Meuse river for the final drive to Antwerp. These
armored divisions were employed in a much more organized and controlled
fashion, and with better leadership, than was the standard in U.S. armies. The
German concept of the armored division involved independent units that carried with them all their supporting elements, making them more mobile, flexi-
ble, and able to concentrate greater force at the point of attack. Shock and high
speed would overwhelm resistance, as did the first drive from the Ardennes in
1940. These tactics made up what was referred to in the press as the blitzkrieg,
or lightning war. This evolution of mechanized attack was more sophisticated
than tactics used by the American army. The German command expected that
the allied high command would take weeks to adjust to the impact.:[334, 340] But
Hitler failed to consider the constricted, winding, often unpaved roads of the
northern Ardennes and vastly underrated the capabilities of the American units
on the northern shoulder.

American innovations and tactics

On the American side, the defense depended on field fortifications, innovative use of light anti-tank weapons like the bazooka and anti-tank mines, and
most importantly the support of a formidable array of indirect fire. American
tanks and anti-tank guns were considered ineffective against the newer German fighting vehicles. This was compensated to some extent by use of the 76

Figure 57: *M7 Self-propelled 105mm ('The Priest')*
near La Gleize, Belgium during the Battle of the Bulge.

mm (76.2 mm) M1A1 gun, designated as the 3-inch cannon, mounted on the Sherman tank and the M18 Hellcat tank destroyer. The British had also designed high velocity anti-armor ammunition for the 57mm anti-tank cannon, which gave this gun a new lease on life against the new heavier German units. American gunners were quick to trade for whatever their allies wanted for this highly effective ammunition.:404 The Americans also adapted the 90mm anti-aircraft gun as an anti-tank cannon, the 90mm cannon, and mounted it on an open turret on the Sherman tank as the M36 Jackson tank-destroyer. This was another innovation effective against German heavy tanks.:167

Since the invasion of Europe, the American army had suffered greater than expected losses, and found slashing German armored counter-attacks particularly difficult.:11 Learning from this, overall American tactics began to include a defense in depth, using mobile armored cavalry squadrons with light tanks and anti-tank guns to screen defensive positions behind them. When attacked, these cavalry units would delay the Germans for a short time, then retreat through stronger positions to their rear. These positions consisted of fortifications set around terrain choke points like villages, passes, and bridges. In the area of Elsenborn Ridge, the twin villages and the area of Domäne Bütgenbach proved to be the best areas for defense. Machine gun and infantry positions would be protected by barbed wire and mine fields. Anti-tank mine "daisy chains" were also prepared. These were composed of a line of mines lashed in

Figure 58: *Aiming the 4.2 inch mortar with a direct sight. An excellent weapon for close support with a respectable range due to its rifled tube.*

a row. This chain of mines would be dragged across a road with a rope when a column of German tanks threatened to advance down the road. This defensive line would be backed by bazooka positions in buildings, dug-in anti-tank guns, and tank destroyers firing from covered positions further in the rear.:[20-1]

Artillery role

As German mobile units stacked up against the American defenses, the U.S. utilized their superior communications and artillery tactics like "time on target", a sequence of firing so that all shells impacted on the target simultaneously. This allowed vast arrays of artillery pieces, distant from the battle, to concentrate unprecedented firepower on attacking German units.:[112]

Also new to the battlefield were artillery proximity fuses. These had been under development and used during selected battles for about a year. Rather than exploding upon direct contact with the target, the shells detonated near an aircraft or before they struck the ground. Shells armed with these fuses were very effective, but the Allies limited their use in Europe. The Pentagon feared that a dud would be recovered by the Germans who would reverse engineer it and use the information to design radar countermeasures and employ it against the Allies' aircraft and troops.

Near Monschau, the 326th Volksgrenadier Division quickly overran the Americans forward positions. Colonel Oscar A. Axelson, commanding officer of the 405th Field Artillery Group, saw a need and ignored orders, and the 196th Battalion was one of the first to use the fuses. The U.S. Army was also lavishly supplied with the self-propelled artillery, aircraft, and the ammunition it took to make these firepower-based tactics successful. When effectively employed and coordinated, these attacks negated the advantage of superior German armor and armored tactics, although at a cost paid by the U.S. infantry, for saturation indirect fire tended to destroy both friend and foe alike.

The Germans had felt relatively safe from timed artillery fire because they thought that the bad weather prevented the Allies from observing their movements accurately. When the Americans employed the POZIT proximity fuse, their artillery fire was far more devastating, decimating German troops caught in the open, causing up to 20% losses. The effectiveness of the new fused shells exploding in mid-air stirred some German soldiers to refuse orders to move out of their bunkers during an artillery attack. U.S. General George S. Patton said that the introduction of the proximity fuse required a full revision of the tactics of land warfare.

The U.S. defense also involved abundant tactical air support, usually by P-47 Thunderbolt fighter bombers. These "flying tanks" were armed with air to surface rockets which were very effective against the thinly armored upper decks of German armored vehicles. Snowstorms prevented the U.S. from utilizing aircraft in the battle until the weather cleared on December 23.[:396]

Legacy

Medal of Honor recipients

Pfc José M. López a machine gunner with Company K, 393rd Infantry Battalion, was awarded the Medal of Honor for his courage while conducting a fighting withdrawal with his unit from tree to tree.

Sgt Richard Cowan killed about one hundred enemy while covering the retreat of Company I, 393rd Infantry Battalion, and was awarded the Medal of Honor.

T/5 Sgt Vernon McGarity was wounded early in the battle, and after receiving first aid, returned to his unit. As squad leader, he directed and encouraged his soldiers throughout the intense fight which ensued. He repeatedly braved heavy fire to rescue wounded men, attack the advancing Germans, and retrieve supplies.

Pvt Truman Kimbro led a squad that was assigned to mine a key crossroads near Rocherath, Belgium. The road was covered by enemy forces, and he left

his men and although wounded, successfully laid mines across the road before
he was killed by enemy fire.

Sgt William A. Soderman faced German tanks three times on an open road and
destroyed the leading tank with a bazooka, stopping or slowing the German
advance, allowing his fellow troops to safely withdraw.

Cpl Henry F. Warner of the 26th Infantry Regiment, 1st Infantry Division
was posthumously awarded the Medal of Honor for single-handedly disabling
several German tanks during a running battle near Bütgenbach.

Memorials

Monuments were built to commemorate the battle in several locations. Along
with the memorials below, monuments were built in Ligneuville, Stavelot,
Stoumont, and near Cheneaux at the Neufmolin Bridge.[133,134]

Bibliography

- Cavanagh, William. C. C. (November 1, 2004). *The Battle East of Elsen-
  born*. Pen and Sword. p. 192. ISBN 1-84415-126-3.
- Cole, Hugh M. (1964), *The Ardennes:Battle of the Bulge*[135], Office of the
  Chief of Military History Department of the Army
- MacDonald, Charles B. (1985), *A Time for Trumpets, The Untold Story of
  the Battle of the Bulge*, William Morrow and Company, Inc., ISBN 0-688-
  03923-5
- Zaloga, Steven (January 15, 2003), *Battle of the Bulge 1944 (1): St Vith
  and the Northern Shoulder (Campaign)*, Howard Gerrard (Illustrator),
  Osprey Publishing, ISBN 978-1-84176-560-0
- Parker, Danny S. (December 1, 2004). *Battle of the Bulge: Hitler's Ar-
  dennes Offensive, 1944–1945* (First ed.). Cambridge, Massachusetts: Da
  Capo Press. ISBN 978-0306813917.

Ⓐ This article incorporates public domain material from the United States
Army Center of Military History document "The Siegfried Line Campaign"[136].

External links

- European Center of Military History (Belgium)[137]
- Battle of the Bulge : US Troops Fight along the Ridge in Elsenborn Belgium[138]
- The German 560th Heavy Antitank Battalion[139]
- Major General Walter Melville Robertson[140]
- The 2nd Infantry Division Defends the Twin Villages[141]
- The 644th Tank Destroyer Battalion[142]
- Colonel Oscar A. Axelson and the Proximity Fuse[143]

Malmedy massacre

Malmedy Massacre	
Part of the Battle of the Bulge and World War II	
Murdered American soldiers at Malmedy (picture taken on January 14, 1945).	
Malmedy massacre (Belgium)	
Location	Malmedy, Belgium
Coordinates	50°24′14″N 6°3′58.30″E[144]Coordinates: 50°24′14″N 6°3′58.30″E[144]

Date	December 17, 1944
Attack type	Mass murder by firing squad
Deaths	84 American POWs of the 258th Field Artillery Observation Battalion
Perpe- trators	SS-*Obersturmbannführer* Joachim Peiper • Kampfgruppe Peiper, 1st SS Panzer Division Leibstandarte SS Adolf Hitler (1st SS Panzer Division)

The **Malmedy massacre** (1944) was a war crime in which 84 American prisoners of war were killed by their German captors near Malmedy, Belgium, during World War II. The massacre was committed on December 17, 1944, at Baugnez crossroads, by members of *Kampfgruppe Peiper* (part of the 1st SS Panzer Division), a German combat unit, during the Battle of the Bulge.

The term also applies generally to the series of massacres committed by the same unit on the same day and following days, which were the subject of the Malmedy massacre trial, part of the Dachau Trials of 1946. The trials were the focus of some controversy.

Background

Hitler's plans for the Battle of the Bulge gave the main goal (breaking through Allied lines) to the 6th SS Panzer Army, commanded by General Sepp Dietrich. He was to break the Allied front between Monschau and Losheimergraben, cross the Meuse River, and then capture Antwerp.[:5] *Kampfgruppe Peiper*, named after and under the command of SS-*Obersturmbannführer* Joachim Peiper, was composed of armoured and motorised elements and was the spearhead of the left wing of the 6th SS Panzer Army. Once the infantry had breached the American lines, Peiper's role was to advance via Ligneuville, Stavelot, Trois-Ponts, and Werbomont and seize and secure the Meuse bridges around Huy.[:260+] The best roads were reserved for the bulk of the 1st SS Panzer Division *Leibstandarte SS Adolf Hitler*. Peiper was to use secondary roads, but these proved unsuitable for heavy armoured vehicles, especially the Tiger II tanks attached to the *Kampfgruppe*. The success of the operation depended on the swift capture of the bridges over the Meuse. This required a rapid advance through US positions, circumventing any points of resistance whenever possible. Another factor Peiper had to consider was the shortage of fuel: the fuel resources of the Reich had been greatly reduced since the fall of Romania.

Hitler ordered the battle to be carried out with a brutality more common on the Eastern Front, in order to frighten the enemy. Sepp Dietrich confirmed this during the war crimes trial after the war ended. According to one source,

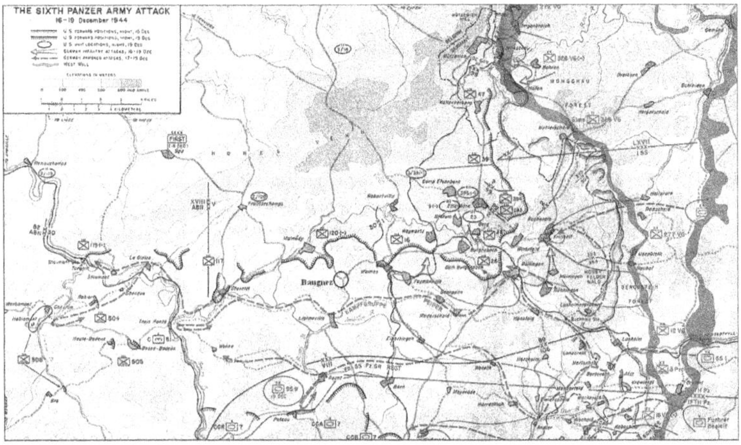

Figure 59: *The route followed by Kampfgruppe Peiper. The crossroads of Baugnez where the Malmedy massacre happened is surrounded by a circle.*

during the briefings before the operation, Peiper stated that no quarter was to be granted, no prisoners taken, and no pity shown towards Belgian civilians.

Peiper advances west

Wikisourcehas original text related to this article:
The Sixth Panzer Army Attack

Figure 60: *SS-Sturmbannführer Joachim Peiper in 1943.*

The Germans' initial position was east of the German-Belgium border and the Siegfried Line near Losheim. SS-*Oberstgruppenführer* Sepp Dietrich's plan was for the Sixth Panzer to advance northwest through Losheimergraben and Bucholz Station and then drive 72 miles (116 km) through Honsfeld, Büllingen, and a group of villages named Trois-Ponts, to connect to Belgian Route Nationale N23, and cross the River Meuse.[70]

Peiper had planned to use the Lanzerath-Losheimergraben road to advance on Losheimergraben immediately following the infantry, who were tasked with capturing the villages and towns immediately west of the International Highway. Unfortunately for the Germans, during their retreat earlier in the year they had destroyed the Losheim-Losheimergraben road-bridge over the railway, which prevented their use of this route. A rail overpass they had planned to use could not bear the weight of the German armour, and German engineers were slow to repair the Losheim-Losheimergraben road, forcing Peiper's vehicles to take the road through Lanzerath to Bucholz Station.[34] Peipers's forces were delayed by massive traffic jams behind the front.

But German military operations on the northern front, the key route for the entire Battle of the Bulge, was troubled by unexpectedly obstinate resistance from American troops. A single platoon of 18 men belonging to an American reconnaissance platoon and four US Forward Artillery Observers held up a battalion of about 500 German paratroopers in the village of Lanzerath, Belgium

Figure 61: *SS-Obergruppenführer Sepp Dietrich in 1943.*

for almost an entire day.[34] Peiper's entire timetable for his advance towards the River Meuse and Antwerp was seriously slowed, allowing the Americans precious hours to move in reinforcements.

The German 9th *Fallschirmjäger* Regiment, 3rd *Fallschirmjäger* Division finally flanked and captured the American platoon at dusk, when they ran low on ammunition and were planning to withdraw. Only one American, a forward artillery observer, was killed, while 14 were wounded: German casualties totalled 92. The Germans paused, believing the woods were filled with more Americans and tanks. Only when Peiper and his tanks arrived at midnight, twelve hours behind schedule, did the Germans learn the woods were empty.

First massacre at Büllingen

At 4:30 on December 17, more than 16 hours behind schedule, the 1st SS Panzer Division rolled out of Lanzerath and headed east for Honsfeld. After capturing Honsfeld, Peiper left his assigned route for several kilometres to seize a small fuel depot in Büllingen, where members of his force killed several dozen American POWs.

Unknown to Peiper, he was in a position to flank the 2nd and the 99th Infantry Divisions. If he had advanced north from Büllingen towards Elsenborn he could have flanked and trapped the Americans, potentially leading to a vastly

Figure 62: *Aftermath of the massacre*

different outcome of the entire battle. But Peiper followed orders. He was more determined to advance west and he stuck to his Rollbahn towards the Meuse River and captured Ligneuville, bypassing Mödersheid, Schoppen, Ondenval, and Thirimont.[145]

The terrain and poor quality of the roads made his advance difficult. Eventually, at the exit of the small village of Thirimont, the spearhead was unable to take the direct road toward Ligneuville. Peiper again deviated from his planned route. Rather than turn left, the spearhead veered right and advanced towards the crossroads of Baugnez, which is equidistant from Malmedy, Ligneuville, and Waimes.

Massacre at Baugnez crossroads

Between noon and 1 pm, the German spearhead approached the Baugnez crossroads, two miles south-east of Malmedy. An American convoy of about thirty vehicles, mainly elements of B Battery of the American 285th Field Artillery Observation Battalion, was negotiating the crossroads and turning right toward Ligneuville and St. Vith, where it had been ordered to join the 7th Armored Division. The spearhead of Peiper's group spotted the American convoy and opened fire, immobilising the first and last vehicles of the column and forcing it to halt. Armed with only rifles and other small arms, the Americans surrendered to the German tank force.

The armoured column led by Peiper continued west toward Ligneuville. The German troops left behind assembled the American prisoners in a field along with other prisoners captured earlier in the day. Many of the survivors testified that about 120 troops were standing in the field when, for unknown reasons, the SS troops suddenly opened fire with machine guns on the prisoners. Several POWs later testified that a few of the prisoners had tried to escape, and others claimed that some prisoners had picked up their previously discarded weapons and shot at the German troops when they attempted to continue toward Ligneuville.[146]Wikipedia:Identifying reliable sources

As soon as the SS machine gunners opened fire, the POWs panicked. Some tried to flee, but most were shot where they stood. Some dropped to the ground and pretended to be dead. SS troops walked among the bodies and shot any who appeared to be alive. A few sought shelter in a café at the crossroads. The SS soldiers set fire to the building and shot any who tried to escape.

Massacre revealed

A few survivors emerged from hiding shortly afterwards and returned through the lines to nearby Malmedy, where American troops still held the town. Eventually, 43 survivors emerged, some who had taken shelter with Belgian civilians.

The first survivors of the massacre were found by a patrol from the 291st Combat Engineer Battalion at about 2:30 p.m. the same day. The inspector general of the First Army learned of the shootings about three or four hours later. By late evening of the 17th, rumours that the enemy was killing prisoners had reached the forward American divisions. One US unit issued orders that "No SS troops or paratroopers will be taken prisoner but will be shot on sight.":261–264 Some American forces may have killed German prisoners in retaliation, like the shooting of German prisoners that took place at Chenogne on January 1, 1945.:261–264

The survivors were interviewed soon after they returned to American lines. Their stories were consistent and corroborated each other, although they had not had a chance to discuss the events with each other.

Bodies recovered

The Baugnez crossroads was behind German lines until the Allied counteroffensive in January. On January 14, 1945, US forces reached the crossroads and massacre site. They photographed the frozen, snow-covered bodies where they lay, and then removed them from the scene for identification and detailed post mortem examinations. The investigation was focused on documenting evidence that could be used to prosecute those responsible for the apparent

Figure 63: *The bodies are taken to Malmedy, where*
the autopsies were performed. 14 January 1945

war crime. Seventy-two bodies were found in the field on January 14 and
15, 1945. Twelve more, lying farther from the pasture, were found between
February 7 and April 15, 1945.Wikipedia:Identifying reliable sources

About 20 of the 84 bodies recovered showed head wounds consistent with a
coup de grâce leaving powder burn residue, indicating a closely administered
and deliberate shot to the head at point-blank range consistent with a massacre
and not self-defense or injuries inflicted while attempting to escape. The bodies
of another 20 showed evidence of small-caliber gunshot wounds to the head
but didn't display powder-burn residue. Some bodies showed only one wound,
in the temple or behind the ear.[147] Ten other bodies showed fatal crushing or
blunt-trauma injuries, most likely from rifle butts. The head wounds were in
addition to bullet wounds made by automatic weapons. Most of the bodies
were found in a very small area, suggesting the victims were gathered close
together before they were killed.[iii][ɔ]

Figure 64: *War correspondent Jean Marin looks at bodies of civilians massacred at the Legaye house in Stavelot, Belgium*

Peiper advances west

The opening forced through the American lines by *Kampfgruppe* Peiper was marked by other murders of prisoners of war, and later of Belgian civilians. Members of his unit killed at least eight other American prisoners in Ligneuville.

Further massacres of POWs were reported in Stavelot, Cheneux, La Gleize, and Stoumont, on December 18, 19, and 20. Finally, on December 19, 1944, between Stavelot and Trois-Ponts, German forces tried to regain control of the bridge over the Amblève River in Stavelot, which was crucial for receiving reinforcements, fuel, and ammunition. Peiper's men killed about 100 Belgian civilians.

American Army engineers blocked Peiper's advance in the narrow Amblève River valley by blowing up the bridges. Additional US reinforcements surrounded the *Kampfgruppe* in Stoumont and la Gleize. Peiper and 800 of his men eventually escaped this encirclement by marching through the nearby woods and abandoning their heavy equipment, including several Tiger II tanks.[376ff]

On December 21, during the battle around La Gleize, the men of *Kampfgruppe* Peiper captured an American officer, Major Harold D. McCown, who was leading one of the battalions of the 119th US Infantry Regiment.[365ff]

Figure 65: *The bodies of Belgian men, women, and children, killed by the German military during their attack into Belgium, await identification before burial.*

Having heard about the Malmedy massacre, McCown personally asked Peiper about his fate and that of his men. McCown testified that Peiper told him neither he nor his men were at any risk and that he (Peiper) was not accustomed to killing his prisoners. McCown noted that neither he nor his men were threatened in any manner, and he testified in Peiper's defence during the 1946 trial in Dachau.

Once re-equipped, *Kampfgruppe* Peiper rejoined the battle, and other killings of POWs were reported on December 31, 1944, in Lutrebois, and between January 10 and 13, 1945, in Petit Thier, where killings were personally ordered by Peiper. The precise number of prisoners of war and civilians massacred attributable to *Kampfgruppe* Peiper is still not clear. According certain sources, 538 to 749 POWs had been the victims of war crimes perpetrated by Peiper's men. These figures are not corroborated by the report of the United States Senate subcommittee that later inquired into the subsequent trial; according to the Committee. According to this report, the count of POWs or civilians killed at different places is as follows:

Place	Prisoners of war	Civilians
Honsfeld	19	

Büllingen	59	1
Baugnez	86	
Ligneuville	58	
Stavelot	8	93
Cheneux	31	
La Gleize	45	
Stoumont	44	1
Wanne		5
Trois-Ponts	11	10
Lutrebois		1
Petit Thier	1[148]	
Total	362	111

Aftermath and trial

On January 13, 1945, American forces recaptured the site where the killings had occurred. The cold had preserved the scene well. The bodies were recovered on January 14/15, 1945. The memorial at Baugnez bears the names of the murdered soldiers.

In addition to the effect the event had on American combatants in Europe, news of the massacre greatly affected the United States. This explains why the alleged culprits were deferred to the Dachau Trials, which were held in May and June 1946, after the war.

In what came to be called the "Malmedy massacre trial", which concerned all of the war crimes attributed to *Kampfgruppe Peiper* during the Battle of the Bulge, the highest-ranking defendant was General Sepp Dietrich, commander of the 6th SS Panzer Army, to which Peiper's unit had belonged. Joachim Peiper and his principal subordinates were defendants. The tribunal tried more than 70 persons and pronounced 43 death sentences (none of which were carried out) and 22 life sentences. Eight other men were sentenced to shorter prison sentences.

After the verdict, the way in which the court had functioned was disputed, first in Germany (by former Nazi officials who had regained some power due to anti-Communist positions with the occupation forces), then later in the United States (by Congressmen from heavily German-American areas of the Midwest). The case was appealed to the Supreme Court of the United States, which made no decision. The case then came under the scrutiny of a sub-committee of the United States Senate.

Figure 66: *A preserved Tiger II tank left by the Kampfgruppe Peiper at La Gleize in December 1944*

Figure 67: *The memorial of the Malmedy massacre at Baugnez. Each black stone embedded into the wall represents one of the victims.*

This drew attention to the trial and the judicial irregularities that had occurred during the interrogations that preceded the trial. But, before the United States Senate took an interest in this case, most of the death sentences had been commuted, because of a revision of the trial carried out by the US Army. The other life sentences were commuted within the next few years. All the convicted war criminals were released during the 1950s, the last one to leave prison being Peiper in December 1956.

A distinct lawsuit about the war crimes committed against civilians in Stavelot was tried on July 6, 1948, in front of a Belgian military court in Liege, Belgium. The defendants were 10 members of Kampfgruppe Peiper; American troops had captured them on December 22, 1944, near the spot where one of the massacres of civilians in Stavelot had occurred. One man was discharged; the others were found guilty. Most of the convicts were sentenced to 10 years' imprisonment; two officers were sentenced to 12 and 15 years.

Death of Peiper

Peiper lived in France following his 1956 release from jail. In 1974 he was identified by a former Communist resistance member of the region who issued a report for the French Communist Party. In 1976 a Communist historian, investigating the STASI archives, found the Peiper file. On June 21, tracts denouncing his presence were distributed in Traves. A day later, an article in the Communist publication *L'Humanité* revealed Peiper's presence in Traves, and he received death threats. Because of the death threats, Peiper sent his family back to Germany, but he remained in Traves. During the night of July 13/14, 1976, a gunfight took place at Peiper's house and his house was set on fire. Peiper's charred corpse was later found in the ruins with a bullet in his chest. The perpetrators were never identified, but were suspected to be former members of the World War II French Resistance or Communists. Peiper had just started writing a book about Malmedy and what followed.

In popular culture

The massacre has been dramatised in three films: *Judgment at Nuremberg* (1961), in which Marlene Dietrich plays the widow of a fictional German general tried and put to death for the massacre, the *Battle of the Bulge* (1965) and *Saints and Soldiers* (2003). The trial was also dramatised in the play *Malmedy Case 5-24* by C.R. (Chuck) Wobbe, published by the Dramatic Publishing Company (1969). The British television series *Foyle's War*, episode "Sunflower", is based on elements of the massacre.

Notes

<templatestyles src="Template:Refbegin/styles.css" />

^ **i:** In Cole's history of World War II, footnote 5 on page 264 reads, *Thus Fragmentary Order 27. issued by Headquarters, 328th Infantry, on 21 December for the attack scheduled the following day says: "No SS troops or paratroopers will be taken prisoner but will be shot on sight."*

^ **ii:** That article includes a diagram showing where the bodies were discovered.

Further reading

- Steven P. Remy, *The Malmedy Massacre: The War Crimes Trial Controversy* (Harvard University Press, 2017), x, 342 pp.

External links

- Mortuary Affairs Operations At Malmedy – Lessons Learned From A Historic Tragedy[149], by Major Scott T. Glass. *Quartermaster Professional Bulletin*, Autumn 1997
- Battle of the Bulge on the Web, Malmedy Massacre resources[150]
- "Massacre at Malmédy during the Battle of the Bulge"[151] (reprint of an article in *World War II* [2003] by M. Reynolds)
- Gettysburg Daily article on 65th anniversary of the Malmedy Massacre.[152]
- Fatal Crossroads: The Untold Story of the Malmédy massacre at the Battle of the Bulge[153], Book by Danny S. Parker, November 2011

333rd Field Artillery Battalion (United States)

The **333rd Field Artillery Battalion** was a racially segregated United States Army unit of African-American troops during World War II. The unit was organized during World War I but never saw combat. In World War II, they landed at Normandy in early July 1944 and saw continuous combat as corps artillery throughout the summer. Beginning in October 1944 it was located in Schoenberg, Belgium as part of the U.S. VIII Corps.

The unit was partially overrun by Germans during the onset of the Battle of the Bulge on 17 December 1944. While most of the 333rd FA Battalion withdrew west towards Bastogne, in advance of the German assault, Service and

Figure 68: *Memorial to the Wereth 11*

C Batteries remained behind to cover the advance of the 106th Infantry Division. The unit suffered heavy casualties, and eleven men of the 333rd were massacred near the Belgian hamlet of Wereth. After the war, the battalion was deactivated and reactivated during various Army reorganizations.

Unit formation and history

Organized as the 333rd Field Artillery (FA) Regiment on 5 August 1917 and subordinated to the 161st Field Artillery Brigade, 86th Infantry Division. The regiment subsequently served in France during World War I, but did not see action. The regiment was demobilized in January 1919 at Camp Grant, Illinois.

The regiment was part of the Organized Reserves in Chicago from 1930 through 1937, at which time it was inactivated until World War II.[154]

On 5 August 1942, the 333rd FA Regiment was activated at Camp Gruber, Oklahoma. As part of an army-wide artillery reorganization, the 1st Battalion was retitled the 333rd FA Battalion and the 2nd Battalion became the 969th FA Battalion. Regimental Headquarters became Headquarters and Headquarters Battery of the 333rd FA Group on 12 February 1943. The group subsequently served in Normandy, Brittany, participated in the siege of Brest and battled across Northern France before arriving in the Ardennes sector as part of the corps artillery of the U.S. VIII Corps.

Figure 69: *Honor guard for the Wereth 11 in 2007.*

Ardennes Offensive

The 333rd Field Artillery Group and the 969th were equipped with 155mm howitzers, and the 771st Field Artillery Battalions was equipped with 4.5-inch guns. They initially supported the 2nd Infantry Division and its replacement, the 106th Infantry Division. At the onset of the Battle of the Bulge they were 11 miles (18 km) behind the front lines. With the rapid advance of the Germans, the 333rd FA Battalion, except for C and Service Batteries, was ordered to withdraw west. C and Service Batteries stayed behind to give covering fire to the retreating 106th Division.

As was typical of segregated units in World War II, white officers commanded black enlisted men. The unit arrived in the small village of Schonberg, near St. Vith, Belgium, in October, 1944. The Service battery was situated west of the Our River while howitzer Batteries A, B, and C were located on the east side of the river to support Army VII Corps. In the early morning hours of December 16, German artillery began shelling the Schonberg area. By the afternoon, there were reports of rapid German infantry and armored progress. The 333rd FAB was ordered to displace further west but the 106th Division artillery commander requested that 'C' Battery and Service Battery remain in position to support the 14th Cavalry Regiment and 106th Division.

By the morning of December 17, the Germans had captured Schonberg and controlled the bridge across the river that connected to St. Vith. The Service

Battery tried to displace to St. Vith through the village and were hit by heavy German armored and small arms fire. Many were killed and those that remained were captured. As the men were being herded to the rear, the column was attacked by an American aircraft. During the ensuing confusion, eleven men escaped into the woods. They were by this time on the east side of the river and forced to sneak their way overland in a northwest direction, hoping they would reach American lines. At about 3 pm, they approached the first house in the nine-house hamlet of Wereth, Belgium, owned by Mathias Langer. A friend of the Langer's was also present.

Wereth 11 Massacre

On 17 December Battery C was flanked and overrun. Most of the troops were killed or captured. Eleven soldiers became separated from the unit after it was overrun early on the second day of the battle. They tried to find the American lines but were unable to and when they reached the hamlet of Wereth, Belgium, farmer Mathias Langer, offered them shelter. The portion of Belgium they were in had been German territory prior to World War I and three of the nine homes in the village were loyal to Germany. The wife of a German soldier who lived in the town told members of the 1st SS Division about the black American GIs hiding in the town. The Germans captured the troops and took them to a nearby field, where they tortured, maimed, and shot all 11 soldiers.

The remains of the 11 troops were found by Allied soldiers six weeks later, in mid-February, after the Allies re-captured the area. The Germans had battered the soldiers' faces, cut their fingers off, broken their legs, used bayonetts to stab them, and shot at least one soldier while he was bandaging a comrade's wounds.

The remnants of the 333rd FAB were ordered to Bastogne and incorporated into its sister unit the 969th Field Artillery Battalion. Both units provided fire support for the 101st Airborne Division in the Siege of Bastogne, subsequently being awarded the Presidential Unit Citation.

The 333rd Field Artillery Battalion suffered more casualties during the Battle of the Bulge than any other artillery unit in the VIII Corps. Six officers (including the commanding officer) and 222 enlisted men were casualties or became prisoners of war. The 333rd FA Group subsequently served in the Central Europe campaign until the end of the war, while the 333rd FA Battalion subsequently served in the Rhineland Campaign.

Names

The troops killed were:

Rank	Name	From	Service number	Buried	Awards
Staff Sergeant (Mess sergeant)	Forte, Thomas J.[155]	Jackson, Mississippi	34046992	Henri-Chapelle plot C, row 11, grave 55.	Purple Heart
Technician Fourth Grade	Pritchett, William Edward[156]	Camden, Alabama	34552760	McCaskill Cemetery[157], Wilcox County, Alabama	
Technician Fourth Grade	Stewart, James A.[158]	Piedmont, West Virginia	35744547	Henri-Chapelle, plot C, row 11, grave 2	Purple Heart
Corporal	Bradley, Mager[159]	Bolivar County, Mississippi	34046336	Fort Gibson National Cemetery, Fort Gibson, Oklahoma, plot 6, 0, 2698-E	
Private First Class	Davis, George[160]	Jefferson County, Alabama	34553436	Henri-Chapelle, plot D, row 10, grave 61	Purple Heart
Private First Class	Leatherwood, James L.[161]	Pontotoc, Mississippi	34481753	College Hill Cemetery[162], Pontotoc County, Mississippi, Plot C Row 9 Grave 57	
Private First Class	Moten, George W.[163]	Hopkins County, Texas	38304695	Henri-Chapelle, plot E, row 10, grave 29	Purple Heart
Private First Class	Turner, Due W.[164]	Emerson, Arkansas	38383369	Henri-Chapelle, plot F, row 5, grave 9	Purple Heart
Private (medic)	Adams, Curtis[165]	South Carolina	34511454	Henri-Chapelle, plot C, row 11, grave 41	Purple Heart
Private	Green, Robert Leroy[166]	Upson County, Georgia	34552457	Highland Park Cemetery[167], Highland Hills, Ohio, Section 3, Lot 3, Tier 24, Grave 22	
Private	Moss, Nathaniel[168]	Longview, Texas	38040062	Henri-Chapelle, plot F, row 10, grave 8	Purple Heart

Memorials

On Sep 11, 1994, Hermann Langer, the son of farmer Mattias Langer who attempted to help the soldiers, erected a small stone cross to remember the 11 black GIs. On May 23, 1994, a new memorial was built on the site of the murders and dedicated to the 11 troops and all African-American soldiers who fought in the European theater. It is believed to be the only memorial specifically dedicated to African-American soldiers of World War II in Europe.

In 2006, veterans with the Worcester, Massachusetts chapter of Veterans of the Battle of the Bulge dedicated what is presumed to be the first memorial to the *Wereth 11* on U.S. soil. It was dedicated at the Winchendon Veterans' Memorial Cemetery on 20 August.Wikipedia:Citation needed

Post World War II

The 333rd FA Battalion was inactivated 10 June 1945 in Germany, while the 333rd FA Group was inactivated at Camp Patrick Henry, Virginia on 30 December 1945.[169] Both the 333rd and 969th FA Battalions were later reactivated, although further reorganizations ensued, with the 333rd FA Battalion renumbered as the 446th FA Battalion. On 1 July 1959 the 333rd FA Group was reactivated as the 333rd Artillery Regiment with the 446th and 969th FA Battalions subordinated to it. On 1 September 1971, the regiment was retitled the 333rd Field Artillery Regiment. Four target acquisition batteries of the 333rd Field Artillery served in Operation Desert Storm in 1991. Today, there is only one target acquisition battery in the Army which still bears the number of the 333rd Field Artillery; F TAB, 333rd FAR is stationed at Camp Casey, Korea as part of the 210th Fires Brigade.

External links

- Wereth.org, an organization set up to remember the Wereth 11[170]
- Stars & Stripes account of memorial[171]
- Army lineage for Battery F, 333rd FA[172]
- 333rd FA Battalion[173]
- www.defense.gov[174]
- The Landmark article about the Massachusetts memorial to the Wereth 11[175]
- American Battle Monuments Commission[176]

Operation Stösser

Operation Stösser (English: Operation Auk) was a paratroop drop into the American rear in the High Fens area during the Battle of the Bulge in World War II. Its objective was to take and hold the crossroads at Belle Croix Jalhay N-68 - N-672 until the arrival of the 12th SS Panzer Division. Both roads were main supply routes, the N-68 Eupen to either Malmedy or Elsenborn and the N-672 Verviers up to Belle-Croix hence up to either Malmedy or Elsenborn. The operation was led by Oberst Freiherr Friedrich August Freiherr von der Heydte, who was given eight days to prepare the mission. The majority of the Fallschirmjäger (paratroopers) and pilots assigned to the operation were under-trained and inexperienced. Kampgruppe Von Der Heydte took up a position at Porfays in the forest east of the N-68 and conducted some local skirmishes on small US convoys and made even some POWs. The mission was a failure.

Background

Friedrich August Freiherr von der Heydte, hero of the legendary if ill-fatedWikipedia:Verifiability airborne assault on Crete,[88] was summoned on 8 December and told to prepare for a mission, but not given any details. Heydte was given eight days to prepare. He wanted to use his own regiment, but this was forbidden because its movement might alert the Allies to the impending counterattack. Instead, he was provided with a Kampfgruppe of 800 men. The II Parachute Corps was tasked with contributing 100 men from each of its regiments. Instead of contributing their best men as ordered, the regiments sent their misfits and troublemakers. Heydte could not afford to resist too strongly. A cousin of Claus von Stauffenberg, a central figure in the July 20, 1944 assassination attempt on Hitler, he was under scrutiny.[218]

In loyalty to their command, 150 men from Heydte's own unit, the 6th Parachute Regiment, disobeyed orders and joined him.[130] To avoid alerting the Allied forces, the German command planned to conduct the drop without reconnaissance or current aerial photographs.

Lack of training

The men had little time to establish unit cohesion or train together. Many of the men assigned to Heydte had never jumped out of an airplane before.[88] Heydte later commented, "Never in my entire career had I been in command of a unit with less fighting spirit."[130]

On 13 December, Heydte visited the headquarters of Army Group B near Bad Münstereifel to complain that the resources allocated to him for the operation

Figure 70: *Friedrich August Freiherr von der Heydte commanded the operation*

were wholly inadequate. Field Marshal Walter Model, who had tried to persuade Hitler to attempt a less ambitious counterattack, replied that he gave the
entire Ardennes Offensive less than a 10 percent chance of succeeding. Model
told him it was necessary to make the attempt: "It must be done because this
offensive is the last chance to conclude the war favorably.":[132]

Assault delay and mis-drops

The drop was delayed for a day when the assigned aircraft did not show up.
The new drop time was set for 03:00 on 17 December; the drop zone was 7
miles (11 km) north of Malmedy. Their objective was to seize the crossroads
and hold it for approximately twenty-four hours until relieved by the 12th SS
Panzer Division, hampering the flow of Allied reinforcements and supplies in
the area.:[130]

Just after midnight on 17 December, 112 Ju 52 transport planes with around
1,300 paratroops took off during a powerful snowstorm with strong winds
and considerable low cloud cover. The Luftwaffe was short of experienced
pilots. Many of the pilots had never flown the Ju 52 before, half had never
flown in combat,:[130] nor were they trained to conduct drops at night or to fly
in formation.:[88] Pathfinders from the Nachtschlachtgruppe 20 were supposed

Figure 71: *A patrol of Company F, 3rd Battalion, 18th Infantry Regiment, 1st Infantry Division, searches the woods between Eupen and Butgenbach, Belgium, for German parachutists*

to lead the way, but the pilots were so inexperienced that they flew with their navigation lights on.[132]

Many planes went off course. Two hundred and fifty men were dropped near Bonn, 50 miles (80 km) from the intended drop zone.[89] Some landed with their troops still on board.[161] Strong winds deflected many paratroops whose planes were relatively close to the intended drop zone and made their landings far rougher. Only a fraction of the force landed near the intended drop zone. Since many of the German paratroops were very inexperienced, some were crippled upon impact and died where they fell. Some were found the following spring when the snow melted.[218]

Confusion among Americans

Because of the extensive dispersal of the drop, *Fallschirmjäger* were reported all over the Ardennes, and the Allies believed a major division-sized jump had taken place, causing the Americans much confusion and convincing them to allocate men to secure the rear instead of facing the main German thrust at the front.[88] An entire U.S. infantry regiment of 3000 men (U.S. 18th Infantry) along with an armored combat command of 300 tanks and 2,000 men searched several days for the German force.[136] The 12th SS Panzer Division, unable to defeat the Americans at the Battle of Elsenborn Ridge, never arrived.

By noon on 17 December, Heydte's unit had scouted the woods and rounded up a total of around 300 troops. With only enough ammunition for a single fight, the force was too small to take the crossroads on its own. Heydte first planned to wait for the arrival of the 12th SS Panzer Division when they would suddenly seize the crossroads just before their arrival. After three days of waiting, he abandoned these revised plans and instead converted his mission to reconnaissance. Oberstgruppenführer Sepp Dietrich had scoffed at Heydte's request for carrier pigeons, and none of the unit's radios survived the drop, so he was unable to report the detailed information he gathered.

Withdrawal to Germany

With only a single day's food supply and limited water, on 19 December Heydte withdrew his forces towards the German lines. He used their limited ammunition to attack the rear of the American lines. Only about one-third reached the German rear. Heydte, wounded, frostbitten, and suffering from pneumonia, knocked on doors in Monschau until he found a German family. The next morning he sent a boy with a surrender note to the Allies.[90]

References

Coordinates: 50°30′40"N 6°04′40"E[177]

Chenogne massacre

Chenogne Massacre	
Location	near Chenogne
Coordinates	49.992°N 5.618°E[178] Coordinates: 49.992°N 5.618°E[178]
Date	January 1, 1945
Attack type	Mass murder
Deaths	60 *Wehrmacht* soldiers

The **Chenogne massacre** is the killing of Wehrmacht prisoners by American troops near the village of Chenogne, Belgium, on January 1, 1945. The massacre was carried out shortly after the Malmedy massacre, where captured American soldiers were gunned down by members of the Waffen SS. It was one of several war crimes that took place during the Battle of the Bulge involving the Allies and Axis forces.

The events were covered up at the time and none of the perpetrators were punished. Post war historians believe the killings were based on senior commanders given verbal orders that "no prisoners were to be taken".

Background

On December 17, 1944, during the Battle of the Bulge, soldiers from the Waffen-SS gunned down 80 American prisoners at the Baugnez crossroads near the town of Malmedy. When news of the killings spread among American forces, it aroused great anger among front line troops. One American unit issued orders: "No SS troops or paratroopers will be taken prisoners but will be shot on sight."[179]

Eyewitness

John Fague of B Company, 21st Armored Infantry Battalion (of the 11th Armored Division), in action near Chenogne described United States troops killing of German prisoners:

> Some of the boys had some prisoners line up. I knew they were going to shoot them, and I hated this business.... They marched the prisoners back up the hill to murder them with the rest of the prisoners we had secured that morning.... As we were going up the hill out of town, I know some of our boys were lining up German prisoners in the fields on both sides of the road. There must have been 25 or 30 German boys in each

group. Machine guns were being set up. These boys were to be machine gunned and murdered. We were committing the same crimes we were now accusing the Japs and Germans of doing.... Going back down the road into town I looked into the fields where the German boys had been shot. Dark lifeless forms lay in the snow.

Cover up

The official post-war history published by the United States government states that while "it is probable that Germans who attempted to surrender in the days immediately after the 17th ran a greater risk" of being killed than earlier in the year, even so, "there is no evidence... that American troops took advantage of orders, implicit or explicit, to kill their SS prisoners." However, according to George Henry Bennett and referring to the above statement; "The caveat is a little disingenuous", and he proceeds to note that it is likely the orders to shoot prisoners (given by the 328th Infantry regiment) were carried out, and that other US regiments were likely also given similar orders.[180] But the killing of SS prisoners had become routine at the time for some units. The 90th Infantry Division at the Saar "executed Waffen-SS prisoners in such a systematic manner late in December 1944 that headquarters had to issue express orders to take Waffen-SS soldiers alive so as to be able to obtain information from them".

In July 2018, KQED radio aired an episode of Reveal series called "Take No Prisoners: Inside a WWII American War Crime" in which Chris Harland-Dunaway, a young journalist at that time, investigates the Chenongne massacre. According to his sources, US soldiers did shoot down about 80 German soldiers right after they surrendered (roughly one for one killed in Malmedy massacre), which qualifies as a war crime[181]. Trying to prove that this fact was known among the US officers, Chris refers to General George S. Patton's diary in which the latter confirms that the Americans "...also murdered 50 odd German men" and that he hopes "we can conceal it".

According to a declassified file Chris got access to, a soldier named Max Cohen described seeing roughly 70 German prisoners machinegunned by the 11th Armored Division in Chenongne. With regard to this claim, General Dwight D. Eisenhower demanded a full investigation, but the 11th Armored managed to get away with it basically saying "it's too late; the war is over, the units are disbanded." Ben Ferencz, an American lawyer who served as a prosecutor at the Nuremberg Tribunal, upon acquainting himself with the declassified report said: "it smells to me like a cover-up of course."

Attack in the center

Battle of St. Vith

Battle of St. Vith	
Part of Battle of the Bulge	
St. Vith, Belgium	
Date	16–21 December 1944
Location	St. Vith, Belgium 50°16′55″N 6°7′36″E[182] Coordinates: 50°16′55″N 6°7′36″E[182]
Result	German victory
Belligerents	
▓▓ United States	🔳 Germany
Commanders and leaders	
▓▓ Bruce C. Clarke	🔳 Walter Model 🔳 Hasso von Manteuffel
Units involved	
▓▓ U.S. VIII Corps • 7th Armored Division • 9th Armored Division • 106th Infantry Division	🔳 5th Panzer Army • 116th Panzer Division • Führer Begleit Brigade • 18th Volksgrenadier Division • 62nd Volksgrenadier Division
Strength	

22,000 men[183]	100,000+ men[184,185]
	500 tanks
Casualties and losses	
12,500 KIA, WIA, POW, or MIA: 345,347,487 88 tanks, 25 armored cars	Unknown

The **Battle of St. Vith** was part of the Battle of the Bulge, which began on 16 December 1944, and represented the right flank in the advance of the German center, 5th *Panzer-Armee* (Armored Army), toward the ultimate objective of Antwerp.

The town of St. Vith, a vital road junction, was close to the boundary between the 5th and Sepp Dietrich's Sixth *Panzer* Army, the two strongest units of the attack. *St. Vith* was also close to the western end of the Losheim Gap, a critical valley through the densely forested ridges of the Ardennes Forest and the axis of the entire German counteroffensive. Opposing this drive were units of the U.S. VIII Corps. These defenders were led by the U.S. 7th Armored Division and included the 424th Infantry (the remaining regiment of the 106th U.S. Infantry Division), elements of the 9th Armored Division's Combat Command B and the 112th Infantry of the U.S. 28th Infantry Division. These units, which operated under the command of Generals Robert W. Hasbrouck (7th Armored) and Alan W. Jones (106th Infantry), successfully resisted the German attacks, thereby significantly slowing the German advance.:26–32, 310–21, 374

Under orders from Field Marshal Bernard Montgomery, Clarke gave up *St. Vith* on 21 December 1944; U.S. troops fell back to positions supported by the 82nd Airborne Division to the west, presenting an imposing obstacle to a successful German advance. By 23 December, as the Germans shattered their flanks, the defenders' position became untenable and U.S. troops were ordered to retreat west of the Salm River. As the German plan called for the capture of *St. Vith* by 18:00 on 17 December, the prolonged action in and around it presented a major blow to their timetable.: 468

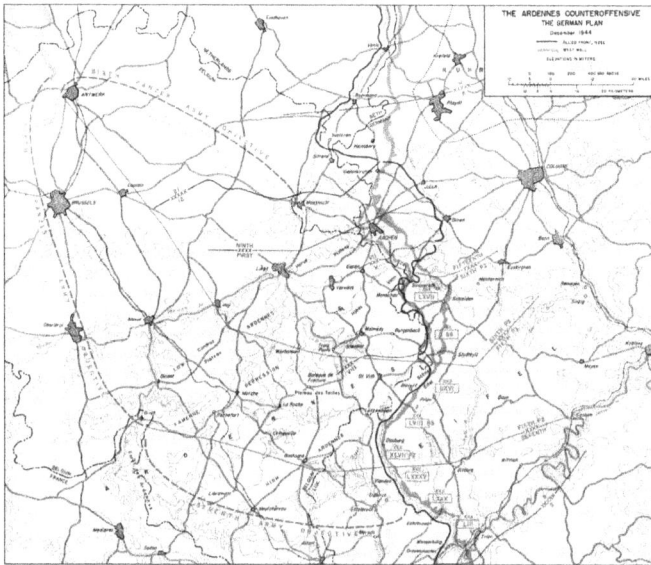

Figure 72: *The German plan - LXVI Corps, 5th Panzer-Armee was assigned the capture of St. Vith.*

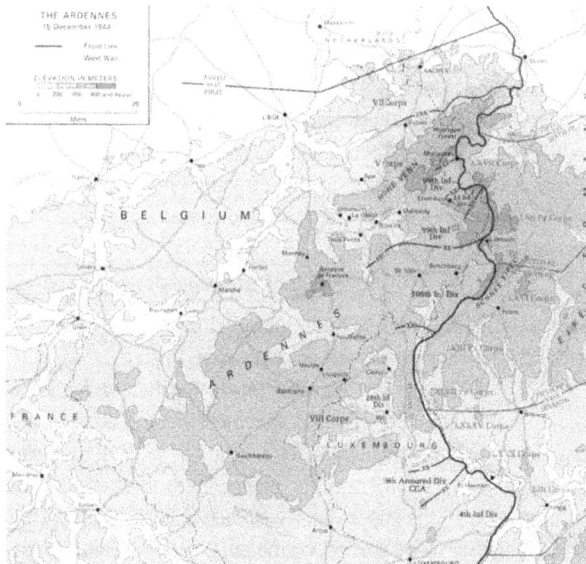

Figure 73: *The Ardennes area of Belgium and Germany just before the German Ardennes counteroffensive, December 15, 1944.*

Background and movement to battle

German preparations: 16 September to 15 December 1944

Adolf Hitler, dictator of the Third Reich, first outlined his plan for a decisive
counteroffensive on the Western Front on 16 September 1944. This assault's
goal was to pierce the thinly held lines of the U.S. First Army between Monschau and Wasserbillig with Army Group B commanded by Field Marshal
(*Generalfeldmarschall*) Walter Model, cross the Meuse between Liege and Dinant, seize Antwerp and the western bank of the Scheldt Estuary. The main
purpose of the counteroffensive was both political and diplomatic. Hitler con-
tended that the alliance between England and the United States in Western
Europe was unnatural and therefore fragile, and would shatter if subjected to
a German drive that would place a wedge between the two nations. Germany
could then make a separate peace with the Western Allies, and concentrate its
armies for a successful drive against the Soviet Union.[20]

In the months following the initial pronouncement, Hitler gathered reserves
for his plan in great secrecy, realizing such a counterattack would have no success unless it was a complete surprise. His chosen commander for the Western Front and figurehead behind which new armies would rally was Gerd von
Rundstedt, an aged field marshal of great reputation and respectability. Under
his banner was recreated a rebuilt Army Group B consisting of three armies,
6th SS Panzer, 5th Panzer and 7th Army. These armies would drive west
through the Ardennes in a repeat of the great western offensive of 1940, splitting the allied armies. The 6th SS Panzer Army would be the strong right arm
of the offensive, on the northern flank and was tasked with driving through
Elsenborn Ridge along the Albert Canal on the most direct route to Antwerp.
The 5th Panzer Army would support the left flank of the 6th, and the less mobile 7th Army would block flanking attacks directed against the southern, or
left flank, of the attacking armies.[22-32]

The center army for the grand offensive was the 5th Panzer Army. It was neither as politically favored nor as well equipped as the 6th SS Panzer Army.
However, the 5th Panzer Army did have an edge in leadership as it was under the command of General der Panzertruppen (General of Armored Forces)
Hasso Eccard von Manteuffel, who was an expert in mechanized warfare from
the Eastern Front. Manteuffel had a reputation for meticulous planning and
daring execution, along with a flair for independent thinking that had led to
trouble in the past with his superiors. As a technical expert, he still retained
enough of a reputation to be trusted with a supporting role in the grand plan.
Though second in power to 6th SS Panzer Army, the 5th Panzer Army still represented considerable mobile strength. Four Panzer Divisions and one Panzer
Brigade were supported by five *Volksgrenadier* (People's Grenadier) divisions.

Supporting these mobile fighting forces were numerous artillery, antiaircraft, and rocket bombardment units.: 101–2, 644–8

After being informed of the nature of the offensive in a meeting with Hitler, von Rundstedt, and Model on 27 October 1944, Manteuffel proceeded to place his personal imprint on the grand plan. At first he supported Model's and Rundstedt's attempt to narrow the scope of the operation to the means that Army Group B could bring to bear. The 1944 offensive could not equal the strength of the 1940 invasion of the west. The number of vehicles and particularly the number of supporting aircraft would be lacking. Therefore, Manteuffel supported what came to be called the "small solution", a limited envelopment that would destroy the American First and Ninth armies. Manteuffel referred to this plan as the "little slam", a title from his love of contract bridge, as opposed to Hitler's "grand slam" plan for the occupation of Antwerp. However, Hitler would not hear of any abbreviation of his goals, so Antwerp remained the official objective, and Manteuffel had to content himself with minor tactical changes.: 35–6

While detailing the deployment of his forces along the Westwall opposite the American lines, Manteuffel performed an extensive reconnaissance of the positions on the German 5th Panzer army front. Based on these observations, performed while disguised in an infantry colonel's uniform, Manteuffel suggested some changes to the attack plan. These changes involved limiting or eliminating the artillery bombardment in areas where American forces were in the habit of withdrawing for the night, or where they were so widely spaced as to allow German troops to advance around them during the night before the attack. He also suggested using searchlights reflecting light indirectly from the clouds to illuminate the advance in the winter darkness preceding the dawn. Hitler agreed to these changes.: 101–2

In planning for the actual attack, Manteuffel had divided his 5th *Panzer* Army into three corps composed of infantry, tanks, and supporting artillery. The main effort, or *schwerpunkt*, would consist of XLVII Panzer Corps and LVIII Panzer Corps advancing west across the River Our at Ouren from the south or left flank of the German army front. They would then occupy the transportation center of Bastogne, before crossing the Meuse River at Namur. The third group, LXVI Corps, would advance west on either side of the Schnee Eifel. This northernmost, or right wing, element would flank and begin an envelopment of the American forces occupying fortifications on the *Schnee Eifel* and then converge on the town of Winterspelt. From there, LXVI Corps would cross the *Our* river and occupy *St. Vith* on the first day of the attack. LXVI Corps was the weakest of the three corps, with no attached tank division or motor transport, but did include an attached assault gun battalion. The *Panzer Lehr* Division (Armor Demonstration Division) and the *Führer Begleit*

Brigade (Führer Escort Brigade) were to be held in reserve, with the *Führer Begleit* only usable with Model's express permission. Manteuffel's preference for the "little slam", or limited solution, was reflected in the absence of planning beyond reaching the Meuse River.: [130]

LXVI Corps comprised two Volksgrenadier divisions. Of the two, the 18th Volksgrenadier Division had been in the area the longest, since October, and was composed for the most part of a *Luftwaffe* (German Air Force) field division with additional troops from the *Kriegsmarine* (German Navy). This division was commanded by Colonel Hoffman-Schonborn and had been formed in Denmark in September. The 62nd Volksgrenadier Division, which was under the command of Colonel Friedrich Kittel, was formed from the remnants of the 62nd Infantry division, which had been destroyed on the Eastern Front, supplemented by Czech and Polish conscripts, most of whom could not speak German. *General der Artillerie* Walter Lucht, commander of LXVI Corps, regarded the 18th *Volksgrenadier* as the more reliable of the two, due to its familiarity with the local terrain, and its German composition. For this reason he trusted the 18th with the most complex components of the plan, and gave it more transport equipment.: [130, 646]

The 18th *Volksgrenadier* Division would have the main role, the *Schwerpunkt*, in a series of envelopments that would cut off the units in the American line and lead to a final convergence of the 18th and 62nd Divisions on *St. Vith*. Manteuffel also made it clear that LXVI Corps's advance would depend on what the Germans called *Stoßtrupptaktik* (thrust troop tactics). This system of attack relied on special shock companies of 80 men that would utilize the rough terrain of the Ardennes to bypass strongpoints and seize key bridges, crossroads, and high ground. Manteuffel also set up a special mechanized combat engineer battalion using halftracks and self-propelled assault guns to clear road blocks and allow for fast flanking attacks.: [104, 137, 314, 321, 469]

American deployment and fortifications: 24 October to 15 December 1944

While Manteuffel's LXVI Corps was gathering for the drive west, the U.S. 1st Army was preparing an attack of its own. In order to advance into Germany, the American high command realized it would have to control the dams that regulated water flow in the Roer River. The attack on the critical dams would be made by the 2nd Infantry Division. This veteran organization had fought its way across Europe from Normandy to the Schnee Eifel. In the process, it had occupied the German fortifications of the *Westwall* and set up fortifications to hold the ridgeline of the Eifel. In order to free-up the 2nd Division for the attack, its place in the defensive line was to be taken over by the newly arrived 106th Infantry Division.: [83]

The 106th Division began replacing the 2nd Infantry Division in the area of St. Vith and the Schnee Eifel on 10 December 1944. Despite the wishes of Major General Walter Melville Robertson, commander of the 2nd Division, the 106th Division would also be deployed for an attack eastward, with most of its force isolated on the Schnee Eifel. In addition, in order not to alert the Germans of the change in divisions, the 106th could not bring any equipment forward and had to rely on equipment left behind by the 2nd Division. The 106th Division came out worse in this deal, for the 2nd had picked up extra communications gear, weapons, and vehicles in the course of its travels across Europe for which the 106th had no equivalent, so the 2nd took most of their equipment with them. The 106th had also suffered significant personnel changes, since sixty percent of its troop strength had been used to make up for higher than expected losses in units already in Europe. These losses had been made up from troops taken from disbanded small units, air cadets in training, and divisions not moving immediately to Europe. The effect of disruptions in organization, training, and equipment made the division relatively ineffective as a combat unit. The American high command believed that the static nature of the Ardennes area would allow time for the 106th to correct its deficiencies.: 116–7

The 106th Division did have supporting units on its flanks and the area of the Losheim Gap to the north. After many requests from General Robertson, the headquarters of the 14th Cavalry Group, commanded by Colonel Mark A. Devine, Jr., was moved into the area. Supporting the 14th were the 820th Tank Destroyer Battalion, with twelve 3" towed anti-tank guns, and the 275th Armored Field Artillery Battalion, with 18 M7 Priest Self-Propelled Howitzers. The headquarters group also brought with it a second cavalry squadron to screen the Losheim Gap, which was on the left flank of the 106th Division. While the two cavalry squadrons, the 14th and 18th, did not represent a lot of firepower, but they did set up fortifications in small villages in the area. This transformed them into isolated strong points guarding road intersections. Most of the supporting firepower came from General Middleton, commander of the American VIII Corps, who arranged for eight of his thirteen reserve artillery battalions to support the area of the Schnee Eifel and the Losheim Gap, the central area of his front line. In late October, the 9th Armored Division had also been added to VIII Corps as a reserve, and part of the division had been moved up to support the 2nd Infantry Division's attack on the Roer River dams.: 83–4, 103–4:228–30

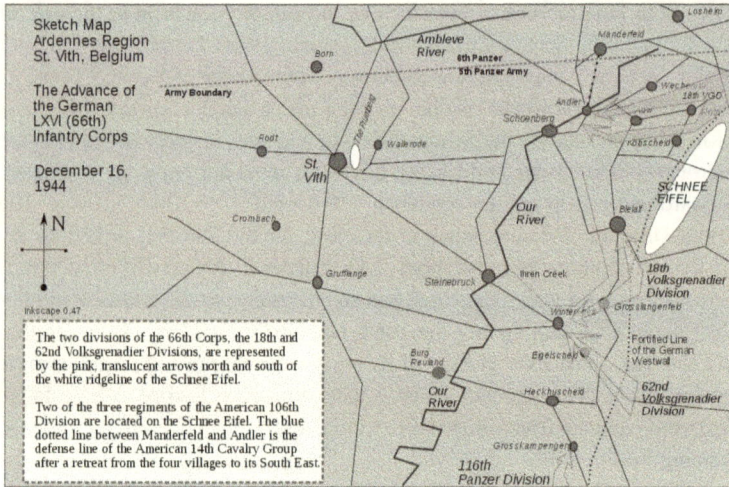

Figure 74: *Sketch map of the first day of the attack of the German LXVI Corps. The furthest German advance has covered about five miles.*

The Battle of St. Vith, 16–22 December 1944

The double envelopement of the *Schnee Eifel*

A little before 5:30 AM, on Saturday, 16 December 1944, a selective artillery bombardment began falling on forward positions of the 106th Division on the *Schee Eifel*, moving gradually back to the division headquarters in *St. Vith*. This attack did not do much damage to troops or fortifications, but did cut up most of the telephone wires the American army used for communications. The Germans also used radio jamming stations that made wireless communications difficult. This had the effect of breaking the defense into isolated positions, and denying corps and army commands information on events at the front line. The most significant aspect of the bombardment is where it did not fall. The villages on the left flank north of the *Schnee Eifel* were not hit at all. Here Manteuffel had found an undefended gap running between *Weckerath* to *Kobscheid*. Into the gaps between the villages marched the 18th *Volksgrenadier* Division, which bypassed the defended villages and headed for *Auw* before the general bombardment began. This movement would coincide with a southern advance of the 18th around the right flank of the *Schnee Eifel* through *Bleialaf* to *Schoenberg* to surround American positions on the *Schnee Eifel* ridge. This double envelopment came as a complete surprise to the American forces as a result of the intelligence failure at First Army level. The high command did not spot the buildup of the German forces for the offensive, and made no preparations to deal with it. This caused a paralyzing lack of situational awareness through the defending forces in front of *St. Vith*. The American commands in the rear found it difficult to abandon their own planned offensive in view of reacting to an unanticipated German attack. They were slow to react on the first day of LXVI Corps attack, giving the initiative to the attackers and multiplying the damage done.: 104–8

After the initial artillery strike, searchlights behind the German line lit up, reflecting an eerie illumination from the clouds and lighting up the front lines. Moving forward with the glow, the 62nd *Volksgrenadier* Division advanced through *Elgelscheid* toward *Winterspelt*. This movement, combined with the advance of a southern column of the 18th *Volksgrenadiers* through *Grosslangenfeld* to meet the 62nd at *Winterspelt* and combine for a capture of *Steinebruck*, with its bridge over the Our River. The capture of *Schoenberg*, (six miles east of *St. Vith*), also with a bridge over the *Our*, and *Steinebruck* would set up LXVI Corps for an envelopment of *St. Vith* itself. The only significant check in the German advance was at *Kobscheid*, where the 18th Cavalry Reconnaissance Squadron had circled the village with barbed wire and dug in machine guns from their armored cars. Here, they held the village for the day; after dark, they destroyed their vehicles and abandoned their positions, withdrawing to *St. Vith*. In the other villages, the cavalry troops were forced to withdraw earlier in the day so as to avoid being surrounded and cut off. The Squadron was directed by Colonel Devine to take-up positions on a new defense line along the ridge running from *Manderfeld* to *Andler*, on the north side of the *Our* River.: 103–10 : 231–6

By the end of the first day, the *Volksgrenadiers* of LXVI Corps had not made it to *St. Vith*, or even the critical bridges on the *Our* River at *Schoenberg* and *Steinebruck*. The American village strong points set up by the cavalry groups and sustained artillery fire from both VIII Corps reserve and the units supporting the 106th division had denied LXVI Corps the roads, but the *Volksgrenadiers* had not been depending on them anyway. Their main problems proved to be the same miserable weather and terrain conditions that prompted the *Ardennes* counteroffensive in the first place. Colonel Friedrich Kittel of the 62nd Division had set up a bicycle battalion to make a fast run on *St. Vith* from *Eigelscheid*, but the snow, ice, and mud had made it ineffective. Expert ski troops could have covered the 11 to 15 miles of snow covered forested ravines from the *Schnee Eifel* to *St. Vith* in one day, but the *Volksgrenadiers* simply did not have that kind of training or equipment. They did not even have the training it took to take full advantage of the motorized assault guns they did have. This was not enough to pull off a carefully timed series of sequential envelopments and advances through rough terrain.: 117–29

On the American side, the significant events were decisions from General
Courtney Hodges, commander of First Army, and General Middleton of VIII
Corps, committing combat commands of the 7th and 9th Armored Divisions
to support the 106th Division defense. Middleton also threw in the 168th
battalion of corps engineers from the Corps reserve. General Alan Walter
Jones, commander of the 106th had also sent reinforcements to *Winterspelt*
and *Schoenberg* around noon. There was also a counterattack by Colonel
Charles C. Cavender of the 423d Regiment, which retook the village of *Bleialf*.
The more significant event was an interruption in communications that led
Jones to believe Middleton did not wish a retreat from the *Schnee Eifel*. Middleton stated to others that Jones would move the 106th west of the *Our* River
about the same time.: 118, 125, 128–9

Before dawn on 17 December, the German LXVI Corps renewed its advance
on the *Our* River. *Winterspelt* fell to the 62nd Volksgrenadiers early in the day.
They then advanced to the critical bridge at *Steinebruck* and advanced past it,
but were thrown back by a counterattack by the American 9th Armored Division's CCB. They were also considering retaking *Winterspelt*, but Middleton
ordered a general withdrawal behind the *Our* River. As German troops were
massing on the opposite bank, the 9th Armored would blow up the bridge on
18 December, and fall back to a defensive line with the 7th Armored Division
on the left and the remaining 424th Regiment of the 106th Division on the
right. The southern arm of the 18th Volksgrenadiers overran *Bleialf* at about
the same time as the attack on *Winterspelt*. The northern arm of the 18th
struck at *Andler*, receiving unexpected help from the 6th SS Panzer Army.
The lavish supply of heavy armored fighting vehicles had proved an embar-
rassment of riches in the area north of 5th Panzer Army - the road net in the
northern area of the attack was unable to support the volume of the attack, so
the vehicles of the *Schwere Panzerabteilung* 506 wandered south into the 5th
Army's area in search of a road west. The super heavy tanks of this unit, the
Tiger II, were slow and of such colossal weight as to endanger any bridge they
crossed. However, in combat they were virtually unstoppable and they easily
routed the light cavalry forces of the 32nd Squadron's Troop B, holding *Andler*. From there, the troops of the 18th Volksgrenadiers swept onward toward
Schoenberg. The heavy tanks of the 506th did not join them, creating a traffic jam in the narrow streets of *Andler*. The jam was expanded by additional
traffic from 6th Panzer Army, blocking the advance far more effectively than
American forces could hope. This jam would be the first of many plaguing
both sides in the paths of the German advance. *Andler*, *Schoenberg*, and the
road west of *St. Vith*, to the west of the town of *Rodt* would all be the scenes
of traffic blockages that would attract the personal intervention of most of the
field commanders in the area of *St. Vith*, all to no avail. General Lucht of

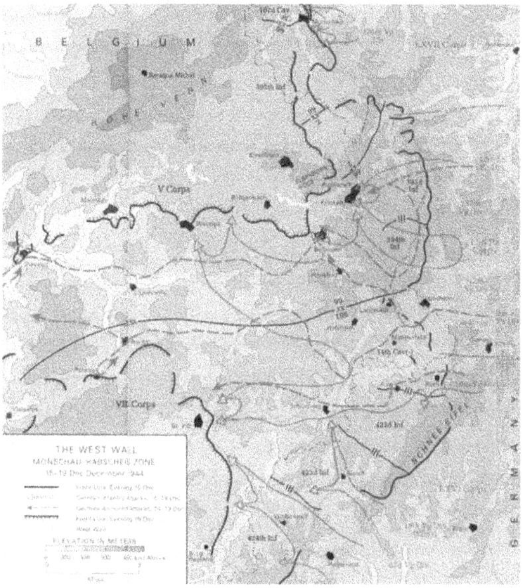

Figure 75: *St. Vith area and surroundings, December 15-19th, 1944. (U.S. Army CMH)*

LXVI Corps was the first commander to waste his efforts clearing the jam at *Andler*, but not the last.: 311, 314, 323, 326, 337, 475

The 18th Volksgrenadiers captured the bridge at *Schoenberg* by 8:45, cutting off American artillery units attempting to withdraw west of the *Our* River. The southern pincer of the 18th, advancing from *Bleialf* against scattered American resistance, was slower than the northern group. As a result, Manteuffel's trap on the *Schnee Eifel* did not close until nightfall on 17 December. General Jones had given the troops east of the *Our* River permission to withdraw at 9:45 AM, but it was too late to organize an orderly withdrawal by that time. This order, and the slow German southern arm, gave more Americans a chance to escape, but since they had newly arrived in the area, and had few compasses or maps, most were unable to take advantage of the opportunity. The American positions east of the *Our* had become the *Schnee Eifel* Pocket.: 314–5, 318, 320

The surrender of the *Schnee Eifel* pocket, 19–21 December 1944

Following the German attacks sweeping around their position, the two regiments of the 106th Division, the 422nd and 423rd had remained in place, since they had heard that the Germans would launch artillery and patrols against

them as they would any new division taking a place on the line. The German activity during the counter offensive seemed to follow this pattern, and
since communication with the division headquarters in *St. Vith* was unreliable
and intermittent, the Americans had remained for the most part inert. The few
messages received indicated they could withdraw, but that counterattacks from
the 7th and 9th Armored divisions would probably clear the Germans out of
the area anyway. It was only at 2:15 AM on 18 December that they received
an order from Jones to break out to the west along the *Bleialf - Schoenberg*
– St. Vith road, clearing the area of Germans in the process. At 10 AM that
morning, the breakout began with Colonel Cavender leading the attack with the
423d Infantry. By nightfall both regiments had covered three miles to the base
of the ridge forming the east side of the *Our* River valley, and were prepared to
attack and capture the bridge at *Schoenberg* at 10 AM the next day. At 9 AM
on the 19th, the American positions came under artillery bombardment, and
the 18th Volksgrenadiers overran the 590th Field Artillery Battalion who were
to provide support for the attack. The attack was launched at 10 AM anyway,
but came under assault gun and anti-aircraft gunfire from armored fighting
vehicles on the ridge to their front. Volksgrenadiers advanced from the flanks
firing small arms. This was bad enough, but then the tanks of the Führer Begleit
Brigade appeared behind them, on their way around the traffic jam at *Schoen-*
berg, it was the last straw. The Americans were under fire from all sides and
running low on ammunition. At this point Colonel Descheneaux, commander
of the 422 decided to surrender the American forces in the pocket. At 4 PM,
this surrender was formalized and the two regiments of the 106th division and
all their supporting units, approximately 7,000 men, became prisoners of the
German Army. A different grouping of scattered American soldiers under the
command of Major Ouellette, numbering some 500 men surrendered later, but
by 8 AM on 21 December, all organized resistance by American forces in the
Schnee Eifel pocket ended. This marked the most extensive defeat suffered by
American forces in the European Theatre.: 338–47

The fall of St. Vith, 21 December 1944

As the trap snapped shut on the *Schnee Eifel* on 17 December, rapid change
was occurring at the headquarters of the 106th Division in *St. Vith*. Brigadier
General Bruce Cooper Clarke, leader of Combat Command-B 7th Armored
Division had arrived in the morning, with news that his command was on the
road to *St. Vith*, but would probably not arrive until later that afternoon. This
was bad news for Jones, who was hoping for a quick deliverance from his
problems by the arrival of organized reinforcements. The situation was not
improved by the appearance of a demoralized Colonel Devine with news that
German Tiger tanks were right on his heels. With the appearance of German
scouts on the hills east of town, Jones decided he had had enough. "I've thrown

Figure 76: *Progress of the German Ardennes
counteroffensive, December 16–25, 1944.*

in my last chips." He told Clarke, and turned over defense of the area to Clarke.
Clarke saw his first task as getting his command into *St. Vith*, and proceeded
to the traffic jams on the *Rodt – St. Vith* road to force his CCB into *St. Vith*.
By midnight of the 17th, he had managed to set up the beginnings of what
was called the "horseshoe defense" of *St. Vith*, a line of units to the north, east
and south of town. These units came mainly from the 7th and 9th Armored
Divisions, but included troops from the 424th Regiment of the 106th Division,
and various supporting artillery, tank, and tank destroyer battalions.: [322-9]

As Clarke was cursing and threatening his way through the traffic jams west of
St. Vith, Model and Manteuffel were doing the same in the traffic jams east of
Schoenberg. Meeting Manteuffel in the confusion, Model ordered him to capture *St. Vith* on the 18th, giving him control of the *Fuhrer Begleit* Brigade to
make sure the objective would be met. It was not to be however, for the armor
brigade had bogged down in the traffic jams, and the 18th and 62nd *Volksgrenadiers* were busy reducing the *Schnee* pocket and rebuilding the bridge
at Steinbruck. The mechanized combat engineer battalion of the 18th *Volksgrenadiers*, with a group from the 1st SS Panzer, did attack from the north,
but were repelled by counterattacks from the 7th and 9th Armored.: [327, 336-7]

The final attack on *St. Vith* was belatedly launched on 21 December, but by
then *St. Vith* had become more of a liability than an asset. Attacks from

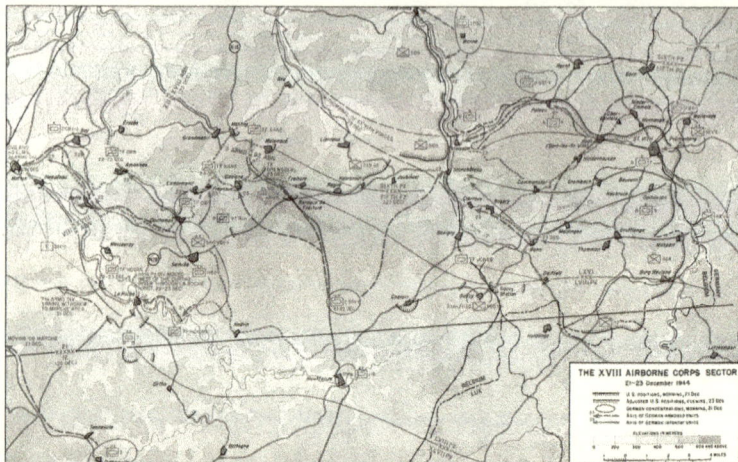

Figure 77: *XVIII Airborne Corps Sector Map, December 21–23, 1944.*
The final withdrawal of American forces from the St. Vith salient.

the 1st SS Panzer Division had cut the Rodt – *St. Vith* road, and the advance of the LVIII Panzer Corps south of *St. Vith* threatened to close a pincer around the entire *St. Vith* salient at *Vielsalm*, eleven miles west of *St. Vith*, trapping most of the First Army. The German attack began at 3 PM with a heavy artillery barrage. The climax of the attack was, once again, the wandering German 506th Heavy Panzer Battalion. Six of these titans attacked from the *Schoenberg – St. Vith* road against American positions on the *Prumberg*. Attacking after dark at 5 PM the Tiger tanks fired star shells into American positions, blinding the defenders, and followed up with armor-piercing shell, destroying all the American defending vehicles. Around 9:30 PM, Clarke, who had earlier stated, "This terrain is not worth a nickel an acre to me." ordered American forces to withdraw to the west. German forces poured into the town, happily looting the remaining American supplies and equipment, in the process creating another traffic jam that prevented pursuit of the American forces.: 329–32, 466, 473–75

Aftermath

<templatestyles src="Template:Quote_box/styles.css" />

As the commander of CCB, I analyzed the situation and decided that the probable objective of the German attack was not just St. Vith or a bridgehead over the Salm River, but rather a decisive objective far to my rear, probably toward the English Channel. Therefore, I could well afford to be forced back slowly, surrendering a few kilometers of terrain at a time to the German forces while preventing the destruction of my command and giving other units to my rear the time to prepare a defense and a counterattack. Therefore, by retiring a kilometer or so a day, I was winning, and the Germans, by being prevented from advancing many kilometers a day, were losing – thus proving my concept that an armored force can be as effectively employed in a defense-and-delay situation as in the offensive.

—General Bruce Clarke,
ARMOR, November-December 1974[186]

While the final battles for *St. Vith* were gathering momentum, the Allied high command was moving to meet the crisis. On 20 December, Field Marshal Bernard Law Montgomery - commander of the 21st Army Group - was given command of all troops north of the German advance. This was done to both improve communications and because Montgomery held the ultimate trump card in the battle, an uncommitted reserve, the British XXX Corps. Also on that day, the forces of the U.S. 82nd Airborne Division, under Major General James M. Gavin, made contact with the 7th Armored Division, meeting the condition General Hodges set for command of the *St. Vith* forces shifting to the U.S. XVIII Airborne Corps under Major General Matthew Ridgway. This was done once again to improve communications and set up a secure supply line to the rear. Ridgeway arrived in *Vielsalm* on 22 December, shortly after American forces were driven from *St. Vith*. He was aware that Montgomery had already decided to withdraw from the *St. Vith* area. Montgomery had seen the threat of a larger encirclement of American forces, and hoped to gather a reserve west of the Meuse River to finally block the German advance while also eliminating vulnerable salients in the allied lines.: [416–22, 478–9]

The American commanders had hoped to use the *St. Vith* salient as the starting point of an attack towards *Malmedy* in Belgium. This would encircle 6th *Panzer* Army and destroy any hope of further German penetrations. Ridgway was still willing to consider holding positions in the area for this purpose, but interviews with the local commanders changed his mind. They had brought up many objections to securing the area: poor roads, unreliable communications and supply, severe combat losses, as well as the imminent danger of being cut off by rapidly moving panzer divisions. General Hoge of the 9th Armored Division even considered it unlikely that any escape from the area could be made. Fortunately for the Americans, the weather came to their assistance for the first time in the campaign. What the Americans called a "Russian High" began blowing on 23 December. A cold wind from the northeast, and clear weather, froze the ground, allowing the free movement of tracked vehicles and the use of allied air superiority. American forces were able to escape to the southwest, cross country to *Crombach, Beho, Bovigny,* and *Vielsalm* west of the Salm River. The Americans were able to outrun the panzers, and join forces with XVIII Airborne Corps by 24 December 1944.: 478–87

The best summation of the fight for *St. Vith* was one given by the architect of the attack, Hasso von Manteuffel, for a documentary series on the battle in 1965. His analysis did not make much of the grand strategies however. His statement described the actions of the common soldier as follows:

> It is the war of the small men, the outpost commanders, the section commanders, the company commanders; those were the decisive people here, who were responsible for success or failure, victory or defeat. We depended upon their courage; they could not afford to get confused, and had to act according to their own decisions, until the higher command was again in a position to take over. I believe I can say, and I have the right to make this judgment, that the Germans did this admirably well, at the same time however, I am also convinced this was the case with the American forces, who after all succeeded in upsetting the entire time schedule, not only of the attacking unit in St. Vith, but also of the 5th and 6th Panzer Armies. That is a fact which cannot be denied.

Documentaries

Documentaries

- The short film *'Tried By Fire Battle of St. Vith - part I'*[187] is available for free download at the Internet Archive The Army Pictorial Center, "Big Picture" Documentary Series (1965)
- The short film *'Battle of St. Vith - part II'*[188] is available for free download at the Internet Archive The Army Pictorial Center, "Big Picture" Documentary Series (1965)
- Battle of *St. Vith* - part I[189] on YouTube The Army Pictorial Center, "Big Picture" Documentary Series (1965)
- Battle of *St. Vith* - part II[190] on YouTube The Army Pictorial Center, "Big Picture" Documentary Series (1965)

External links

> Wikisourcehas original text related to this article:
> **St. Vith is lost**

- Battle for St. Vith[191]
- St. Vith Is Lost[192]

Figure 78: *American 3-inch M5 anti-tank gun near Vielsalm, Belgium, 23 Dec 1944.*

Figure 79: *American M4 Sherman tanks in defensive positions near St. Vith.*

Operation Greif

> Wikisourcehas original text related to this article:
> **The 1st SS Panzer Division's Dash Westward, and Operation Greif**

Operation *Greif* (German: *Unternehmen Greif* [gʁaɪf], meaning "Griffin") was a special operation commanded by Waffen-SS commando Otto Skorzeny during the Battle of the Bulge in World War II. The operation was the brainchild of Adolf Hitler, and its purpose was to capture one or more of the bridges over the Meuse river before they could be destroyed. German soldiers, wearing captured British and US Army uniforms and using captured Allied vehicles, were to cause confusion in the rear of the Allied lines. A lack of vehicles, uniforms, and equipment limited the operation and it never achieved its original aim of securing the Meuse bridges. Skorzeny's postwar trial set a precedent clarifying article 4 of the Geneva Convention: as the German soldiers removed the Allied uniforms before engaging in combat, they were not to be considered francs-tireurs.

There was an earlier military operation that used this name; an anti-partisan operation conducted by the German Army, begun on August 14, 1944, in the vicinity of Orsha and Vitebsk, Soviet Union.

Background

Skorzeny had become one of Hitler's favorites following the success of Operation Panzerfaust in which he had supervised the kidnapping of Miklós Horthy, Jr., the son of Hungary's Regent, Admiral Miklós Horthy to force Horthy's resignation. Following his return to Germany, Skorzeny was summoned to meet Hitler at his headquarters at Rastenburg in East Prussia on 22 October 1944. After congratulating Skorzeny, Hitler outlined the planned Ardennes Offensive and the role he was to play in it.

Skorzeny was to form a special brigade - Panzer Brigade 150 - whose purpose would be to capture one or more of the bridges over the Meuse river before they could be destroyed. Hitler informed him that he had decided this could be accomplished more quickly and with fewer losses if Skorzeny and his men wore U.S. uniforms. Hitler also remarked that small units disguised in enemy uniforms could cause great confusion among the enemy by giving false orders, upsetting communications, and misdirecting troops.

> *I want you to command a group of American and British troops and get them across the Meuse and seize one of the bridges. Not, my dear Skorzeny, real Americans or British. I want you to create special units wearing American and British uniforms. They will travel in captured Allied*

Figure 80: *Skorzeny with the liberated Mussolini – Sept. 12 1943*

tanks. Think of the confusion you could cause! I envisage a whole string of false orders which will upset communications and attack morale.

—Hitler, The Black Angels, 1979

Skorzeny was well aware that under the Hague Convention of 1907, any of his men captured while wearing U.S. uniforms would be executed as spies and this possibility caused much discussion with Generaloberst Jodl and Field Marshal von Rundstedt.

Panzer Brigade 150

The timing of the Ardennes Offensive meant that Skorzeny had only five or six weeks to recruit and train a brand new unit for what Hitler named Operation *Greif* ("Gryphon"). Within four days he sent his plans for Panzer Brigade 150 to Generaloberst Alfred Jodl. Despite asking for 3,300 men he was given an immediate go-ahead and promised full support. The Oberkommando der Wehrmacht issued an order on 25 October requesting suitable soldiers for the operation with "knowledge of the English language and also the American dialect" which was passed on to every headquarters on the Western Front, and this request soon became known to the Allies.[193]

The new brigade needed US Army vehicles, weapons and uniforms; OB West was asked to find 15 tanks, 20 armoured cars, 20 self-propelled guns, 100 jeeps, 40 motorcycles, 120 trucks, and British and US Army uniforms all to be delivered to the brigade's training camp which had been set up at Grafenwöhr

Figure 81: *Knocked-out Panther tank disguised as an M10 Tank Destroyer*

in eastern Bavaria. The equipment delivered fell short of the requirements, including only two Sherman tanks in poor condition, and Skorzeny had to use German substitutes, five tanks (Panzer V "Panther") and six armoured cars. The brigade was also flooded by Polish and Russian equipment sent by units who had no idea what the request was for. Only 10 men who spoke perfect English and had some knowledge of American idioms were found, 30-40 men who spoke English well but had no knowledge of slang, 120-150 who spoke English moderately well, and 200 or so who had learned English at school.

Faced with these setbacks, Skorzeny scaled down Panzer Brigade 150 from three battalions to two and assembled the 150 best English speakers into a commando unit named *Einheit Stielau*. Skorzeny also recruited a company of SS-Jagdverbände "Mitte" and two companies from SS-Fallschirmjäger-Abteilung 600, and was given two Luftwaffe parachute battalions formerly of KG 200, tank crews from Panzer regiments, and gunners from artillery units. A total of 2,500 men were eventually assembled at Grafenwöhr, 800 less than had been hoped.

The final total of equipment assembled was also less than had been hoped; only enough US Army weapons had been found to equip the commando unit, and only four US Army scout cars, 30 jeeps, and 15 trucks were found, the difference being made up with German vehicles painted in US olive drab with

Allied markings applied. Only a single Sherman tank was available, and the brigade's Panther tanks were disguised as M10 tank destroyers by removing their cupolas and disguising their hulls and turrets with thin sheet metal. The problem of recognition by their own forces was crucial, and they were to identify themselves by various methods: displaying a small yellow triangle at the rear of their vehicles; tanks keeping their guns pointing in the nine o'clock position; troops wearing pink or blue scarves and removing their helmets; and flashes from a blue or red torch at night.

As the brigade prepared for action, rumours began to fly that they were to relieve the besieged towns of Dunkirk or Lorient, capture Antwerp, or to capture the Allied Supreme Command at SHAEF at Paris.[194] It was not until 10 December that Skorzeny's own commanders were made aware of the brigade's true plans. Panzerbrigade 150 was to attempt to capture at least two of the bridges over the Meuse river at Amay, Huy, and Andenne before they could be destroyed, the troops to begin their operation when the Panzer advance reached the High Fens, between the Ardennes and the Eifel highlands. The three groups (Kampfgruppe X, Kampfgruppe Y, and Kampfgruppe Z) would then move towards the separate bridges.

Einheit Stielau mission

The *Einheit Stielau* commando unit had been assembled from the brigade's best English speakers, but few of them had much if any experience of undercover operations or sabotage. There was little time to train them properly, but they were given short courses in demolition and radio skills, studied the organization of the US Army and its badges of rank and drill, and some were even sent to POW camps at Küstrin and Limburg to refresh their language skills through contact with US POWs.

Dressed in US Army uniforms (the highest US Army rank used was that of colonel), armed with US Army weapons, and using US Army jeeps, the commandos were given three missions:

- Demolition squads of five or six men were to destroy bridges, ammunition dumps, and fuel stores.
- Reconnaissance patrols of three or four men were to reconnoiter on both sides of the Meuse river and also pass on bogus orders to any US units they met, reverse road signs, remove minefield warnings, and cordon off roads with warnings of nonexistent mines.
- "Lead" commando units would work closely with the attacking units to disrupt the US chain of command by destroying field telephone wires and radio stations, and issuing false orders.

Figure 82: *Battle of the Bulge, Meuse river at the lower left*

Action

On 14 December Panzerbrigade 150 was assembled near Bad Münstereifel and on the afternoon of 16 December it moved out, advancing behind the three attacking Panzer divisions, the 1st SS Panzer Division, the 12th SS Panzer Division, and the 12th Volksgrenadier Division, with the aim of moving around them when they reached the High Fens. However, when the 1st SS Panzer Division failed to reach the start point within two days, Skorzeny realized that Operation *Greif*'s initial aims were now doomed.

As a consequence, on 17 December Skorzeny attended a staff conference at the 6th Panzer Army's HQ, and suggested that his brigade be used as a normal army unit. This was agreed, and he was ordered to assemble south of Malmedy and report to the 1st SS Panzer Division's HQ in Ligneuville.

On 21 December 1944 this brigade, under Skorzeny's command tried to take Malmedy. Several assaults of the Skorzeny brigade were eventually successfully repelled by the American defenders. This would constitute the only noticeable attempt from the Germans to take Malmedy during the battle of the Bulge.

Commandos

Skorzeny described the activities of the *Einheit Stielau* in an interview with the US Army in August 1945 following his surrender. According to him, four units of reconnaissance commandos and two units of demolition commandos were sent out during the first few days of the attack, and three units went with the 1st SS Panzer Division, 12th SS Panzer Division, and 12th Volks Grenadier Division, with another three units accompanying Panzerbrigade 150's three groups. Skorzeny reported that one commando team entered Malmedy on 16 December, and another team managed to persuade a US Army unit to withdraw from Poteau the same day. Another team switched around road signs and sent an entire American regiment in the wrong direction.

As a result, American troops began asking other soldiers questions that they felt only Americans would know the answers to in order to flush out the German infiltrators, which included naming certain states' capitals, sports and trivia questions related to America, etc. This practice resulted in American brigadier general Bruce Clarke being held at gunpoint for some time after he incorrectly said the Chicago Cubs were in the American League[195] and a captain spending a week in detention after he was caught wearing German boots. General Omar Bradley was repeatedly stopped in his staff car by checkpoint guards who seemed to enjoy asking him such questions. The Skorzeny commando paranoia also contributed to tragic instances of mistaken identity which were very common. All over the Ardennes, American soldiers attempted to persuade suspicious American security guards that they were genuine GIs. On 20 December, two American soldiers were killed by a nervous US military policeman. Two more American soldiers were killed and several wounded as late as 2 January 1945 when an armor task force from the US 6th Armored Division moving into the Wardin area of Bastogne opened fire on the US 35th Infantry Division in a case of mistaken identity.[196] (According to Paul Fussell, an uncorrected typographical error on American identity cards could serve as a tell: the top of a genuine card read "NOT A PASS. FOR IDENTIFICATION PURPOSES ONLY." Someone preparing the disguises of the commandos could not resist correcting the spelling on their false cards to read "IDENTIFICATION.")

In all, 44 German soldiers wearing US uniforms were sent through US lines, and all but eight returned, with the last men being sent through the lines on 19 December; after this, the element of surprise had been lost and they reverted to wearing German uniforms. It was not an uncommon practice at the time to send camouflaged reconnaissance units behind enemy lines, but because of the impact of Operation *Greif*, every occurrence of this was attributed to Skorzeny's men. In addition, German infantry often salvaged any items of

US Army clothing they found, thus it was not out of the question that regular German troops might be killed or captured wearing items of US uniforms.[197]

Eisenhower rumor

So great was the confusion caused by Operation *Greif* that the US Army saw spies and saboteurs everywhere. Perhaps the largest panic was created when a German commando team was captured near Aywaille on 17 December. Comprising Unteroffizier Manfred Pernass, Oberfähnrich Günther Billing, and Gefreiter Wilhelm Schmidt, they were captured when they failed to give the correct password. It was Schmidt who gave credence to a rumor that Skorzeny intended to capture General Dwight Eisenhower and his staff.[198] A document outlining Operation *Greif*'s elements of deception (though not its objectives) had earlier been captured by the US 106th Infantry Division near Heckhuscheid, and because Skorzeny was already well known for rescuing Italian dictator Benito Mussolini (Operation Oak or *Unternehmen Eiche*) and Operation Panzerfaust, the Americans were more than willing to believe this story and Eisenhower was reportedly unamused by having to spend Christmas 1944 isolated for security reasons. After several days of confinement, he left his office, angrily declaring he had to get out and that he didn't care if anyone tried to kill him.

Not even British Field Marshal Bernard Montgomery was exempt from Skorzeny's commando paranoia. Upon hearing of Eisenhower's confinement, Montgomery took off in his staff car towards Malmédy to increase his own prestige among American troops. Little did he know that a rumor had been spread in the Ardennes that one of Skorzeny's commandos looked strikingly similar to Montgomery and had identified himself as such at several American checkpoints. When American guards halted his car at the first checkpoint, Montgomery told them that he would not put up with such nonsense and ordered the driver to keep going. The guards angrily shot out his tires and dragged the field marshal to a nearby barn where he was detained for several hours. Montgomery was enraged and called for the court martial of the American privates if they did not release him. He was also insulted that they did not recognize him after the guards demanded his identification. He was only released after a British captain known to the Americans properly recognized the fuming field marshal. An amused Eisenhower got great pleasure from the incident, saying this was the best thing for which Skorzeny had ever been responsible.[199]

Figure 83: *Pernass, Billing, and Schmidt were lined and tied up for execution by firing squad after a U.S. military court found them guilty of espionage. They were captured behind U.S. lines in U.S. uniforms during the Battle of the Bulge.*

Aftermath

Pernass, Billing, and Schmidt were given a military trial at Henri-Chapelle on 21 December and were sentenced to death and executed by a firing squad on 23 December. Three more Germans were also tried on 23 December and shot at Henri-Chapelle on 26 December, seven more men were tried on 26 December and executed at Henri-Chapelle on 30 December, and three others were tried on 31 December and executed at Huy on 13 January 1945. These executions were carried out by the U.S. First Army. All of these commissions were appointed by Lieutenant General Courtney Hodges, Commanding General of the U.S. First Army pursuant to authority delegated to him by General Omar Bradley, Commanding General of the Twelfth U.S. Army Group on the instructions of General Dwight Eisenhower, commanding the European Theater of Operations, U.S. Army.

The team's leader of Operation *Greif*, Günther Schulz, was tried by a military commission sometime in May 1945 and executed near the German city of Braunschweig on 14 June. It is not known why his trial was delayed until May 1945, and nor is it clear who ordered his death sentence to be carried out. His execution was carried out by the U.S. Ninth Army.

After World War II, Skorzeny was tried as a war criminal at the Dachau Trials in 1947 for allegedly violating the laws of war during the Battle of the Bulge. He and nine officers of the Panzerbrigade 150 were charged with improperly using American uniforms "by entering into combat disguised therewith and treacherously firing upon and killing members of the armed forces of the United States." They were also charged with participation in wrongfully obtaining U.S. uniforms and Red Cross parcels consigned to American prisoners of war from a prisoner-of-war camp. Acquitting all defendants, the military tribunal drew a distinction between using enemy uniforms during combat and for other purposes including deception; it could not be shown that Skorzeny had actually given any orders to fight in U.S. uniforms.[200] Skorzeny said that he was told by German legal experts that as long as he didn't order his men to fight in combat while wearing U.S. uniforms, such a tactic was a legitimate ruse of war. A surprise defense witness was F. F. E. Yeo-Thomas, a former Allied SOE agent, who testified that he and his operatives wore German uniforms behind enemy lines.

In popular culture

- The German deception operation is featured in the 1949 film *Battleground*.
- *The Last Blitzkrieg* is a 1959 World War II film which is a fictional account of Operation *Grief*. Technical advisor to the film was Major John W. McClain who was a company commander with the 23rd Infantry. A novelization of the screenplay was written by Walter Freeman.
- A 1964 episode of *Kraft Suspense Theatre* about the operation as titled *Operation Greif*.
- The German deception operation is featured prominently in the 1965 film *Battle of the Bulge*.
- The beginning of 2002 film *Hart's War,* set during the Battle of the Bulge, involves a scene where German soldiers are dressed as American MPs.
- In *Die Hard with a Vengeance*, it was mentioned to John that Simon Gruber was a member of an infiltration unit similar to Operation Greif and The Battle Of The Bulge. Only Simon is using his skills to rob the Federal Reserve.
- "The Second Objective", Mark Frost's novel based on Operation Greif weaves a thriller narrative around Hitler's last attempt to defeat the allies.
- The video game *Call of Duty: WWII* featured Operation Grief (Under the title Operation Griffin) as a map as part of its Multiplayer War Gamemode.

Sources

- Pallud, Jean-Paul; David Parker; Ron Volstad (1987). *Ardennes, 1944: Peiper and Skorzeny*. Osprey Publishing. p. 29. ISBN 0-85045-740-8.

External links

- Tony Paterson (2 May 2004). "Revealed: Farce of plot to kidnap Eisenhower"[201]. *The Telegraph*. Berlin.
- Koessler, Maximilian (1959). "International Law on Use of Enemy Uniforms As a Stratagem and the Acquittal in the Skorzeny Case"[202]. *Missouri Law Review*. **24** (1).

Attack in the south

Siege of Bastogne

Siege of Bastogne	
Part of the Ardennes Offensive (World War II)	

101st Airborne Division troops watch as C-47s
drop supplies over Bastogne, 26 December 1944

Date	20–27 December 1944
Location	Bastogne, Belgium 50°00′00″N 5°43′17″E[203]Coordinates: 50°00′00″N 5°43′17″E[203]
Result	American victory

Belligerents	
▄▄ United States	🔷 Germany

Commanders and leaders	
▄▄ Anthony McAuliffe (101st Airborne) ▄▄ William L. Roberts (Combat Command B (CCB), 10th Armored Division) ▄▄ Creighton Abrams (37th Tank Battalion, 4th Armored Division) ▄▄ George S. Patton (Third Army)	🔷 Hasso von Manteuffel (5th Panzer Army) 🔷 Heinrich Freiherr von Lüttwitz (XLVII Panzer Corps) 🔷 Wilhelm Mohnke (I SS Panzer Corps)

Units involved	

191

Initially parts of:	Initially parts of:
101st Airborne Division	26th Volksgrenadier Division
CCB of the 10th Armored Division	5th Parachute Division
CCR of the 9th Armored Division	Panzer Lehr Division
705th Tank Destroyer Battalion	2nd Panzer Division
35th and 158th Combat Engineer Battalions	**Total:** All or parts of 7 divisions
58th and 420th Armored Field Artillery Battalions	**Eventual Participants:**
755th and 969th Field Artillery Battalions of 8th	1st SS Panzer Division Leibstandarte
Corps	SS Adolf Hitler[205]
Team SNAFU[204]	Führerbegleitbrigade
Eventual Participants:	12th SS Panzer Division Hitlerjugend
4th Armoured Division	9th SS Panzer Division Hohen-
26th Infantry Division	staufen[204]
6th Armoured Division	
11th Armoured Division	
35th Infantry Division	
87th Infantry Division	
90th Infantry Division[204]	
Strength	
101st: 11,000 enlisted + 800 officers	54,000+ men
Remaining units: 11,000+	
Total: 22,800+ men	
Casualties and losses	
3,000+ total casualties (2,000 in the 101st)	12,000 casualties

File:Belgium location map.svg
Location within Belgium

The **Siege of Bastogne** was an engagement in December 1944 between American and German forces at the Belgian town of Bastogne, as part of the larger
Battle of the Bulge. The goal of the German offensive was the harbour at
Antwerp. In order to reach it before the Allies could regroup and bring their
superior air power to bear, German mechanized forces had to seize the road-
ways through eastern Belgium. Because all seven main roads in the densely
wooded Ardennes highlands converged on Bastogne (*Bastnach* in German),
just a few miles away from the border with neighbouring Luxembourg, control of its crossroads was vital to the German attack. The siege was from 20 to

27 December, until the besieged American forces were relieved by elements of General George Patton's Third Army.

Background

After the successful invasion of Normandy and the subsequent eastward push through France, the Allied front lines extended from Nijmegen in the north down to neutral Switzerland in the south. The valuable port city of Antwerp had been captured during the push, and by the time winter arrived, the Allies even had control of German territory near the city of Aachen. Adolf Hitler soon laid out a plan to attack the Allied lines in Belgium and Luxembourg; 25 divisions would launch a surprise attack through the Ardennes, with the aim of crossing the Meuse River (called *Maas* in German and Dutch) and recapturing Antwerp. Despite major misgivings from his senior commanders, including Gerd von Rundstedt and Walther Model, the plan was not modified and the jump-off date was eventually set as 16 December 1944. Meanwhile, the Allied commanders considered the Ardennes area to be unsuitable for a large-scale German attack, mainly because of terrain issues. In addition, intelligence reports suggested that the only German divisions stationed in the area were weary, and in the weeks leading up to the assault, no Allied commander saw reason to believe that an attack was imminent. Bastogne, a hub city that commanded several important roads in the area, was defended mainly by the 28th Infantry Division, which had seen continuous fighting from 22 July to 19 November, before being assigned to this relatively quiet area. The Allies believed only an infantry division was present opposite the 28th Infantry, and they believed any attack along this sector would be limited in scale. The seven roads in and out of Bastogne were critical to the movement of German armor, making Allied retention of the roads imperative.

Hasso von Manteuffel—commanding the 5th Panzer Army—gave Heinrich Freiherr von Lüttwitz's XLVII Panzer Corps the responsibility of capturing Bastogne, before crossing the Meuse near Namur. Lüttwitz planned to attack a 7 mi (11 km) front with three divisions: the 26th Volksgrenadier and the 2nd Panzer would lead the assault, with the *Panzer-Lehr-Division* behind them. Opposing this significant force were two battalions of the 110th Infantry Regiment (the third was held back as a division reserve), responsible for a 9 mi (14 km) front along the Our River which forms the border between Germany and neighbouring Luxembourg. The Allied forces were gathered into small groups at major Luxembourgish villages, with outposts along the river manned only during the daytime. The forces were too thin to maintain an even battle line, they focused their attention on the four roads that crossed the Our. Due to heavy rain preceding the German attack, only one of the roads was in good enough condition to be used as a crossing point—the northernmost road, which

crossed the Our at Dasburg on its way to the Luxembourgish town of Cler-
vaux (in German: *Klerf*, in Luxembourgish: *Klierf*) and Bastogne. The 2nd
Panzer Division was assigned to cross the river along this road, while the 26th
Volksgrenadier Division would construct a bridge near Gemünd for its crossing. Lüttwitz realized the importance of the road network of Bastogne—he
knew that the town had to be captured before his corps could venture too far
westward. Therefore, he ordered the *Panzer-Lehr* Division' to push forward
to Bastogne as soon as his other troops had crossed the Clerf River in Northern
Luxembourg.

Prelude

The attack

On the evening of 15 December, the 26th Volksgrenadier established an out-
post line on the west bank of the Our, something they did routinely during
the nighttime. At 03:00, engineers began ferrying men and equipment over
the river where they began assembling at the departure point, quite close to
the American garrisons. At 05:30, the German artillery began bombarding
the American positions, knocking out telephone lines, as the infantry started
to advance. The Germans attacked swiftly, their advances made possible by
sheer weight of numbers. In the Luxembourgish village of Weiler, one American company, supported by some mortars and a platoon of anti-tank guns,
lasted until nightfall against repeated attacks from multiple German battalions.
German engineers completed bridges over the Our before dark, and armor began moving to the front, adding to the Germans' vast numerical superiority.
But in the end, the Germans were significantly delayed by the American defenders—their plan to cross the Clerf River by nightfall on the first day was
delayed by two days.

On 19 December, the 28th Division command post transferred to Bastogne
from Wiltz, a large Luxembourgish town to the southeast. At Wiltz, the division put up its last stand; 3rd Battalion of the 110th—supported by armor
and artillery—arrived at the town around noon of that day. The 44th Engineer Battalion was set up north of the town, but they were soon overwhelmed
and retreated into the town, blowing up a bridge behind them. This small
force—numbering no more than 500 in total—held out until the evening, when
their position became completely untenable and they retreated to the west.
With the 110th Infantry completely destroyed as an effective combat unit, it
would be up to the rest of the Allied army to defend Bastogne.

Commitment of reserves

Despite several notable signs in the weeks preceding the attack, the Ardennes Offensive achieved virtually complete surprise. By the end of the second day of battle, it became apparent that the 28th Infantry was near collapse. Major General Troy H. Middleton, commander of VIII Corps, was given Combat Command B of the 10th Armored Division to assist in the defense of Bastogne. CCB consisted of the 3rd Tank Battalion, 20th Armored Infantry Battalion, C Company 21st Tank Battalion, B Company 54th Armored Infantry Battalion, C Company, 609th Tank Destroyer Battalion, 420th Armored Field Artillery Battalion, and three companies of support troops. General George S. Patton, commander of the U.S. Third Army was not happy about giving up the unit right before he planned an offensive near Mainz but General Omar Bradley, commander of the 12th Army Group, ordered General Patton to release the unit. Meanwhile, General Dwight D. Eisenhower, the Supreme Allied Commander, ordered forward the SHAEF reserve, composed of the 82nd Airborne Division, commanded by Major General James Gavin, and the 101st Airborne Division, temporarily under command of Brigadier General Anthony McAuliffe, at Reims. These were veteran troops that had served with distinction since the parachute drops in Normandy and were resting and re-equipping after two months of combat in the Netherlands after Operation Market Garden. Both divisions were alerted on the evening of 17 December, and not having transport automatically assigned for their use, began arranging trucks for movement forward. The 82nd—longer in reserve and thus better re-equipped—moved out first. The 101st left Camp Mourmelon on the afternoon of 18 December, with the order of march of the division artillery, division trains, 501st Parachute Infantry Regiment (PIR), 506th PIR, 502nd PIR, and 327th Glider Infantry Regiment (GIR). Much of the convoy was conducted at night in drizzle and sleet, using headlights despite threat of air attack to speed the movement, and at one point the combined column stretched from Bouillon, Belgium, back to Reims, a distance of 120 kilometres (75 mi).

The 101st Airborne was originally supposed to go to Werbomont on the northern shoulder but was rerouted to Bastogne, located 107 miles (172 km) away on a 1,463 feet (446 m) high plateau, while the 82nd Airborne, because it was able to leave sooner, went to Werbomont to block the critical advance of the *Kampfgruppe Peiper* ("Combat Group Peiper"). The 705th Tank Destroyer Battalion—in reserve 60 miles (97 km) to the north—was ordered to Bastogne to provide anti-tank support to the armor-less 101st Airborne on 18 December and arrived late the next evening. The first elements of the 501st PIR entered the division assembly area 4 miles (6.4 km) west of Bastogne shortly after midnight of 19 December, and by 09:00 the entire division had arrived.

Brigadier General Anthony McAuliffe sent the 501st PIR southeast through
Bastogne at 06:00 to develop the situation. By 09:00, it had advanced and
deployed on either side of the highway to Magéret and Longvilly, where the
Panzer-Lehr-Division (*Armored Training Division*) was engaged in an all-day
action to destroy the armor-infantry combat teams assigned to slow the German
advance. The 506th followed shortly thereafter, its 1st Battalion was sent to
Noville to re-enforce Major Desobry's team from the 10th Armored CCB while
the other two battalions were ordered to act as reserves north of Bastogne. The
502nd PIR marched north and northwest to establish a line from Champs east
to Recogne, while the 327th GIR, newly arrived, protected the division service
area southwest of Bastogne until German intentions could be deciphered.

Initial combat at Noville

On 19–20 December, the 1st Battalion of the 506th PIR was ordered to support
Team Desobry (Maj. William R. Desobry), a battalion-sized tank-infantry task
force of the 10th Armored Division assigned to defend Noville located north-
northeast of both Foy and of Bastogne just 4.36 mi (7.02 km) away. With just
four[206] M18 Hellcat tank destroyers of the 705th Tank Destroyer Battalion to
assist, the paratroopers attacked units of the 2. *Panzerdivision*, whose mission
was to proceed by secondary roads via Monaville (just northwest of Bastogne)
to seize a key highway and capture, among other objectives, fuel dumps—for
the lack of which the overall German counter-offensive faltered and failed.
Worried about the threat to its left flank in Bastogne, it organized a major
combined arms attack to seize Noville. Team Desobry's high speed highway
journey to reach the blocking position is one of the few documented cases in
which the top speed of the M18 Hellcat (55 mph (89 km/h)) was actually used
to get ahead of an enemy force as envisioned by its specifications.

The attack of 1st Battalion and the M18 Hellcat tank destroyers of the 705th
TD Battalion together destroyed at least 30 German tanks and inflicted 500-
1,000 casualties on the attacking forces in what amounted to a spoiling at-
tack.Wikipedia:Citation needed The 3rd Battalion was ordered forward from
a reserve position north of Bastogne to ease the pressure on 1st Battalion by
occupying a supporting position in Foy to the south.

The heavy losses inflicted by the tank-destroyers deceived the German commander into believing the village was being held by a much stronger force and
he recoiled from further attacks on the village, committing a strategic error
while seeking tactical advantage—significantly delaying the German advance
and setting the stage for the Siege of Bastogne just to the south. This delay also gave the 101st Airborne Division enough time to organize defenses
around Bastogne. After two days, the 2nd Panzer Division finally continued

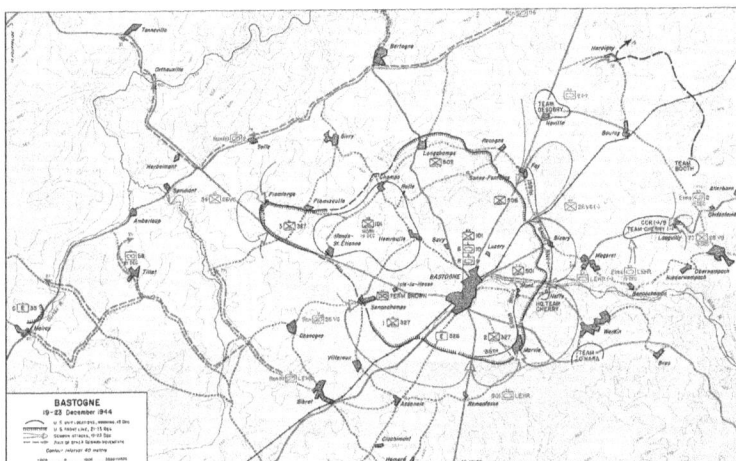

Figure 84: *19–23 December 1944*

on its original mission to the Meuse River. As a consequence of its involve-
ment at Bastogne, and its failure to dislodge the airborne forces, the column
ultimately ran out of fuel at Celles, where it was destroyed by the U.S. 2nd
Armored Division and the British 29th Armoured Brigade.

By the time the 1st Battalion pulled out of Noville on the 20th, the village of
Foy half-way to Bastogne center had been captured from the 3rd Battalion by
a separate attack, forcing the 1st Battalion to then fight its way through Foy.
By the time 1st Battalion made it to the safety of American lines, it had lost 13
officers and 199 enlisted men, out of about 600 troops, and was assigned as the
division reserve. Team Desobry lost a quarter of its troops and was reduced to
just four medium tanks when it passed through the lines of 3rd Battalion.

Battle

The 101st Airborne formed an all-round perimeter using the 502nd PIR on
the northwest shoulder to block the 26th Volksgrenadier, the 506th PIR to
block entry from Noville, the 501st PIR defending the eastern approach, and
the 327th GIR scattered from Marvie in the southeast to Champs in the west
along the southern perimeter, augmented by engineer and artillery units plugging gaps in the line. The division service area to the west of Bastogne had
been raided the first night, causing the loss of almost its entire medical company, and numerous service troops were used as infantry to reinforce the thin
lines. CCB of the 10th Armored Division, severely weakened by losses to its
Team Desobry (Maj. William R. Desobry), Team Cherry (Lt. Col. Henry

T. Cherry), and Team O'Hara (Lt. Col. James O'Hara) in delaying the Germans, formed a mobile "fire brigade" of 40 light and medium tanks (including survivors of CCR 9th Armored Division and eight replacement tanks found unassigned in Bastogne).

Three artillery battalions were commandeered and formed a temporary artillery group. Each had twelve 155 mm (6.1 in) howitzers, providing the division with heavy firepower in all directions restricted only by its limited ammunition supply. Col. Roberts, commanding CCB, also rounded up 600+ stragglers from the rout of VIII Corps and formed Team SNAFU as a further stopgap force.

As a result of the powerful American defense to the north and east, XLVII Panzer Corps commander Gen. von Lüttwitz decided to encircle Bastogne and strike from the south and southwest, beginning the night of 20/21 December. German *Panzer* reconnaissance units had initial success, nearly overrunning the American artillery positions southwest of Bastogne before being stopped by a makeshift force. All seven highways leading to Bastogne were cut by German forces by noon of 21 December, and by nightfall the conglomeration of airborne and armored infantry forces were recognized by both sides as being surrounded.

The American soldiers were outnumbered approximately 5-1 and were lacking in cold-weather gear, ammunition, food, medical supplies, and senior leadership (as many senior officers, including the 101st's commander—Major General Maxwell Taylor—were elsewhere). Due to the worst winter weather in memory, the surrounded U.S. forces could not be resupplied by air nor was tactical air support available due to cloudy weather.

However, the two Panzer divisions of the XLVII Panzer Corps—after using their mobility to isolate Bastogne, continued their mission towards the Meuse on 22 December, rather than attacking Bastogne with a single large force. They left just one regiment behind to assist the 26th Volksgrenadier Division in capturing the crossroads. The XLVII Panzer Corps probed different points of the southern and western defensive perimeter in echelon, where Bastogne was defended by just a single airborne regiment and support units doubling as infantry. This played into the American advantage of interior lines of communication; the defenders were able to shift artillery fire and move their limited *ad hoc* armored forces to meet each successive assault.

It was on the 22nd of December that General von Lüttwitz submitted the following demand for surrender to his American counterpart commanding the American forces in Bastogne, Brigadier General Anthony McAuliffe:

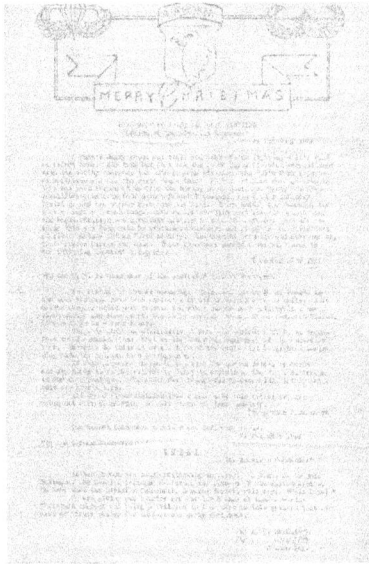

Figure 85: *Letter from General McAuliffe on Christmas Day to the 101st Airborne troops defending Bastogne.*

To the U.S.A. Commander of the encircled town of Bastogne.

The fortune of war is changing. This time the U.S.A. forces in and near Bastogne have been encircled by strong German armored units. More German armored units have crossed the river Our near Ortheuville, have taken Marche and reached St. Hubert by passing through Hompre-Sibret-Tillet. Libramont is in German hands.

There is only one possibility to save the encircled U.S.A. troops from total annihilation: that is the honourable surrender of the encircled town. In order to think it over a term of two hours will be granted beginning with the presentation of this note.

If this proposal should be rejected one German Artillery Corps and six heavy A. A. Battalions are ready to annihilate the U.S.A. troops in and near Bastogne. The order for firing will be given immediately after this two hours term.

All the serious civilian losses caused by this artillery fire would not correspond with the well-known American humanity.

The German Commander.

Shortly thereafter, McAuliffe sent the following communication to von Lüttwitz in response to the German demand:[207]

To the German Commander.

NUTS!

The American Commander

The commander of the 327th GIR interpreted it to the German truce party as
"Go to hell!".[208]

Despite the defiant American response to the surrender demand, the 26th VG
received one Panzergrenadier regiment from the 15th Panzergrenadier Division on Christmas Eve for its main assault the next day. That night, at about
7:00 PM, Luftwaffe bombers attacked Bastogne, killing 21 in an aid station.
Because it lacked sufficient troops and those of the 26th VG Division were
near exhaustion, the XLVII Panzer Corps concentrated its assault on several
individual locations on the west side of the perimeter in sequence rather than
launching one simultaneous attack on all sides. The assault—led by 18 tanks
carrying a battalion of infantry—pierced the lines of the 327th's 3rd Battalion
(officially, the 1st Battalion, 401st Glider Infantry), and advanced as far as the
battalion command post at Hemroulle.

However, the 327th held its original positions and repulsed infantry assaults
that followed, capturing 92 Germans. The panzers that had achieved the penetration divided into two columns, one trying to reach Champs from the rear,
and were destroyed in detail by two companies of the 1st Battalion 502nd PIR
under Lt. Col. Patrick F. Cassidy and four tank destroyers of the 705th Tank
Destroyer Battalion.

Allied control of Bastogne was a major obstacle to the German armored advance, and the morale of Allied forces elsewhere on the Western Front was
boosted by news of the stubborn defence of the besieged town.

333rd Field Artillery Battalion – The Black Battalion

A rarity in the World War II era American Army, the 333rd Battalion was
a combat unit composed entirely of African American soldiers, led by white
officers. At the start of the Battle of the Bulge, the 333rd was attached to the
106th Infantry Division. Prior to the German offensive, the 106th division
was tasked with holding a 26-mile (41.8 kilometers) long length of the front,
despite the Army Field manual stating that a single infantry division could hold
no more than 5 miles (8 kilometers) of front. As a result, in the initial days of
the assault, two of the division's three overstretched regiments were brushed
aside by the German Army, yielding 6000 prisoners. The 333rd was badly
affected, losing nearly 50% of its soldiers including its commanding officer.
Eleven of its soldiers were cut off from the rest of the unit and attempted to
escape German capture, but were massacred on sight by the Waffen SS. The

Figure 86: *A Panzer IV H of Kampgruppe Peiper of the 1st SS Panzer Division Leibstandarte SS Adolf Hitler. The 101st Airborne Division fought this elite Waffen SS division when the 101st attacked towards Bourcy, northeast of Bastogne, on 13 January 1945.*

remnants of the battalion retreated to Bastogne where they linked up the 101st. The vestiges of the 333rd were attached to its sister unit the 969th Battalion. The remains of the 333rd were given carbines and assigned to defend the town. Despite low supplies of food and ammunition, and being limited to only 10 artillery rounds per day, the 333rd fought tenaciously, successfully holding their sector of the front despite repeated German assaults. For their heroism, the 333rd was awarded the Presidential Unit Citation.

Breaking the encirclement

Elements of General George Patton's Third Army succeeded in reaching Bastogne from the southwest, arriving from the direction of Assenois. The spearhead reached the lines of the 326th Engineers on the day after the Christmas attack at approximately 16:50. The 101st's ground communications with the American supply dumps were restored on 27 December, and the wounded were evacuated to the rear. Gen. Taylor reached Bastogne with the 4th Armored Division and resumed command.

With the encirclement broken, the men of the 101st expected to be relieved, but were given orders to resume the offensive. The 506th attacked north and re-captured Recogne on 9 January 1945, the Bois des Corbeaux (*Crows' Wood*), to the right of Easy Company, on 10 January, and Foy on 13 January. The 327th attacked towards Bourcy, northeast of Bastogne, on 13 January and en-countered stubborn resistance. The 101st Airborne Division faced the elite of the German military which included such units as 1st SS Panzer Division Leibstandarte SS Adolf Hitler, Führerbegleitbrigade, 12th SS Panzer Division Hitlerjugend, and the 9th SS Panzer Division Hohenstaufen.[204] The 506th re-took Noville on 15 January and Rachamps the next day. The 502nd reinforced the 327th, and the two regiments captured Bourcy on 17 January, pushing the Germans back to their point of advance on the day the division had arrived in Bastogne. The next day the 101st Airborne Division was relieved.

Aftermath

The 101st Airborne Division's casualties from 19 December 1944 to 6 January 1945 were 341 killed, 1,691 wounded, and 516 missing. The 10th Armored Division's CCB incurred approximately 500 casualties.

Augusta Chiwy, a nurse who administered aid to the wounded during the siege, was honoured with the Civilian Award for Humanitarian Service by the Am-bassador to Belgium Howard Gutman in December 2011.[209]

Gallery

Figure 87: *Map of troop movements during the battle of the Bulge. Bastogne is near the middle.*

Figure 88: *101st Airborne troops picking up air-dropped supplies during the siege.*

Figure 89: *44th Armored Infantry soldiers and 6th Armored Division tanks near Bastogne, 31 December 1944*

Figure 90: *General Patton's jeep in Bastogne, 1 January 1945.*

Figure 91: *Members of C Company, 9th Engineers, conduct a memorial service for those killed during the siege, 22 January 1945.*

Figure 92: *Infantry of relief force near Bastogne, December 1944.*

References

- Stephen E. Ambrose (1993). *Band of Brothers: E Company, 506th Regiment, 101st Airborne: From Normandy to Hitler's Eagle's Nest.* Touchstone Books. ISBN 978-0-671-86736-2.
- Turow, Scott (2005). *Ordinary Heroes: A Novel.* Macmillan. ISBN 978-0-374-18421-6.
- Winters, Richard D., Cole C. (Cole Christian) Kingseed, and Inc ebrary. *Beyond Band of Brothers: The War Memoirs of Major Dick Winters.* New York: Berkley Caliber, 2006. Web. 26 October 2012.
- Atkinson, Rick. *The Guns at Last Light,* 2013
- *101st Airborne: The Screaming Eagles in World War Two* by Mark Bando

Further reading

- Evans, Major Gary F. (22 June 1972). *The 501st Parachute Infantry at Bastogne, Belgium December 1944*[210]. United States Army Center of Military History Historical Manuscripts Collection 8-3.1 BB 2. Retrieved June 9, 2010.
- Marshall, Colonel S. L. A. (1946). *Bastogne: The Story of the First Eight Days in Which the 101st Airborne Division Was Closed within the Ring of German Forces*[211] (1988 reprint ed.). United States Army Center of Military History. CMH Pub 22-2. Retrieved June 9, 2010.
- R. V. Cassill (1955), *The General Said "Nuts": The Exciting Moments of Our History—As Recalled by Our Favorite American Slogans,* New York: Birk.
- Collins, Michael; King, Martin (2013). *The Tigers of Bastogne: Voices of the 10th Armored Division in the Battle of the Bulge.* Casemate. ISBN 9781612001814.

External links

> Wikisourcehas original text related to this article:
> **THE ARDENNES:**
> **BATTLE OF THE BULGE.**
> **CHAPTER XIX:**
> **THE BATTLE OF BASTOGNE**

- Summary of the battle[212]
- The Battle of the Bulge – Fortunes of War[213]
- Battle of the Bulge – 4th Armored Division Help End the Siege of Bastogne[214]

- The Battle of Bastogne on YouTube[215]
- Map: The Western Front – 3 January 1945[216]
- "The Ardennes Offensive: Air resupply by paradrops and gliders (23–27 Dec. 1944)"[217]. National WWII Glider Pilots Association, Inc.

German counterattack

Operation Bodenplatte

<table>
<tr><td colspan="2" align="center">**Operation *Bodenplatte***</td></tr>
<tr><td colspan="2" align="center">Part of the Battle of the Bulge, World War II</td></tr>
<tr><td colspan="2" align="center"></td></tr>
<tr><td colspan="2">A Fw 190D-9 of 10./JG 54 *Grünherz*, pilot (Leutnant Theo Nibel), downed by a partridge which flew into the nose radiator near Brussels on 1 January 1945.</td></tr>
<tr><td>**Date**</td><td>1 January 1945</td></tr>
<tr><td>**Loca-tion**</td><td>Belgium, the Netherlands and France</td></tr>
<tr><td>**Result**</td><td>German operational failure[218,219]
• Pyrrhic German tactical success[220,221,222]
• Strategic German exhaustion[223,224]
• End of the *Luftwaffe* as a major fighting force</td></tr>
<tr><td colspan="2" align="center">**Belligerents**</td></tr>
<tr><td>United Kingdom
United States
Canada
New Zealand
Poland[225,226]</td><td>Germany</td></tr>
<tr><td colspan="2" align="center">**Commanders and leaders**</td></tr>
<tr><td>Arthur Coningham
Jimmy Doolittle
Hoyt Vandenberg</td><td>Werner Kreipe
Joseph Schmid
Dietrich Peltz
Karl Hentschel
Gotthard Handrick</td></tr>
<tr><td colspan="2" align="center">**Units involved**</td></tr>
</table>

🏴 2nd Tactical Air Force ▬ Eighth Air Force ▬ Ninth Air Force	II. *Jagdkorps* 3. *Jagddivision* 5. *Jagddivision*
Casualties and losses	
See Aftermath and casualties	See Aftermath and casualties

Operation *Bodenplatte* (Baseplate), launched on 1 January 1945, was an attempt by the Luftwaffe to cripple Allied air forces in the Low Countries during the Second World War. The goal of *Bodenplatte* was to gain air superiority during the stagnant stage of the Battle of the Bulge so that the German Army and *Waffen-SS* forces could resume their advance. The operation was planned for 16 December 1944, but was delayed repeatedly due to bad weather until New Year's Day, the first day that happened to be suitable.[227]

Secrecy for the operation was so tight that not all German ground and naval forces had been informed of the operation and some units suffered casualties from friendly fire. British signals intelligence (Ultra) recorded the movement and buildup of German air forces in the region, but did not realise that an operation was imminent.

The operation achieved some surprise and tactical success, but was ultimately a failure. A great many Allied aircraft were destroyed on the ground but replaced within a week. Allied aircrew casualties were quite small, since the majority of Allied losses were grounded aircraft. The Germans, however, lost many pilots who could not be readily replaced.[223]

Post-battle analysis suggests only 11 of the Luftwaffe's 34 air combat *Gruppen* (groups) made attacks on time and with surprise.[223] The operation failed to achieve air superiority, even temporarily, while the German ground forces continued to be exposed to Allied air attack. *Bodenplatte* was the last large-scale strategic offensive operation mounted by the Luftwaffe during the war.[228]

Background

The armies of the Western Allies were supported by the Allied Air Forces as they advanced across Western Europe in 1944. The Royal Air Force (RAF) and its Second Tactical Air Force—under the command of Air Marshal Arthur Coningham—moved No. 2 Group RAF, No. 83 Group RAF, No. 84 Group RAF and No. 85 Group RAF to continental Europe in order to provide constant close air support. The RAF harassed the German air, sea and ground forces by hitting strong points and interdicting their supply lines while reconnaissance units apprised the Allies of German movements. With Allied air superiority, the German Army could not operate effectively. The *Luftwaffe*, equally, found it difficult to provide effective air cover for the German Army.

Figure 93: *Focke-Wulf Fw 190A shot down by a fighter of the USAAF XXIX Tactical Air Command in 1944 or 1945. German losses were very heavy by late 1944.*

Although German aircraft production peaked in 1944 the *Luftwaffe* was critically short of pilots and fuel, and lacked experienced combat leaders.[229]

The land battles moved towards the River Rhine, to the east of which lay the German heartland. Most of France had been liberated, as had the Belgian cities Brussels and Antwerp. Although Operation *Market Garden* had failed in 1944, by 1945 the Allies had overrun most of the southern Netherlands and the Scheldt Estuary. As the ground forces moved across Europe, the Allied tactical air forces moved into new bases on the continent, to continue providing close support. The only limiting factor for the Allies was the weather. As winter came, the rains and mud turned airfields into quagmires, so large-scale air and land operations came to a halt.[230]

The situation might well have continued until the spring thaw had the German High Command (*Oberkommando der Wehrmacht*) not launched *Unternehmen Wacht am Rhein* (Operation *Watch on the Rhine*) on 16 December 1944. The land offensive was to improve the German military position by capturing Antwerp and separating the British Army from United States Army forces. Part of the planning for the German land operation required the attack to be conducted under the cover of bad winter weather, which kept the main Allied asset, the Tactical Air Forces, on the ground. It initially succeeded, but the weather also grounded the *Luftwaffe* for the most part. Nevertheless, the

Luftwaffe did manage to put 500 aircraft into the air on 16 December, more than had been achieved for a long time. This first day had been the originally planned date for the strike against Allied airfields, named Operation *Bodenplatte*.[231] However, the weather proved particularly bad and operations were shut down.[232]

The offensive achieved surprise and much initial success. To counter the attack from the air, the United States Army Air Forces (USAAF) handed operational control of its XXIX Tactical Air Command and part of its Ninth Air Force, under the command of Major General Hoyt Vandenberg, to the RAF and Arthur Coningham. On 23 December, the RAF Second Tactical Air Force provided the American forces with much needed support, and helped prevent a German capture of Malmedy and Bastogne. This left the Germans with only the logistical bottleneck of St. Vith to support their operations. The German attack faltered.[232]

The *Luftwaffe* had been far from absent over the front in December. It flew several thousand sorties over the theatre. Its encounters with the RAF and USAAF had meant heavy losses in *matériel* and pilots. On the eight days of operations between 17 and 27 December 1944, 644 fighters were lost and 227 damaged. This resulted in 322 pilots killed, 23 captured and 133 wounded. On the three days of operations 23–25 December, 363 fighters were destroyed. None of the *Geschwaderkommodoren* expected any large-scale air operations by the end of the month.[233]

Plan

In September 1944, Adolf Hitler resolved to recover Germany's deteriorating fortunes by launching an offensive in the West. On 16 September, Hitler directed *Generalleutnant* Werner Kreipe—Chief of the General Staff—to prepare the necessary aircraft for the offensive. On 21 October, Kreipe ordered the air fleet defending the Greater German *Reich* (*Luftflotte Reich*) to hand over seven *Jagdgeschwader* and *Schlachtgeschwader* to Air Command West (*Luftwaffenkommando West*) for a future offensive.[234]

On 14 November, Hermann Göring—Commander-in-Chief of the *Luftwaffe*—ordered the 2. *Jagddivision* and the 3. *Jagddivision* to prepare their units for a large-scale ground attack operation in the Ardennes. Preparations were to be complete by 27 November. The attack was to be carried out on the first day of the offensive.[235]

Generalmajor Dietrich Peltz was to plan the operation having been appointed C-in-C of II. *Fliegerkorps* on 8 December. *Luftwaffenkommando* West had ordered all units—except *Jagdgeschwader 300* and 301—to attend the main planning meeting in Flammersfeld on 5 December. On 14 December, Peltz officially initiated plans for a major blow against the Allies in northwest Europe. Peltz was not a fighter pilot; his combat record was as a dive bomber pilot, flying the Junkers Ju 87 *Stuka*. His experiences in Poland, in France, and during the early campaigns on the Eastern Front had moulded him into an outstanding ground attack specialist, making him an ideal candidate for planning *Bodenplatte*.[236]

On 15 December, this plan was worked out with the help of the *Luftwaffe's Jagd-Geschwaderkommodore*, among them Gotthard Handrick (*Jagdab-schnittsführer Mittelrhein*; Fighter Sector Leader Middle Rhein), Walter Grabmann and Karl Hentschel, commanders of 3. and 5. *Jagddivision* respectively. It was originally scheduled to support the Battle of the Bulge, the German Army's offensive, which began 16 December 1944. However, the same bad weather that prevented the RAF and USAAF from supporting their own ground forces also prevented the *Luftwaffe* from carrying out the operation. It was therefore not launched until 1 January 1945. By this time, the German Army had lost momentum owing to Allied resistance and clearing weather, which allowed Allied Air Forces to operate. The German Army attempted to restart the attack by launching Operation *Northwind* (*Unternehmen Nordwind*). The *Luftwaffe* was to support this offensive through *Bodenplatte*.[236]

The plan of *Bodenplatte* called for a surprise attack against 16 Allied air bases in Belgium, the Netherlands and France.[236] The object was to destroy or cripple as many Allied aircraft, hangars and airstrips as possible. Every fighter and fighter-bomber *Geschwader* (Wing) currently occupied with air defence along the Western Front was redeployed. Additional night-fighter units (*Nachtjagdgeschwader*) and medium bomber units (*Kampfgeschwader*) acted as pathfinders. The strike formations themselves were mostly single-engine Messerschmitt Bf 109 and Focke-Wulf Fw 190 fighters.[218]

However, in a blunder, the planners had set flight paths that took many units over some of the most heavily defended areas on the continent, namely the V2 launch sites around The Hague. These sites were protected by large numbers of German anti-aircraft artillery (AAA) units. At the turn of 1944/45 Air Command West had 267 heavy and 277 medium or light AAA batteries, and in addition to this there were 100 *Kriegsmarine* AAA batteries along the Dutch coast. Most of these lay in the sector of the 16th AAA Division, with its control station at Doetinchem, 15 mi (24 km) northeast of Arnhem.[237] Some of the AAA units been warned about the air operation but were not kept up to date with developments about changing timetables and the flight plan of German formations. As a result, one quarter of the German fighter units lost aircraft to friendly fire before the attacks could be initiated.[238]

After five years of war and heavy attrition many of the *Luftwaffe's* pilots were inexperienced and poorly trained, deficient in marksmanship and flight skills. There was a shortage of experienced instructors, and many of the training units were forced to fly front-line operations in order to bolster the front-line *Jagdgeschwader*.[239] Aviation fuel supplies were also at a premium, limiting the duration of training. Long-range Allied fighters exacerbated this situation by shooting down many training aircraft. By late 1944 there were no safe areas in which pilots could be trained without the possibility of air attack. The result was a "vicious circle": poorly trained pilots were quickly lost in combat or accidents, and the need to replace them put more pressure on the training system. Allied personnel who witnessed the attacks remarked on the poor aim of the strafing aircraft, and many of the *Luftwaffe* aircraft shot down by Allied anti-aircraft fire were caught because they were flying too slowly and too high.[240]

The plan called for strict radio silence and secrecy in order to maintain surprise. Maps were also only half complete, identified only enemy installations, and left out flight paths, lest the document fall into Allied hands enabling them to trace the whereabouts of German fighter bases. Most commanders were also refused permission to brief their pilots until moments before take-off. This created operational confusion. Commanders managed to get across only the bare essentials of the plan. When the operation got under way, many German pilots still did not understand what the operation was about, or what exactly was required of them.[218,241] They were convinced it was just a reconnaissance in force over the front, and were happy to follow their flight leaders on this basis.[218]

Targets and order of battle

It is unclear whether all of the following were deliberately targeted. Evidence suggests that Grimbergen, Knocke and Ophoven were targeted in error,[242] as was Heesch.[243] In all, the *Oberkommando der Luftwaffe* (OKL) deployed 1,035 aircraft[244] from several *Jagdgeschwader* (JG — fighter wings) *Kampfgeschwader* (KG — bomber wings), *Nachtjadggeschwader* (NJG — night fighter wings) and *Schlachtgeschwader* (SG — ground attack wings); of these, 38.5% were Bf 109s, 38.5% Fw 190As, and 23% Fw 190Ds.[245]

Below is the German target list:[246,247]

Target	Target Code (Allied)	Allied Air Force	Main aircraft type(s) targeted	Luftwaffe combat wing
Deurne, Belgium	B.70	RAF	Hawker Typhoon/Supermarine Spitfire/North American Mustang	JG 77
Asch	Y-29	USAAF	Republic P-47 Thunderbolt/P-51 Mustang	JG 11
Brussels—Evere	B.56	USAAF / RAF	Supermarine Spitfire	JG 26 and JG 54
Brussels—Grimbergen	B.60	USAAF	Boeing B-17 Flying Fortress/P-51 Mustang[248]	JG 26 and JG 54
Brussels—Melsbroek	B.58	RAF	North American Mitchell[248]	JG 27 and JG 54
Eindhoven	B.78	RAF / RCAF	Hawker Typhoon/Supermarine Spitfire	JG 3
Ghent/Sint-Denijs-Westrem	B.61	RAF / Polish Wing	Supermarine Spitfire	JG 1
Gilze en Rijen	B.77	RAF	Supermarine Spitfire/NA Mustang	KG 51 and JG 3
Heesch	B.88	RCAF	Supermarine Spitfire	JG 6
Le Culot	A-89	USAAF	P-38 Lightning	JG 4
Maldegem	B.65	PAF /- RNZAF / RAF	Supermarine Spitfire	JG 1
Metz—Frescaty	A-90	USAAF / RAF	P-47 Thunderbolt	JG 53
Ophoven	Y-32	RAF	Supermarine Spitfire	JG 4
Sint-Truiden	A-92	USAAF	P-47 Thunderbolt	SG 4 and JG 2
Volkel	B.80	RAF	Hawker Typhoon/Hawker Tempest	JG 6
Woensdrecht	B.79	RAF	Supermarine Spitfire	JG 77
Ursel	B.67	USAAF /RAF	de Havilland Mosquito/Avro Lancaster/B-17 (small numbers)[249]	JG 1

Codenames

Following the *Unternehmen Bodenplatte* raids, the Allies retrieved several log-books from crashed German aircraft. In several of these, the entry *"Auftrag Hermann 1.1. 1945, Zeit: 9.20 Uhr"* was translated as "Operation Hermann to commence on 1 January 1945, at 9:20am." This led the Allies to believe the

operation itself was named Hermann for *Reichsmarschall* Hermann Göring.[250]
Five further different codes were used for the attack:

* *Varus*: Indicating that the operation was "a go" and that it would take
  place within 24 hours of the *Varus* order being given.
* *Teutonicus*: Authority to brief the pilots and to arrange for the aircraft to
  be armed and ready at the edge of the airfield.
* *Hermann*: Giving the exact date and time of the attack.
* *Dorothea*: Indicating a delay in the attack.
* *Spätlese*: Cancelling of the attack after formations are airborne.

Allied intelligence

Allied intelligence failed to detect the German intention. In Ultra transcripts,
there are only a few indications of what was happening on the other side of the
front. On 4 December 1944, II *Jagdkorps* had ordered stockpiling for naviga-
tional aids, such as "golden-rain" flares and smoke bombs. Allied intelligence
made no written observations of this communication. They also disregarded
communications to Junkers Ju 88 groups regarding the use of flares when leading formations. Intelligence concluded that these instructions were designed
for a ground support mission rather than an interception operation. This was
reasonable, but no indications of possible ground targets were given.

On 20 December, a 3. *Jagddivision* message was intercepted confirming that
the locations for emergency landing grounds during a "special undertaking"
had remained unchanged. This was a clear indication that something was
amiss, but Allied intelligence did not comment on it. It also ignored more
messages indicating that low-level attacks were being practised. Allied intelligence, by 16 December, had monitored the reshuffling of both German Army
and *Luftwaffe* formations opposite the American-held front at the Ardennes.
Yet nothing major was suspected.[251]

Battle

Maldegem, Ursel and St. Denijs Westrem

Units	I, II, III./JG 1
Aircraft	71
Aircraft lost	29
Damaged	unknown
Pilots killed or captured	25

Jagdgeschwader 1 (JG 1) was responsible for the attack on the Ursel and Maldegem airfields. *Oberstleutnant* Herbert Ihlefeld led the *Geschwader*. The formation was mixed; Stab., (headquarters flight or *Stabschwarm*, attached to every *Geschwader*), I. and II./JG 1 operated the Fw 190 while the III./JG 1 flew the Bf 109. I./JG 1 lost four of their number to friendly anti-aircraft fire. Three of the four pilots were killed.[252]

The attacks at Maldegem and Ursel began at 08:30. Both I and II./JG 1 became involved in intense dogfights. III./JG 1 had lost only one aircraft over the target (and not to enemy fire).[253] I./JG lost a further Fw 190 to friendly anti-aircraft fire as it made its way to Ursel. III./JG 1 lost at least two further Fw 190s to friendly anti-aircraft fire.[254] Casualties could have been heavier, had the British anti-aircraft defences of Maldegem airfield not been moved in December.[255]

Stab. and I./JG 1 lost 13 Fw 190s and nine pilots were missing; five were killed and four were captured. Thus the loss rates in personnel and *matériel* were 39 and 56%, respectively. III./JG 1 lost only three Bf 109s with one pilot dead and two captured. I./JG 1 claimed 30 British Spitfires on the ground and two shot down over Maldegem. At Maldegem, 16 aircraft were destroyed, and at Ursel only six were lost. The claims of I./JG 1 were actually more in line with British total losses at both Maldegem and Ursel. No. 131 Wing RAF / Polish Wing lost 13 Spitfires plus two damaged beyond repair, a total of 15 lost.[256] At Ursel, six aircraft were destroyed, including, a B-17, two Lancasters and a Mosquito. I. and III./JG 1 lost a total of 16 aircraft and 12 pilots — not a good return.[257]

II./JG 1 attacked the airfield at St. Denis Westrem. Of the 36 II./JG 1 Fw 190s that took off, 17 were shot down, a staggering 47% loss rate. Among the pilots lost were several experienced fliers. In exchange, the Germans shot down two Spitfires, and seven forced-landed. At St. Denis 18 Spitfires were destroyed on the ground.[258,259]

Altogether JG 1 lost 25 pilots and 29 aircraft. This return for around 60 enemy aircraft (54 on the ground) cannot be considered a complete success, although the damage at St. Denijs Westrem and Maldegem had been significant.[260] Just nine of the fighters lost by JG 1 are confirmed to have been shot down in combat with Spitfires. It is possible a further three were shot down by Spitfires, or perhaps ground fire.[261] Two Spitfires were shot down and destroyed, with two more damaged.[262] One pilot of each Squadron (308 and 317) was killed. The total Spitfire losses were perhaps 32.

Sint-Truiden

Units	I, II, III./JG 2 and SG 4
Aircraft	144
Aircraft lost	46
Damaged	12
Pilots killed or captured	23

Schlachtgeschwader 4 and *Jagdgeschwader* 2 (SG 4 and JG 2) were to strike
at Sint-Truiden airfield. JG 2 was commanded by Kurt Bühligen. I./JG 2's
ground crews managed to make ready 35 of 46 Fw 190s, 29 of which were
Fw 190D. Only 33 pilots were fit for operations. So the *Gruppe* reported only
33 Fw 190s ready. II./JG 2 could field 20 of 29 Bf 109s. Stab./JG 2 had
three Fw 190s ready for the mission. It is not clear whether Bühligen took
part in the mission. III./JG 2 reported 40 Fw 190s operational, 34 of them Fw
190Ds. However, only 28 of the 43 pilots in the unit were fit for operations
and the formation fielded only 28 fighters. In total, 84 aircraft were ready on
31 December, including 28 Fw 190D-9s.[263]

SG 4 was led by Alfred Druschel. It had 152 machines on strength, of which
just 60 were operational, yet the 129 pilots were fit for action. Stab./SG 4 had
three Fw 190s and two pilots. I./SG 4 had 21 Fw 190s operational and 27
pilots ready. II./SG reported 27 Fw 190s ready, but pilot strength is unknown.
III./SG reported 24 Fw 190s, but only 16 were available at the forward airfields. Pilot strength is unknown. Best estimations make it around 60 Fw 190s
operational, of which 55 took part.[264]

At 09:12, JG 2 crossed the front line at Malmedy and was greeted by an enormous volume of Allied ground fire. The entire area was heavily defended by
anti-aircraft artillery, since the area had been the scene of heavy fighting, but
also had been attacked by V-1 and V-2 missiles. I./JG 2 lost at least seven fighters to ground fire alone. III./JG 2 lost 10 fighters. A possible seven Bf 109s
from II./JG 2 were also lost to ground fire. JG 2 attacked Asch and Ophoven
airfields by mistake.[265]

JG 2's mission was a disaster. I./JG 2 lost 18 Fw 190s and six more were
damaged by ground fire and enemy aircraft. This represented 73% of their
force. Of the 15 pilots missing, six would survive as POWs. II./JG 2 lost five
Bf 109s and three were damaged a loss rate of 40%. Pilot losses were three
missing, one dead and one wounded. III./JG 2 lost 19 Fw 190s and three were
damaged, a loss rate of 79%. Nine pilots were killed, two were wounded and
four were captured.[266] JG 2 losses, according to another source, amounted to
40% of its force. Pilot losses were 24 killed or posted missing, 10 captured and

four wounded.[267] Another source asserts that pilot losses stood at 23 killed or missing.[268]

SG 4's mission was also a disaster. During the assembly phase, they flew across JG 11's flight path, and the formation was broken up. Some of the pilots joined JG 11 in the confusion. Unable to recover the formation, I and II./SG 4 then decided to head home. The *Kommodore*, Druschel, had continued with five other pilots from III./SG 4 who had lost contact with their *Gruppe*. They crossed the front near Hürtgenwald around 09:10. As they did so, American anti-aircraft batteries opened fire, claiming seven aircraft in the next 30 minutes. Only six of the 50 Fw 190s of SG 4 carried out an attack, against airfields near Aachen and the Asch aerodrome. Of these six, four did not return. Druschel himself was reported missing.[269]

Volkel and Heesch

Units	I, II, III./JG 6
Aircraft	78
Aircraft lost	27
Damaged	5
Pilots killed or captured	23

The target of *Jagdgeschwader* 6 (JG 6) was Volkel. I and III./JG 6 were to attack while II./JG 6 was to provide cover against Allied fighters. I./JG 6 managed to get 29 of its 34 Fw 190s ready, while 25 of II./JG 6's fighters took part. Overall, most of the 99 Fw 190s were made available for the operation. III./JG 6 received orders to target petrol installations on the airfield only. Only 78 Fw 190s took off.[270]

While on course, JG 6 approached the airfield of Heesch and some of its pilots assumed it to be Volkel airfield. It is unlikely that the Heesch strip, built in October 1944, was known to the *Luftwaffe*. No. 126 Wing RCAF was based there and had dispatched its 411 and 442 Squadrons on recce missions early that morning so the majority of its units were airborne. Its 401 Squadron was readying for takeoff when JG 6 appeared at 09:15. Most of the German pilots had failed to notice the airfield, concentrating on keeping formation at low altitude. 401 Squadron scrambled. Some of the German fighters were authorised to engage, while the main body continued to search for Volkel. Stab., and II./JG 6 stumbled on another strip at Helmond, which contained no aircraft. Several German pilots believed it to be Volkel and attacked, losing several of their number to ground fire.[271] II./JG 6 suffered severely from Spitfire and Tempests based at Helmond. Very little damage was done at Heesch or Helmond.[272]

In the event, all four *Gruppen* failed to find Volkel and its Hawker Tempests remained untouched.[273] The only success JG 6 had was I./JG's erroneous attack on Eindhoven, which claimed 33 fighters and six medium bombers. Like Volkel, Helmond and Heesch had escaped damage. In the dogfights over Helmond, JG 6 claimed six victories. In fact, only two Spitfires were shot down and one badly damaged. Only one further fighter, a Hawker Typhoon, was shot down. Stab./JG 6 lost the *Kommodore*, Kogler, as a POW. Of I./JG's 29 Fw 190s, seven were lost and two damaged; of II./JG 6's 25 Fw 190s, eight were destroyed and two damaged; III./JG 6 lost 12 out 20 Bf 109s. In total, JG 6 lost 43% of its strength and suffered 16 pilots killed or missing and seven captured. As well as Kogler, one other commanding officer was lost—*Gruppenkommandeure* Helmut Kühle. Three *Staffelkapitäne* were lost: *Hauptmann* Ewald Trost was captured, *Hauptmann* Norbert Katz was killed and Lothar Gerlach was posted missing presumed killed.[274],[275]

Antwerp-Deurne and Woensdrecht

Units	I, II, III./JG 77
Aircraft	59
Aircraft lost	11
Damaged	–
Pilots killed or captured	11

Deurne airfield was to be destroyed by *Jagdgeschwader* 77 (JG 77). Antwerp housed the largest Allied contingent of nine Squadrons. It had been incessantly attacked by V-1 cruise missiles and V-2 SRBM ballistic missiles, and had been given a strong anti-aircraft defence.[276]

At 08:00, two formations 18 Bf 109s of I and III./JG 77, led by *Major* Siegfried Freytag, took off with their pathfinders. At the same time 23 Bf 109s of II./JG 77 took off. Around the Bocholt area they formed up with the other two *Gruppen*. Heading south and still north of Antwerp, JG 77 passed Woensdrecht airfield. It was home to No. 132 Wing RAF and its five Spitfire squadrons; No. 331 Squadron RAF, No. 332 Squadron RAF (Norwegian), No. 66 Squadron RAF and No. 127 Squadron RAF, and No. 322 Squadron RAF (Dutch). Some pilots from II./JG 77 either mistakenly believed it to be Antwerp, or thought the opportunity was too good to pass up. Two German fighters were claimed shot down, and one pilot captured. However, none of the JG 77 casualties fit this description.[277]

The main body continued to Antwerp. Some 12–30 German fighters attacked the airfield from 09:25 to 09:40. The ground defences were alert and the

Figure 94: *Destroyed P-47s at Y-34 Metz-Frescaty airfield.*

German formations attacked in a disorganised manner. 145 Wing RAF was missed completely and considering the large number of targets the destruction was light; just 12 Spitfires were destroyed.[278]

In total, 14 Allied aircraft were destroyed and nine damaged. JG 77 lost 11 Bf 109s and their pilots were lost. Six were killed and five captured according to Allied sources. However, German records show the loss of only 10 pilots. Four are listed as captured.[279,280]

Metz-Frescaty

Units	Stab., II., III., IV./JG 53
Aircraft	80
Aircraft lost	30
Damaged	8
Pilots killed or captured	17

Jagdgeschwader 53 (JG 53) was tasked with the operation against the USAAF airfield at Metz-Frescaty Air Base. Stab., II., III., and IV./JG 53 were available.[281] III./JG 53 was to destroy anti-aircraft installations in the Metz area, while the other *Gruppen* knocked out the airfields.[282]

The USAAF XIX Tactical Air Command had established a strong presence in northeast France and was supporting the U.S. 3rd Army. JG 53 was to knock out its airfields.[283] Some 26 Bf 109s took off but were intercepted by 12 P-47s of the 367th Fighter Squadron, 358th Fighter Group. The P-47s claimed 13 destroyed, one probable and six damaged for no losses. On the way home at 09:20, III./JG 53 were intercepted by 366th Fighter Squadron. Altogether, III./JG 53 lost 10 Bf 109s and one damaged to the 358th Fighter Group.[284] Of the 25 III./JG 53 Bf 109s that took part, 11 were shot down representing 40% of the attacking force. The 358th Fighter Group received the Distinguished Unit citation for preventing the attack on the 362nd Fighter Groups airfield.[285]

Although III./JG 53 failed, the main attack was a success by comparison. Stab,. II. and IV./JG 53 encountered no difficulties on the outward leg. The Germans caused significant damage among the parked USAAF fighters on the field. When the attack against the Metz airfield was over, the three JG 53 *Gruppen* reported the loss of 20 Bf 109s and seven damaged. This represented more than 50 percent of the attacking 52 fighters. Some 13 pilots were missing; three were killed, six remain missing as of today, and four were captured. A further three were wounded. JG 53 claimed 27 USAAF fighters on the ground and eight damaged. Added to this total is four aerial victories. In total JG 53 lost 30 Bf 109s and eight damaged in the two operations. This was a total loss of 48%.[286] The losses of the USAAF were 22 destroyed, 11 damaged (all P-47ts).[287] However, the negative effects of *Bodenplatte* on JG 53 outweighed any advantages gained.

Le Culot and Ophoven

Units	I, II, III./JG 4
Aircraft	55—75
Aircraft lost	25—26
Damaged	~ 6
Pilots killed or captured	17

Le Culot airfield (later known as Beauvechain) was 45 km (28 mi) northeast of Charleroi and was the target of *Jagdgeschwader* 4 (JG 4). The main strip (A-89) was known locally as Beauvechain, and an auxiliary field known as Le Culot East (Y-10), known to the locals as Burettes, was nearby. It was known to the *Luftwaffe* because several of its units had operated there.[288]

Geschwaderkommodore Major Gerhard Michalski commanded the force. Five pilots were shot down by ground fire. Another pilot got lost during the flight and ended up near Eindhoven where he was shot down and killed. Reduced in number, 8–10 fighters of IV./JG 4 continued to their target. After 10 minutes, they located a fairly large airfield and attacked, believing it to be Le Culot. It was in fact Sint-Truiden.[289]

The mistake was easy to make, Le Culot was located nearby. Sint-Truiden housed the 48th Fighter Group and 404th Fighter Group. The 492nd Fighter Squadron was readying to take off at 09:20. JG 4 hit the airfield at 09:15. Several P-47s taxiing out were abandoned by pilots and strafed to destruction.[290] The small-scale attack by JG had achieved considerable damage. Total American losses were 10 destroyed and 31 damaged. The Germans lost eight fighters, including seven Bf 109s, and three damaged.[291] No damage was done at Le Culot airfield.[292]

II (Sturm)./JG 4 took off for Le Culot at 08:08. Getting lost, they stumbled upon Asch airfield and claimed one P-47 destroyed and two twin-engine aircraft damaged, as well as two trains and trucks destroyed. The unit claimed an Auster reconnaissance aircraft shot down. The machine was probably a Stinson L-1 Vigilant of the 125th Liaison Squadron, U.S. Army. However, virtually the entire *Gruppe* of 17 Fw 190s was wiped out.[293]

I. and III./JG 4 were to strike Le Culot together. Taking off at 08:20 and heading northwest, they comprised a force of 35 Bf 109s (nine from III./JG 4). Two Ju 88G-1s of II./NJG 101 lead as pathfinders. Some of I./JG 4 attacked No. 125 Wing RAF Spitfires at Ophoven airfield. Spitfire losses are unclear. Two P-47s and a B-17 were destroyed. I./JG 4 reported two Bf 109s missing, one damaged and one destroyed. Just a hangar, one P-47 and several vehicles were claimed, and the anti-aircraft battery was silenced. The attack on the Spitfires at Ophoven and the mentioned B-17 and two P-47s are not included in the total.[294] Another source suggests two Spitfires destroyed and 10 damaged at Ophoven.[295]

According to one source, JG 4's losses were 25 fighters of the 55 that took part. With 17 pilots killed or missing and seven captured,[296] JG 4 suffered a 42% loss rate.[297] A more recent source claims a total of 75 aircraft of JG 4 took part, with only 12 attacking ground targets. Two Ju 88 pathfinders were lost, as well as 26 fighters with six more damaged.[298]

Asch

Units	Stab. I, II, III./JG 11
Aircraft	61
Aircraft lost	28
Damaged	unknown
Pilots killed or captured	24

The Asch Airfield had been constructed in November 1944 and was home to the 352nd Fighter Group, 8th Air Force, and the 366th Fighter Group, Ninth Air Force.[299] *Jagdgeschwader* 11 (JG 11) was to destroy the airfield. I./JG 11 had only 16 Fw 190s on strength and only six fit and operational pilots. Only six of I./JG 1's pilots took part, and just four of Stab./JG 1's pilots participated. III./JG 11 had more aircraft than pilots, and so other *Staffel* made up the numbers.[300] Just 41 Fw 190s of JG 11 took part in *Bodenplatte*; four from the Stab., six from I *Gruppe* and 31 of III *Gruppe*. The 20 fighters from II. *Gruppe* were Bf 109s.[301]

The plan called for a low-level strike by I and III./JG 11, while II./JG 11 flew as top cover against USAAF fighters. The pilots were shown maps and photographs of the airfield, but were not told the targets' identity until the morning of the attack. After crossing Allied lines, four fighters were lost to AAA fire. The course of JG 11 took it directly over Ophoven. Large formations of JG 11 attacked, in the mistaken belief it was Asch. The other half continued to Asch. Ophoven housed No. 125 Wing RAF, just 5 km (3.1 mi) north of Asch. About half, or some 30 Fw 190s and Bf 109s attacked the airfield.[302,303]

Asch was notable for a chance event. The 390th Squadron of the 366th Fighter Group had launched two fighter sweeps that morning, which played a crucial role in the failure of JG 11's attack.[304] The leader of the 487th squadron, 352nd Fighter Group, John Charles Meyer, anticipated German activity and had a flight of 12 P-51s about to take off on a combat patrol when the attack began. They took off under fire.[305]

Several pilots made "Ace" status that day. No P-51s were lost; two were damaged and one was damaged on the ground. The 336th Fighter Group lost one P-47.[306] The 366th was credited with eight enemy aircraft, and AAA claimed seven more. However, overclaiming is likely. *Luftwaffe* records indicate JG 11 lost 28 fighters. Four German pilots (two wounded) made it back to German-held territory, while four were captured and the remaining twenty were killed.[307] Some 24 of the Bf 109s and Fw 190s lost were lost over enemy lines.[308] German ace Günther Specht was among those German pilots killed.[309]

Figure 95: *Kurt Tank and Major Günther Specht (left) inspecting the rudder of his Bf 109. Specht's loss was a bitter blow for JG 11.*

Little is known about the claims of JG 11. According to one German document, 13 fighters, two twin-engine and one four-engine aircraft were claimed destroyed. Five fighters were claimed damaged on "Glabbeek airfield" — in reality it was Ophoven. Ten aerial victories and one probable were also claimed. But U.S. Fighter Group losses indicate these claims are excessive.[310]

The Americans claimed 35 German aircraft destroyed.[311] Only 14 can be judged with a degree of certainty to have been shot down by USAAF fighters, and possibly two more. Four are confirmed to have been shot down by AAA fire. Total JG 11 losses were 28.[312,313] The air battle over Asch had lasted 45 minutes.[314]

Brussels-Evere/Grimbergen

Units	Stab., I, II, III./JG 26 and III./JG 54
Aircraft	127
Aircraft lost	40
Damaged	unknown
Pilots killed or captured	30

Jagdgeschwader 26 (JG 26) and the III. *Gruppe* of *Jagdgeschwader* 54 (JG 54) were to strike at Brussels-Evere. At the end of December, II./JG 26 had 39 D-9s and III./JG 26 had 45 Bf 109s.[315] Records of available aircraft indicate 110 aircraft of JG 26 flew that day; all but 29 were Fw 190s, the remainder were Bf 109s. 17 Fw 190s from III./JG 54 took part with JG 26.

Unknown to the *Luftwaffe* the Grimbergen Airfield was almost completely abandoned. The Evere airfield was located to the south. It was one of the most densely populated airfields in Belgium and had plenty of targets. The main force consisted of 60 Spitfire XVIs of No. 127 Wing RAF. Also present were B-17s and B-24s of the Eighth Air Force. Overall, well over 100 aircraft were on the field.[316]

At 08:13, the first formations took off. In total, 64 Fw 190D-9s participated. Before the target was reached, some 14 D-9s were forced to turn back due to AAA damage or mechanical difficulties. Three Fw 190s were lost to German AAA fire. At 09:10, when the front was reached, Allied heavy AAA units began to engage the formation and another five were shot down. Most of the fire was from British Naval AAA defences defending the Scheldt Estuary. As the formation crossed the Dutch and Belgian border, I./JG 26 and III./JG 54 were intercepted by Spitfires. Five of the Fw 190s were shot down. I./JG 26 destroyed or damaged the few aircraft at the airfield. AAA defences claimed five kills and I./JG 26 reported two Fw 190s lost to Spitfires. Several others were lost over the airfield. Other losses occurred against friendly fire again on the return flight.[317]

The raid was a disaster. Just six machines were destroyed at Grimbergen for the loss of 21 Fw 190s and two damaged. Another eight sustained minor damage. Some 17 pilots were missing, eight of whom would survive as prisoners.[318]

Only II. and III./JG 26 hit Evere. Between 44 and 52 Fw 190s from these units took off. II. and III./JG 26 knocked out the flak towers and destroyed anything combustible: hangars, trucks, fuel dumps and aircraft.[319] 127 Wing RCAF lost one Spitfire in the air and 11 on the ground; 11 vehicles were damaged and one was destroyed. A total of 60–61 Allied aircraft were destroyed

Figure 96: *Fire crews attempt to save an Avro Lancaster from burning at Melsbroek, Belgium. This aircraft had landed at Melsbroek with the number 3 (starboard inner) engine out of action, its propeller feathered.*

at Evere.[320] A large number of transports were located there and attracted the attention of German pilots, which left many more Spitfires undamaged. Given the number of Spitfires on the field, the Canadian wing suffered "low" losses. The Canadian Wing Commander—Johnnie Johnson—blamed the poor marksmanship of German pilots for failing to achieve further success.[321,322]

Allied losses are given at Evere as 32 fighters, 22 twin-engine aircraft and 13 four-engine aircraft destroyed, plus another nine single, six twin and one four-engine aircraft damaged. In total, II./JG 26 losses included 13 Fw 190s destroyed and two damaged. Nine of its pilots were missing; five were killed and four captured. III./JG 26 lost six Bf 109s and four pilots. Only one of them was captured, the remainder were killed. The amount of damage the Germans inflicted made up for the losses; the Evere strike was a success.

Brussels-Melsbroek

Units	I, II, III./JG 27 and IV./JG 54
Aircraft	43
Aircraft lost	21

Damaged	1
Pilots killed or captured	17

Jagdgeschwader 27 and IV./*Jagdgeschwader* 54 (JG 27 and JG 54) targeted Melsbroek airfield. On 31 December, JG 27 could only muster the following operational pilots and aircraft: 22 (22) from I., 19 (13) from II., 13 (15) from III., and 16 (17) from IV. *Gruppe*.[323,324,325] *Geschwaderkommodore* Wolfgang Späte had rebuilt IV./JG 54. It had only 21 pilots and 15 of its 23 Fw 190s were operational. Altogether 28 Bf 109s of JG 27 and 15 Fw 190s of JG 54 took off. Seven fighters were lost to enemy aircraft and friendly AAA fire before they reached the target.[326]

The Germans hit Melsbroek hard. According to Emil Clade (leading III./JG 27), the AAA positions were not manned, and aircraft were bunched together or in lines, which made perfect targets. The attack caused considerable damage among the units based there and was a great success. The Recce Wings had lost two entire squadrons worth of machines. No. 69 Squadron RAF lost 11 Vickers Wellingtons and two damaged. No. 140 Squadron RAF lost four Mosquitoes, the losses being made good the same day. At least five Spitfires from No. 16 Squadron RAF were destroyed. No. 271 Squadron RAF lost at least seven Harrow transports "out of action". A further 15 other aircraft were destroyed. 139 Wing reported five B-25s destroyed and five damaged. Some 15 to 20 USAAF bombers were also destroyed.[327,328] Another source states that 13 Wellingtons were destroyed, as were five Mosquitoes, four Auster and five Avro Ansons from the Tactical Air Forces 2nd Communications Squadron. Three Spitfires were also lost and two damaged.[329] At least one RAF Transport Command Douglas Dakota was destroyed.

The pilots of JG 27 and 54 claimed 85 victories and 40 damaged. German reconnaissance was able to confirm 49. JG 27 suffered unacceptable losses; 17 Bf 109s, 11 pilots killed, one wounded and three captured. IV./JG 54 lost two killed and one captured. Three Fw 190s were lost and one damaged.[330,331]

Gilze-Rijen and Eindhoven

Units	Stab. I., III., IV./- JG 3 and KG 51
Aircraft	81
Aircraft lost	15–16
Damaged	Unknown
Pilots killed or captured	15–16

Jagdgeschwader 3 (JG 3) and *Kampfgeschwader* 51 (KG 51) were tasked with eliminating the Allied units at the Eindhoven base and Gilze-Rijen airfield. The field contained three Spitfire Squadrons and eight Typhoon units of the RAF and RCAF.[332] Some 22 Bf 109s of I./JG 3 took off,[333] along with four from Stab./JG 3, 15 from III./JG 3 and 19 Fw 190s from IV./JG 3. KG 51 contributed some 21 of their 30 Messerschmitt Me 262 jets to the action.[334] Some histories mistakenly include *Kampfgeschwader* 76 (KG 76) on the order of battle, but KG 76 did not take part in the mission.[335]

Each *Staffel* was expected to make at least three firing passes. I./JG 3 took off and joined the lead *Gruppe*, IV Sturm./JG 3, with III./JG 3 following in the rear. The Bf 109s and Fw 190s of the *Geschwader* reached the area at about 09:20. *Geschwaderkommodore* Heinrich Bär led the attack. Some pilots made four passes, destroying AAA emplacements, fuel storage stations and vehicles.[336] Nearly 300 aircraft were on the field, along with huge stores of equipment and fuel. The attack caused fires all over the airfield.[337]

JG 3 claimed 53 single-engine and 11 twin-engine aircraft destroyed. Five fighters and one four-engine bomber were also claimed damaged.[338] Four Typhoons, three Spitfires, one Tempest and another unidentified aircraft were claimed shot down. All in all, JG 3 managed to destroy 43 aircraft according to British records, and damage a further 60, some seriously. The *Geschwader* believed it had destroyed 116. JG 3 did not come away unscathed. I./JG 3 lost nine of its aircraft and pilots, a 50% loss rate. Damage to the returning *Gruppe* aircraft meant the entire unit was unserviceable. RAF AAA were credited with shooting down five.[339] JG 3 lost, altogether, 15 of the 60 fighters sent, a 25% loss rate. Some 15 pilots were missing; nine were killed and five captured, and another pilot was posting as missing in action and his fate remains unknown.[340] Another source says 16 pilots; ten killed or missing and six captured.[341]

The damage done to Eindhoven was significant and can be considered a victory for JG 3. It was also assisted by elements of JG 6 which had misidentified Eindhoven as one their targets. The greatest losses were amongst the Recce Wing and the Canadian 124 Wing RCAF, which suffered 24 aircraft destroyed or damaged. The visiting 39 Wing RAF lost 30 aircraft destroyed or damaged. 143 Wing RCAF lost 29 damaged or destroyed.[342] It is likely that I./JG 3 was responsible for about 2/3 of the damage. Another source gives 47 aircraft destroyed and 43 damaged.[343]

Possible V-2 missile launch attempts

At least one V-2 missile on a mobile *Meillerwagen* launch trailer was observed being elevated to launch position by a USAAF 4th Fighter Group pilot over the northern German attack route near the town of Lochem on 1 January 1945. Possibly on account of the launch crew sighting the American fighter, the rocket was quickly lowered from a near launch-ready 85° elevation to 30°.[344]

Results of raid

The results of the raid are difficult to judge given the confusion over loss records. It is likely more aircraft were destroyed than listed. The Americans failed to keep a proper record of their losses and it appears the U.S. 8th Air Force losses were not included in loss totals. When these estimates and figures are added to the losses listed in the table below, it is likely that the correct figures are 232 destroyed (143 single-engine, 74 twin-engine and 15 four-engine) and 156 damaged (139 single-engine, 12 twin-engine and five four-engine). Researching individual squadron records confirms the destruction of even more USAAF aircraft. This suggests at least a further 16 B-17s, 14 B-24s, eight P-51s, and at least two P-47s were destroyed on top of that total. A total of 290 destroyed and 180 damaged seems a more realistic summation than the conservative figures given by the USAAF, RAF, and RCAF. Including the 15 Allied aircraft shot down and 10 damaged in aerial combat, 305 destroyed and 190 damaged is the sum total of the attack.[345]

The results of the attacks are listed:[346]

little to no damage

light damage

medium damage

heavy damage

Target	Target Code (Allied)	Luftwaffe unit (wing)	Allied forces	Effect on Allied Squadrons (according to official figures)
Antwerp—Deurne	B-70	JG 77	No. 146 Wing RAF, No. 145 Wing RAF and USAAF Bomb Group also present[347]	One aircraft confirmed destroyed, around 15 damaged, including three possibly destroyed.[348][349]
Asch	Y-29	JG 11	USAAF 366th Fighter Group, 352nd Fighter Group.[350]	One abandoned B-17 destroyed, three damaged.

Brussels—Evere	B-56	JG 26 and JG 54	No. 127 Wing RAF, Second Tactical Air Force Communication Squadron, and visiting units No. 147 Squadron RAF and No. 271 Squadron RAF. USAAF 361st Fighter Group and 358th Fighter Group elements also present.[351]	34 destroyed, 29 damaged.[352]
Brussels—Grimbergen	B-60	JG 26 and JG 54	Only six aircraft were present	All six aircraft destroyed.[248]
Brussels—Melsbroek	B-58	JG 27, JG 54 and JG 4	No. 34 Wing RAF, No. 139 Wing RAF, TAF Communications Squadron and No. 85 Group RAF Communications squadron.	35 destroyed, 9 severely damaged.[353]
Eindhoven	B-78	JG 3	No. 124 Wing RCAF, No. 143 Wing RCAF and 39 Wing RAF. No. 400 Squadron RCAF, No. 414 Squadron RCAF and No. 430 Squadron RCAF were also present.[354]	26 Typhoons destroyed, plus around 30 damaged.[355] A further five reconnaissance Spitfires were destroyed (400 Squadron), one of which was destroyed via a collision with a shot down Fw 190.[356]
Ghent/Sint-Denijs-Westrem	B-61	JG 1	No. 131 (Polish) Wing RAF	16 destroyed, several damaged.[249]
Gilze—Rijen	B-77	JG 3 and KG 51	No. 35 Recce Wing RAF	One destroyed and one damaged.
Heesch	B-88	JG 6	No. 401 Squadron RCAF, No. 402 Squadron RCAF, No. 411 Squadron RCAF, No. 412 Squadron RCAF, No. 442 Squadron RCAF.[357]	No losses
Le Culot	A-89	JG 4	USAAF 36th Fighter Group, 373d Fighter Group, 363rd TRG	No damage
Maldegem	B-65	JG 1	No. 485 Squadron RNZAF and No. 349 Squadron RAF	13 destroyed, two damaged beyond repair.[358]
Metz—Frescaty	A-90	JG 53	USAAF. IX Tactical Air Force; 354th Fighter Group, 362nd Fighter Group, 40th Fighter Group, 406th Fighter Group, 425th Fighter Group, 367th Fighter Group, 368th Fighter Group, 361st Fighter Group. XII Tactical Air Force's 64th Fighter Wing; 1 ere, Escadre of the French Air Force, 50th Fighter Group, 358th Fighter Group	22 destroyed, 11 damaged (all P-47 Thunderbolts).

Ophoven	Y-32	JG 4	No. 130 Squadron RAF, No. 350 Squadron RAF	One destroyed, about six damaged.[359]
Sint—Truiden	A-92	JG 2, JG 4 and SG 4	USAAF 48th Fighter Group and 404th Fighter Group	10 destroyed, 31 damaged.
Volkel	B-80	JG 6	No. 56 Squadron RAF, No. 486 Squadron RNZAF	One aircraft destroyed.
Woensdrecht	B-79	JG 77	No. 132 Wing RAF	No effect
Ursel	B-67	JG 1	USAAF 486th Bomb Group and No. 61 Squadron RAF	Three aircraft destroyed.

Aftermath and casualties

The operation achieved tactical surprise,[360] but it was undone by poor execution due to low pilot skill resulting from poor training. The operation failed to achieve its aim[218] and that failure was very costly to German air power. Some of the units of the RAF, RCAF and USAAF on the receiving end of *Bodenplatte* had been badly hit, others not so badly, but most had sustained some losses. The Germans, however, launched *Bodenplatte* under a set of conditions, such as poor planning and low pilot skill, which clearly indicated any advantage gained would be outweighed by possible losses.[361] *Bodenplatte* weakened the *Jagdwaffe* past any hope of rebuilding.[223] *General der Jagdflieger* Adolf Galland said, "We sacrificed our last substance".[362]

The *Luftwaffe* lost 143 pilots killed and missing, while 70 were captured and 21 wounded including three *Geschwaderkommodore*, five *Gruppenkommandeure*, and 14 *Staffelkapitäne*—the largest single-day loss for the *Luftwaffe*.[363] Many of the formation leaders lost were experienced veterans, which placed even more pressure on those who were left. Thus, *Bodenplatte* was a very short-term success but a long-term failure. Allied losses were soon made up, while lost *Luftwaffe* aircraft and especially pilots were irreplaceable. German historian Gerhard Weinberg wrote that it left the Germans "weaker than ever and incapable of mounting any major attack again".[364]

In the remaining 17 weeks of war the *Jagdwaffe* struggled to recover sufficiently from the 1 January operation to remain an effective force. In strategic terms, German historian Werner Girbig wrote, "Operation Bodenplatte amounted to a total defeat".[365] The exhausted German units were no longer able to mount an effective defence of German air space during Operation *Plunder* and Operation *Varsity*, the Allied crossing of the Rhine River, or the overall Western Allied invasion of Germany. Subsequent operations were insignificant as a whole, and could not challenge Allied air supremacy. The only service in the *Luftwaffe* capable of profitable sorties was the night fighter force.[366]

In the last six weeks of the war the *Luftwaffe* was to lose another 200 pilots killed.[367] Girbig wrote, "it was not until the autumn of 1944 that the German fighter forces set foot down the sacrificial path; and it was the controversial Operation *Bodenplatte* that dealt this force a mortal blow and sealed its fate. What happened from then on was no more than a dying flicker".[224]

References

Bibliography

<templatestyles src="Template:Refbegin/styles.css" />

- Caldwell, Donald and Muller, Richard. *The Luftwaffe Over Germany: Defense of the Reich*. Greenhill books. ISBN 978-1-85367-712-0
- Caldwell, Donald. *JG 26; Top Guns of the Luftwaffe*. New York: Ballantine Books, 1991. ISBN 0-8041-1050-6
- de Zeng, H.L; Stanket, D.G; Creek, E.J. *Bomber Units of the Luftwaffe 1933–1945; A Reference Source, Volume 1*. Ian Allen Publishing, 2007. ISBN 978-1-85780-279-5
- de Zeng, H.L; Stanket, D.G; Creek, E.J. *Bomber Units of the Luftwaffe 1933–1945; A Reference Source, Volume 2*. Ian Allen Publishing, 2007. ISBN 978-1-903223-87-1
- Forsythe, Robert. *JV 44; The Galland Circus*. Burgess Hill, West Sussex, UK: Classic Publications, 1996. ISBN 0-9526867-0-8
- Forsythe, Robert & Laurier, *Jagdverband 44: Squadron of Experten*. Osprey. Oxford. 2008. ISBN 978-1-84603-294-3
- Franks, Norman *The Battle of the Airfields: 1 January 1945*. Grub Street, London, 1994. ISBN 1-898697-15-9
- Franks, Norman *Fighter Command Losses of the Second World War: Volume 3, Operational Losses, Aircraft and Crews 1944–1945. Incorporating Air Defence Great Britain and 2nd TAF* Midland. London, 2000. ISBN 1-85780-093-1
- Girbig, Werner. *Start im Morgengrauen*. Germany: Pietsch-Verlag Paul Pietsch Verlage GmbH + Co, 1997. ISBN 3-613-01292-8
- Girbig, Werner. *Six Months to Oblivion: The Eclipse of the Luftwaffe Fighter Force Over the Western Front, 1944/45*. Schiffer Publishing Ltd. 1975. ISBN 978-0-88740-348-4
- Johnson, J.E. *Wing Leader* (Fighter Pilots). London: Goodall Publications Ltd. 2000 (original edition 1956). ISBN 0-907579-87-6.
- Manrho, John & Pütz, Ron. *Bodenplatte: The Luftwaffe's Last Hope-The Attack on Allied Airfields, New Year's Day 1945*. Ottringham, United Kingdom. Hikoki Publications. ISBN 1-902109-40-6

- Peszke, Michael Alfred *A Synopsis of Polish-Allied Military Agreements During World War Two* The Journal of Military History. October 1980. Volume 44. Number 3, pp. 128–134
- Parker, Danny S. *To Win The Winter Sky: The Air War Over the Ardennes, 1944–1945*. Da Capo Press, 1998. ISBN 0-938289-35-7.
- Prien, Jochen & Stemmer, Gerhard. *Jagdgeschwader 3 "Udet" in World War II*. Atlgen, Germany: Schiffer Military History, 2002. ISBN 0-7643-1681-8
- Weal, John. *Jagdgeschwader 27 'Afrika'*. Osprey, Oxford. 2003. ISBN 1-84176-538-4
- Weal, John. *Focke-Wulf Fw 190 Aces of the Western Front*. Osprey, Oxford. 1996. ISBN 978-1-85532-595-1
- Weal, John. *Bf 109 Defence of the Reich Aces*. Osprey, Oxford. 2006. ISBN 1-84176-879-0
- Weinberg, Gerhard. *A World At Arms*, Cambridge University Press: 2 edition, 2005, ISBN 978-0-521-61826-7

External links

- Squadron Log 1 January 1945[368]
- Operation Strength of JG 1 at the time of Unternehmen Bodenplatte[369]
- To win the Winter Sky by Danny S. Parker[370]

<indicator name="good-star"> ⊕ </indicator>

Operation Nordwind

Operation North Wind	
Part of the Western Front of World War II	
Operation *Nordwind*	
Date	31 December 1944 - 25 January 1945
Location	Alsace and Lorraine, France and Rhineland-Palatinate, Germany
Result	German operational failure, Tactical German victory
Belligerents	
United States France	Germany
Commanders and leaders	
Jacob L. Devers Alexander Patch Jean de Lattre de Tassigny	Johannes Blaskowitz Hans von Obstfelder Heinrich Himmler Siegfried Rasp
Units involved	

Seventh Army
 • XV Corps
  • 103rd Infantry Division
  • 44th Infantry Division
  • 100th Infantry Division
  • 63rd Infantry Division
 • VI Corps
  • 42nd Infantry Division
  • 45th Infantry Division
  • 70th Infantry Division
  • 79th Infantry Division
 French 1st Army
 I Corps
 • 1st Infantry Division
 • 2nd Armored Division
 • 3rd Algerian Division
	1st Army
	 • 25th Panzergrenadier Division
	 • 21st Panzer Division
	 • 6th SS Mountain Division
	 XIII SS Corps
	 • 19th Volksgrenadier Division
	 • 36th Volksgrenadier Division
	 • 17th SS Panzergrenadier Division
	 XC Corps
	 • 559th Volksgrenadier Division
	 • 257th Volksgrenadier Division
	 LXXXIX Corps
	 • 361st Volksgrenadier Division
	 • 245th Infantry Division
	 • 256th Volksgrenadier Division
	 German 19th Army
	 • 10th SS Panzer Division

II Corps	LXIV Corps
• 1st Armored Division	• 189th Infantry Division
• 1st Colonial Division	• 198th Infantry Division
• 3rd Moroccan Division	• 708th Volksgrenadier Division
• 4th Moroccan Division	LXIII Corps
• 5th Armored Division	• 159th Infantry Division
• 10th Infantry Division	• 716th Infantry Division
▰ XXI Corps	• 269th Infantry Division
• 36th Infantry Division	
• 12th Armored Division	
• 14th Armored Division	
Strength	
▰ 295,000 men ▰ 200,000 men	?
Casualties and losses	
▰ United States 14,000[371] ▰ France 2,000[:922]	23,000[:922]

Operation North Wind (German: *Unternehmen Nordwind*) was the last major German offensive of World War II on the Western Front. It began on December 31, 1944 in Rhineland-Palatinate, Alsace and Lorraine in southwestern Germany and northeastern France, and ended on 25 January 1945.

Objectives

In a briefing at his military command complex at Adlerhorst, Adolf Hitler declared in his speech to his division commanders on 28 December 1944 (three days prior to the launch of Operation *Nordwind*): "This attack has a very clear objective, namely the destruction of the enemy forces. There is not a matter of prestige involved here. It is a matter of destroying and exterminating the enemy forces wherever we find them."[:499]

The goal of the offensive was to break through the lines of the U.S. Seventh Army and French 1st Army in the Upper Vosges mountains and the Alsatian Plain, and destroy them, as well as the seizure of Strasbourg, which Himmler had promised would be captured by January 30th. This would leave the way open for Operation Dentist (*Unternehmen Zahnarzt*), a planned major thrust into the rear of the U.S. Third Army which would lead to the destruction of that army.[:494]

Offensive

On 31 December 1944, German Army Group G—commanded by Generaloberst Johannes Blaskowitz—and Army Group Oberrhein ("Upper Rhein")—commanded by Reichsführer-SS Heinrich Himmler—launched a major offensive against the thinly stretched, 110 kilometres (68 mi)-long front line held by the U.S. 7th Army. Operation Nordwind soon had the under-strength U.S. 7th Army in dire straits. The 7th Army—at the orders of U.S. General Dwight D. Eisenhower—had sent troops, equipment, and supplies north to reinforce the American armies in the Ardennes involved in the Battle of the Bulge.

On the same day that the German Army launched Operation Nordwind, the *Luftwaffe* (German Air Force) committed almost 1,000 aircraft in support. This attempt to cripple the Allied air forces based in northwestern Europe was known as Operation Bodenplatte, which failed without having achieved any of its key objectives.

The initial Nordwind attack was conducted by three Corps of the German 1st Army of Army Group G, and by 9 January, the XXXIX Panzer Corps was heavily engaged as well. By 15 January at least seventeen German divisions (including units in the Colmar Pocket) from Army Group G and Army Group Oberrhein, including the 6th SS Mountain, 17th SS Panzergrenadier, 21st Panzer, and 25th Panzergrenadier Divisions were engaged in the fighting. Another, smaller, attack was made against the French positions south of Strasbourg, but it was finally stopped. The U.S. VI Corps—which bore the brunt of the German attacks—was fighting on three sides by 15 January.

The 125th Regiment of the 21st Panzer Division under Col. Hans von Luck aimed to sever the American supply line to Strasbourg, by cutting across the eastern foothills of the Vosges at the northwest base of a natural salient in a bend of the River Rhine. Here the Maginot Line ran east-west, and now "showed what a superb fortification it was". On January 7 Luck approached the Line south of Wissembourg at the villages of Rittershoffen and Hatten. Heavy American fire came from the 79th Infantry Division, the 14th Armoured Division, plus elements of the 42nd Infantry Division. On January 10 Luck reached the villages. Two weeks of heavy fighting followed. Germans and Americans each occupying parts of the villages while civilians sheltered in cellars. Luck later said that the fighting around Rittershoffen had been "one of the hardest and most costly battles that ever raged".[372]

Eisenhower, fearing the outright destruction of the U.S. 7th Army, had rushed already battered divisions hurriedly relieved from the Ardennes, southeast over 100 km (62 mi), to reinforce the 7th Army. But their arrival was delayed, and on 21 January with supplies and ammunition short, Seventh Army ordered the much depleted 79th and 14th Divisions to retreat from Rittershoffen and fall back on new positions on the south bank of the Moder River.

On 25 January the German offensive was halted, after the US 222nd Infantry Regiment stopped their advance near Haguenau, and earning the Presidential

Unit Citation in the process. This was the same day that the reinforcements began to arrive from the Ardennes. Strasbourg was saved but the Colmar Pocket
was a danger which had to be eliminated.

The German offensive was a failure, failing to destroy the enemy's forces.

Bibliography

- Bonn, Keith E. *When the Odds Were Even: The Vosges Mountains Cam-
  paign, October 1944-January 1945*. Novato, CA: Presidio, 2006.
- Engler, Richard. *The Final Crisis: Combat in Northern Alsace, January
  1945*. Aberjona Press. 1999. ISBN 978-0-9666389-1-2
- *Nordwind* & the US 44th Division * Battle History of the 44th I.D.[373]
- Whiting, Charles (1992). *The Other Battle of the Bulge: Operation
  Northwind*. Avon Books. ISBN 0380716283. OCLC 211992045[374].
- Citino, Robert (2017), *The Wehrmacht's Last Stand: The German Cam-
  paigns of 1944-1945*, University Press of Kansas, ISBN 978-0-7006-
  2494-2

External links

- Cirillo, Roger. *The Ardennes-Alsace*[375]. The U.S. Army Campaigns of
  World War II. United States Army Center of Military History. CMH Pub
  72-26.
- The NORDWIND Offensive (January 1945)[376] on the website of the
  100th Infantry Division Association contains a list of German primary
  sources on the operation.

Appendix

References

[1] Bergström 2014, p. 428.

[2] Bergström 2014, p. 358.

[3] Includes two parachute divisions.

[4] Miles 2004.

[5] Parker, "Battle of the Bulge" p. 292

[6] Vogel 2001, p. 632.

[7] Ellis 2009, p. 195.

[8] 10,749 dead; 34,225 wounded; 22,487 captured<ref name="FOOTNOTEVogel2001632">Vogel 2001, p. 632.

[9] Parker p. 293

[10] Bergström 2014, p. 426, including 20 Tiger II tanks, 194 Panther tanks, 158 Panzer IV tanks and 182 assault guns and tank destroyers.

[11] Schrijvers 2005, p. xiv.

[12] Cirillo 2003, p. 4.

[13] Eggenberger 1985 cites the official name as Ardennes-Alsace campaign; David Eggenberger describes this battle as the "Second Battle of the Ardennes".

[14] Stanton 2006.

[15] Cirillo 2003, p. 53.

[16] MacDonald 1998, p. 618.

[17] Operation Overlord planned for an advance to the line of the Seine by D+90 (i.e., the 90th day following D-Day) and an advance to the German frontier sometime after D+120.

[18] Shirer 1990, pp. 1088–1089.

[19] Shirer 1990, p. 1086.

[20] Ryan 1995, p. 68.

[21] Shirer 1990, p. 1085.

[22] Parker 1994, pp. 122–123.

[23] Weinberg 1964.

[24] Shirer 1990, p. 1091.

[25] Shirer 1990, p. 1092.

[26] Shirer 1990, p. 1090.

[27] The Ardennes offensive was also named Rundstedt-Offensive, but von Rundstedt strongly objected "to the fact that this stupid operation in the Ardennes is sometimes called the 'Rundstedt-Offensive'. This is a complete misnomer. I had nothing to do with it. It came to me as an order complete to the last detail. Hitler had even written on the plan in his own handwriting 'not to be altered'". (Jablonsky, David (1994), *Churchill and Hitler: Essays on the Political-Military Direction of Total War*, Taylor & Francis, p. 194, ISBN 978-0-7146-4119-5).

[28] Wacht am Rhein was renamed Herbstnebel after the operation was given the go-ahead in early December, although its original name remains much better known (Parker 1991, pp. 95–100; Mitcham 2006, p. 38; Newton 2006, pp. 329–334).

[29] Parker 1994, p. 118.

[30] MacDonald 1984, p. 40.

[31] & Cole 1964, p. 21.

[32] O'Donnell Patrick K., *Dog Company: The Boys of Pointe du Hoc—the Rangers Who Accomplished D-Day's Toughest Mission and Led the Way across Europe*, Da Capo Press, 2012.

[33] & MacDonald 1984, pp. 86–89.

[34] & Toland 1999, p. 16, 19.

[35] Parker 2004, p. 132.

[36] Quarrie 1999.

[37] MacDonald 1984, p. 410.

[38] Cole 1964, pp. 1–64.

[39] Cavanagh 2004, p. 8.
[40] Parker 2004, p. 69.
[41] & Cole 1964, p. 83.
[42] Cole 1964, pp. 75–106.
[43] MacDonald 1984.
[44] Toland 1999, p. 382.
[45] MacDonald 1984, p. 210.
[46] Quarrie 1999, p. 31.
[47] Bouwmeester 2004, p. 106.
[48] Bouwmeester 2004, p. 107.
[49] Toland 1999, p. 103, 104.
[50] Bouwmeester 2004, p. 108.
[51] Bouwmeester 2004, p. 109.
[52] Bouwmeester 2004, p. 111.
[53] Bouwmeester 2004, p. 112.
[54] MacDonald 1984, p. 461, 463.
[55] Eisenhower 1969, p. 224.
[56] & Cole 1964, pp. 259–260.
[57] Goldstein, Dillon & Wenger 1994, p. 88.
[58] Parker 2004, p. 130.
[59] Parker 2004, p. 137.
[60] Schrijvers 2005, p. 303f.
[61] Sorge 1986, p. 147.
[62] Liddell Hart 1970, p. 653.
[63] Zaloga 2004, pp. 76–83.
[64] Ambrose 1998, p. 208.
[65] MacDonald 1984, p. 422.
[66] Marshall 1988, p. 177.
[67] Ambrose 1992, c. "Bastogne".
[68] Nuts can mean several things in American English slang. In this case it signified rejection, and was explained to the Germans as meaning "Go to Hell!"
[69] Zaloga 2004, pp. 84–86.
[70] Weinberg 1995, p. 769.
[71] Clarke & Smith 1993, p. 527.
[72] A footnote to the U.S. Army's official history volume "Riviera to the Rhine" makes the following note on U.S. Seventh Army casualties: "As elsewhere, casualty figures are only rough estimates, and the figures presented are based on the postwar 'Seventh Army Operational Report, Alsace Campaign and Battle Participation, 1 June 1945' (copy CMH), which notes 11,609 Seventh Army battle casualties for the period, plus 2,836 cases of trench foot and 380 cases of frostbite, and estimates about 17,000 Germans killed or wounded with 5,985 processed prisoners of war. But the VI Corps AAR for January 1945 puts its total losses at 14,716 (773 killed, 4,838 wounded, 3,657 missing, and 5,448 nonbattle casualties); and Albert E. Cowdrey and Graham A. Cosmas, *The Medical Department: The War Against Germany*, draft CMH MS (1988), pp. 54–55, a forthcoming volume in the United States Army in World War II series, reports Seventh Army hospitals processing about 9,000 wounded and 17,000 'sick and injured' during the period. Many of these may have been returned to their units, and others may have come from American units operating in the Colmar area but still supported by Seventh Army medical services."
[73] "U.S. infantrymen fire at German troops in the advance to relieve the surrounded paratroopers in Bastogne. In foreground a platoon leader indicates the target to a rifleman by actually firing on the target. In Bastogne the defenders were badly in need of relief, they were attacked nightly by German aircraft, supplies were critically low in spite of the airdrops, and the wounded could not be given proper attention because of the shortage of medical supplies. After an advance which had been slow, U. S. relief troops entered Bastogne at 1645 on 26 December 1944." <ref>
[74] Schneider 2004, p. 274.
[75]

[76]

[77] Dupuy, appendix E

[78] "Initial" is the sum total of all unit rosters of the respective combatants at the point at which those units entered the battle, while "Final" reflects the state of those units on 16 January 1945. For the strength of the opposing sides at any one time, see table above.

[79] MacDonald 1985, pp. 77–79.

[80] MacDonald 1985, pp. 21–22.

[81] The Memoirs of Field-Marshall Montgomery – 1958, P. 308

[82] Urban 2005, p. 194.

[83] Gallagher 1945.

[84] Bradley 1951, p. 58.

[85] Ryan 1995, pp. 204–205.

[86] *The Memoirs of Field-Marshall Montgomery* – 1958, p. 311–314

[87] Bradley 1983, pp. 382–385.

[88] *The Struggle for Europe*, p. 611

[89] Montgomery, Brian, *A Field Marshal in the Family*, Pen and Sword, 2010, p.296.

[90] Delaforce 2004, p. 318.

[91] Parker p. 293

[92] Bergström 2014, p. 425.

[93] Bergström 2014, p. 424.

[94] "American Military History, Volume 2" http://www.history.army.mil/books/AMH-V2/AMH%20V2/chapter5.htm#b10. US Army Center of Military History. Washington DC. Page 157.

[95] Bergström 2014, p. 426.

[96] Parker p. 292

[97] Dupuy, p. 501. The US 2nd Armored Division put on perhaps the best performance for the Allies, achieving a Combat Efficiency Value of 1.48 when it smashed the 2nd Panzer Division (0.52) at Celles in late December.

[98] Sandler 2002, p. 101.

[99] Harry Hinsley's words, in *Codebreakers: The Inside Story of Bletchley Park*, eds. F. H. Hinsley & Alan Strip (Oxford 1993), p.11

[100] Pearson, Joss ed. *Neil Webster's Cribs for Victory: The Untold Story of Bletchley Park's Secret Room* Polperro Heritage Press 2011 p.66-67

[101] Calvocoressi to Neil Leslie Webster, in Pearson, Joss ed. *Neil Webster's Cribs for Victory: The Untold Story of Bletchley Park's Secret Room* (2011), p.67

[102] Millward, William, 'Life in and out of Hut 3' in Codebreakers: The Inside Story of Bletchley Park, eds. F. H. Hinsley & Alan Strip (Oxford 1993), p.24

[103]

[104]

[105] Strong, K. W. D., *Intelligence at the Top: the recollections of an Intelligence Officer* (London, 1968), p.175-6

[106]

[107] 'Peter Calvocoressi: Political writer who served at Bletchley Park and assisted at the Nuremberg trials', independent.co.uk https//www.independent.co.uk

[108] Units Entitled to Battle Credit http://armypubs.army.mil/epubs/pdf/go4863.pdf

[109] Boardgamegeek https://boardgamegeek.com/boardgamefamily/25084/world-war-2-battle-bulge

[110] //en.wikipedia.org/w/index.php?title=Battle_of_the_Bulge&action=edit

[111] http://cgsc.contentdm.oclc.org/cdm/singleitem/collection/p4013coll2/id/181/rec/4

[112] http://www.airpower.au.af.mil/airchronicles/apj/apj89/win89/carter.html

[113] http://www.history.army.mil/brochures/ardennes/aral.htm

[114] https://web.archive.org/web/20081206183021/http://www.history.army.mil/brochures/ardennes/aral.htm

[115] http://www.history.army.mil/books/wwii/7-8/7-8_cont.htm

[116] //lccn.loc.gov/65060001

[117] http://cgsc.cdmhost.com/cdm4/document.php?CISOROOT=/p4013coll8&CISOPTR=130&REC=2

[118] https://news.google.com/newspapers?nid=1129&dat=19450108&id=x6FhAAAAIBAJ&sjid=L2oDAAAAIBAJ&pg=5911,1918615

[119] http://www.history.army.mil/books/wwii/Bastogne/bast-fm.htm

[120] https://web.archive.org/web/20081204013505/http://www.history.army.mil/books/wwii/Bastogne/bast-fm.htm

[121] http://archive.defense.gov/news/newsarticle.aspx?id=24591

[122] //doi.org/10.2307/1842933

[123] //www.jstor.org/stable/1842933

[124] http://www.history.army.mil/books/70-7_20.htm

[125] http://www.history.army.mil/books/70-7_0.htm

[126] http://www.army.mil/botb

[127] https://purl.fdlp.gov/GPO/gpo46222

[128] http://www.bulge1944.com/battle-of-the-bulge-museums/

[129] http://www.veteransofthebattleofthebulge.org/vbob/wp-content/uploads/2010/12/go1141.pdf

[130] //tools.wmflabs.org/geohack/geohack.php?pagename=Battle_of_Elsenborn_Ridge&params=50_26_47_N_6_15_51_E_region:BE_scale:50000_type:event

[131] Lone Sentry http://www.lonesentry.com/gi_stories_booklets/99thinfantry/

[132]

[133] Walden, Gregory A. On the Trail of Kampfgruppe Peiper Part 2 https://web.archive.org/web/20101117012442/http://www.ss501panzer.com/Peiper_Trail_Part_2.htm Retrieved September 15, 2015. Archived November 17, 2010

[134] Walden, Gregory A. On the Trail of Kampfgruppe Peiper Part 3 https://web.archive.org/web/20101117012515/http://www.ss501panzer.com/Peiper_Trail_Part_3.htm Retrieved September 15, 2015. Archived November 17, 2010

[135] http://www.history.army.mil/books/wwii/7-8/7-8_cont.htm

[136] https://web.archive.org/web/20100615174621/http://www.history.army.mil/books/wwii/Siegfried/Siegfried%20Line/siegfried-fm.htm

[137] http://www.eucmh.com

[138] https://web.archive.org/web/20061030042035/http://www.historynet.com/wars_conflicts/world_war_2/3031946.html

[139] http://www.wwiivehicles.com/germany/tank-hunters/jagdpanther.asp

[140] http://www.ww2awards.com/person/34753

[141] http://www.heroesforever.nl/William%20R%20Hinsch%20Jr.htm

[142] http://www.644td.com/

[143] http://en.allexperts.com/q/Military-History-669/WWII-artillery-ammo-fitted.htm

[144] //tools.wmflabs.org/geohack/geohack.php?pagename=Malmedy_massacre&params=50_24_14_N_6_3_58.30_E_type:event_region:BE_scale:50000

[145] Cole (1965). Statement of General Lauer "the enemy had the key to success within his hands, but did not know it."

[146] Wholesale Slaughter at Baugnez-lez-Malmedy, Willy D. Alenus http://members.cox.net/honorguard2/Battle_of_the_Bulge.html

[147] Roger Martin, L'Affaire Peiper, Dagorno, 1994, p. 76

[148] http://forum.axishistory.com/viewtopic.php?f=6&t=116977&start=30

[149] https://web.archive.org/web/20040721233353/http://www.qmfound.com/malmedy.htm

[150] https://web.archive.org/web/20050207205350/http://isidore-of-seville.com/bulge/13.html

[151] http://www.historynet.com/wwii/blmassacreatmalmedy/

[152] http://www.gettysburgdaily.com/?p=6297/

[153] http://dannyparker.com/books/fatal-crossroads/

[154] Steven E. Clay, U.S. Army Order of Battle 1919 - 1941, Volume 2, p. 860. Fort Leavenworth: Combat Studies Institute Press, 2010.

[155] https://www.findagrave.com/memorial/56281210/thomas-j.-forte

[156] https://www.findagrave.com/memorial/62167686/william-edward-pritchett

[157] https://www.findagrave.com/cemetery/24296/mccaskill-cemetery

[158] https://www.findagrave.com/memorial/56285888/james-aubrey-stewart

[159] https://www.findagrave.com/memorial/399650/mager-bradley

[160] https://www.findagrave.com/memorial/56280514/george-davis

[161] https://www.findagrave.com/memorial/62167448/jimmie-lee-leatherwood
[162] https://www.findagrave.com/cemetery/58705/college-hill-cemetery
[163] https://www.findagrave.com/memorial/56283980/george-washington-moten
[164] https://www.findagrave.com/memorial/56286276/due-w.-turner
[165] https://www.findagrave.com/memorial/56278937/curtis-adams
[166] https://www.findagrave.com/memorial/62167928/robert-leroy-green
[167] https://www.findagrave.com/cemetery/41411/highland-park-cemetery
[168] https://www.findagrave.com/memorial/56283978/nathaniel-moss
[169] Shelby Stanton, *World War II Order of Battle*, New York: Galahad Books, 1991
[170] http://www.wereth.org/
[171] http://www.stripes.com/article.asp?section=104&article=42807&archive=true
[172] http://www.history.army.mil/html/forcestruc/lineages/branches/fa/0333faregbty-f.htm
[173] http://tmg110.tripod.com/usarmyh8.htm
[174] https://web.archive.org/web/20120308210020/http://www.defense.gov/news/newsarticle.aspx?id=33014
[175] http://www.thelandmark.com/news/2006-07-06/Paxton_News/052.html
[176] http://www.abmc.gov/search/wwii_unit_detail.php
[177] //tools.wmflabs.org/geohack/geohack.php?pagename=Operation_St%C3%B6sser&params=50_30_40_N_6_04_40_E_region:BE_type:mountain_source:kolossus-frwiki
[178] //tools.wmflabs.org/geohack/geohack.php?pagename=Chenogne_massacre&params=49.992_N_5.618_E_type:event_region:BE_scale:50000
[179] This incident described was from the writing of John Fague.
[180] p.78
[181] https://www.revealnews.org/episodes/take-no-prisoners-inside-a-wwii-american-war-crime/
[182] //tools.wmflabs.org/geohack/geohack.php?pagename=Battle_of_St._Vith&params=50_16_55_N_6_7_36_E_region:BE_type:event_scale:50000
[183] Samuel W. Mitcham: *Panzers in Winter: Hitler's Army And the Battle of the Bulge*, Greenwood Publishing Group, 2006, , page 122 https://books.google.com/books?id=3ZNVME6-LHAC&pg=PA122.
[184] Trevor Nevitt Dupuy, David L. Bongard, Richard C. Anderson (Jr.), Richard Claire Anderson: *Hitler's last gamble: the Battle of the Bulge, December 1944-January 1945*, HarperCollins, 1994, , page 155.
[185] Edited by Walt Cross Foreword by Gen. Hasbrouck: *From the Beaches to the Baltic: The Story of the 7th Armored Division in World War II*, 2006, , page 56 https://books.google.com/books?id=Eotg4qz40LEC&pg=PA56.
[186] http://www.benning.army.mil/armor/eARMOR/content/issues/2014/OCT_DEC/Clarke.html
[187] https://archive.org/details/gov.dod.dimoc.30182
[188] https://archive.org/details/gov.dod.dimoc.30183
[189] https://www.youtube.com/watch?v=_Tdy_O81rLw
[190] https://www.youtube.com/watch?v=9JozuB1NFtg
[191] http://stvith.tripod.com/
[192] http://www.history.army.mil/books/wwii/7-8/7-8_17.htm
[193] Pallud, p. 4
[194] Delaforce, p. 60
[195] https//books.google.com
[196] German Special Operations in the 1944 Ardennes Offensive. http://www.dtic.mil/dtic/tr/fulltext/u2/a284495.pdf
[197] Pallud, p. 14
[198] Pallud, p. 15
[199] *Operation Greif* and the Trial of the "Most Dangerous Man in Europe." http://www.wiu.edu/cas/history/wihr/pdfs/BednarWIHRSp09.pdf
[200] TRIAL OF OTTO SKORZENY AND OTHERS http://www.ess.uwe.ac.uk/WCC/skorzeny.htm
[201] https://www.telegraph.co.uk/news/worldnews/europe/germany/1460846/Revealed-Farce-of-plot-to-kidnap-Eisenhower.html
[202] http://scholarship.law.missouri.edu/cgi/viewcontent.cgi?article=1627&context=mlr

[203] //tools.wmflabs.org/geohack/geohack.php?pagename=Siege_of_Bastogne&params=50.0_N_5.7214_E_type:event_region:BE_scale:50000

[204] Bando P.188

[205] Bando P.188-189

[206]

[207] S.L.A. Marshall, *Bastogne: The First Eight Days* http://www.history.army.mil/books/wwii/Bastogne/bast-14.htm, Chapter 14, describing the incident in detail and sourcing it.

[208] S.L. A. Marshall, *Bastogne: The First Eight Days* http://www.history.army.mil/books/wwii/Bastogne/bast-14.htm, Chapter 14, detailing and sourcing the incident.

[209] WWII Belgian nurse Augusta Chiwy honoured by US army https://www.bbc.co.uk/news/world-us-canada-16136007

[210] http://www.history.army.mil/documents/WWII/501PIRBulge.htm

[211] http://www.history.army.mil/books/wwii/Bastogne/bast-fm.htm

[212] http://www.101airborneww2.com/warstories3.html

[213] http://www.militaryhistoryonline.com/wwii/articles/bastogne.aspx

[214] https://web.archive.org/web/20070930210627/http://www.historynet.com/historical_conflicts/3031921.html

[215] https://www.youtube.com/watch?v=J9FktEyCpwM

[216] http://www.ibiblio.org/hyperwar/USA/USA-E-Last/maps/USA-E-Last-I.jpg

[217] http://www.ww2gp.org/ardennessituation.php

[218] Girbig 1975, p. 73.

[219] Prien & Stemmer 2002, p. 349.

[220] Franks 1994, pp. 163–165.

[221] Zaloga 2004, p. 61.

[222] Girbig 1975, p. 114.

[223] Caldwell 2007, p. 262.

[224] Girbig 1975, p. 12.

[225] Peszke 1980, p. 134

[226] Agreement #4 of the 11 June 1940 between the United Kingdom and Poland recognised the Polish Navy and Army as sovereign but that of the Air Force was refused. Agreement #7 reversed this decision in June 1944, and the Polish Air Force was "returned" to full Polish jurisdiction (with the exception of combat assignments, although the Poles retained the right to veto). UNIQ-ref-0-fb09c08bed4faa6f-QINU

[227] Girbig 1975, p. 74.

[228] Franks 1994, no page (inside cover)

[229] Franks 1994, p. 10.

[230] Franks 1994, pp. 10–11.

[231] Price 2001, p. 113.

[232] Franks 1994, p. 11.

[233] Manrho & Pütz 2004, p. 10.

[234] Manrho & Pütz 2004, p. 7.

[235] Manrho & Pütz 2004, p. 8.

[236] Franks 1994, p. 13.

[237] Girbig 1975, p. 75.

[238]

[239] Caldwell & Muller 2007, p. 205.

[240] Johnson 2000, pp. 294–95.

[241] Parker 1998, p. 375.

[242] Girbig 1975, p. 77.

[243] Manrho 2004, p. 125.

[244] Girbig 1975, p. 76. (given in footnote)

[245] Franks 1994, p. 188.

[246] Parker 1998, p. 377.

[247] Parker 1998, p. 381.

[248] Franks 1994, p. 198.

[249] Franks 1994, p. 197.

[250] Johnson 2000, p. 291.
[251] Caldwell 2007, pp. 257–258.
[252] Manrho & Pütz 2004, pp. 16–18.
[253] Manrho & Pütz 2004, pp. 18–22.
[254] Manrho & Pütz 2004, pp. 22–28.
[255] Franks 1994, p. 75.
[256] Girbig 1975, p. 83.
[257] Manrho & Pütz 2004, p. 28.
[258] Manrho & Pütz 2004, p. 34.
[259] Girbig 1975, p. 85.
[260] Manrho & Pütz 2004, p. 39.
[261] Manrho & Pütz 2004, p. 278.
[262] Manrho & Pütz 2004, p. 290.
[263] Manrho & Pütz 2004, pp. 51–52.
[264] Manrho & Pütz 2004, p. 277.
[265] Manrho & Pütz 2004, pp. 54–59.
[266] Manrho & Pütz 2004, p. 62.
[267] Girbig 1975, p. 88.
[268] Parker 1994, p. 416.
[269] Manrho & Pütz 2004, pp. 63–64.
[270] Manrho & Pütz 2004, pp. 276, pp. 123–24.
[271] Manrho & Pütz 2004, pp. 125–35.
[272] Manrho & Pütz 2004, p. 137.
[273] Parker 1998, p. 396.
[274] Weal 1996, p. 83.
[275] Manrho & Pütz 2004, pp. 137–38.
[276] Manrho & Pütz 2004, p. 251.
[277] Manrho & Pütz 2004, pp. 253–54.
[278] Manrho & Pütz 2004, pp. 254–56.
[279] Girbig 1975, p. 108.
[280] Manrho & Pütz 2004, p. 259.
[281] Manrho & Pütz 2004, p. 221.
[282] Franks 1997, p. 139.
[283] Manrho & Pütz 2004, pp. 224–25.
[284] Manrho & Pütz 2004, pp. 228–35.
[285] Manrho & Pütz 2004, p. 233.
[286] Manrho & Pütz 2004, p. 245.
[287] Manrho & Pütz 2004, p. 294.
[288] Manrho & Pütz 2004, pp. 94–95.
[289] Manrho & Pütz 2004, pp. 96–97.
[290] Manrho 2004, pp. 98–99.
[291] Manrho & Pütz 2004, p. 104.
[292] Girbig 1975, p. 93.
[293] Manrho & Pütz 2004, pp. 107–11.
[294] Manrho & Pütz 2004, pp. 111–14.
[295] Franks 2000, p. 135.
[296] Girbig 1975, p. 95.
[297] Franks 1994, p. 128.
[298] Manrho & Pütz 2004, p. 117.
[299] Manrho & Pütz 2004, p. 140.
[300] Manrho & Pütz 2004, p. 143.
[301] Manrho & Pütz 2004, p. 276.
[302] Manrho & Pütz 2004, p. 146.
[303] Parker 1998, p. 388.
[304] Manrho & Pütz 2004, p. 147.
[305] Scutts 1994, p. 78.

[306] Manrho & Pütz 2004, p. 148.
[307] Manrho & Pütz 2004, pp. 281–84.
[308] Manrho & Pütz 2004, p. 162.
[309] Manrho & Pütz 2004, p. 149.
[310] Manrho & Pütz 2004, pp. 164–65.
[311] Franks 1994, p. 136.
[312] Manrho & Pütz 2004, p. 281.
[313] Parker 1998, pp. 385–91.
[314] Parker 1998, p. 391.
[315] Manrho & Pütz 2004, p. 169.
[316] Manrho & Pütz 2004, pp. 173–74.
[317] Manrho & Pütz 2004, pp. 174–79.
[318] Manrho & Pütz 2004, p. 180.
[319] Manrho & Pütz 2004, pp. 187, 190.
[320] Manrho & Pütz 2004, p. 193.
[321] Manrho & Pütz 2004, p. 195.
[322] Parker 1994, p. 440.
[323] Manrho & Pütz 2004, p. 200.
[324] Weal 2003, p. 116.
[325] Franks 1994, p. 109.
[326] Manrho & Pütz 2004, pp. 201, 205, 206.
[327] Manrho & Pütz 2004, p. 217.
[328] Weal 2003, p. 117.
[329] Franks 2000, p. 134.
[330] Manrho & Pütz 2004, p. 219.
[331] Franks 1994, p. 117.
[332] Prien & Stemmer 2002, pp. 348–49.
[333] Manrho & Pütz 2004, p. 75.
[334] de Zeng *et al* Vol. 1, 2007, p. 147.
[335] de Zeng *et al* Vol. 2, 2007, p. 243.
[336] Manrho & Pütz 2004, p. 76.
[337] Manrho & Pütz 2004, p. 77.
[338] Manrho & Pütz 2004, p. 85.
[339] Manrho & Pütz 2004, p. 80.
[340] Manrho & Pütz 2004, p. 91.
[341] Girbig 1975, p. 92.
[342] Manrho & Pütz 2004, pp. 86–88.
[343] Franks 2000, pp. 132–34.
[344] Ordway & Sharpe 1979, p. 256.
[345] Manrho & Pütz 2004, p. 272.
[346] Girbig 1975, p. 78.
[347] Manrho & Pütz 2004, p. 291.
[348] Franks 1994, p. 193.
[349] Other sources say as many as 10 were destroyed along with another five possibles. Another nine confirmed damaged plus another few damaged.Girbig 1975, p. 73.
[350] Manrho & Pütz 2004, p. 289.
[351] Manrho & Pütz 2004, p. 293.
[352] Franks 1994, p. 195.
[353] Franks 1994, p. 196.
[354] Manrho & Pütz 2004, p. 71.
[355] Franks 1994, p. 204.
[356] Parker 1994, p. 402.
[357] Manrho & Pütz 2004, p. 288.
[358] Franks 1997, p. 196.
[359] Manrho & Pütz 2004, p. 295.
[360] Johnson 2000, p. 292.

[361] Franks 1994, pp. 163–65.

[362] Parker 1998, p. 486.

[363] Manrho & Pütz 2004, p. 272–73

[364] Weinberg 2005 p. 769.

[365] Girbig 1975, p. 112.

[366] Girbig 1975, p. 123.

[367] Girbig 1975, p. 137.

[368] http://www.rcaf.com/439squadron/1a.htm

[369] https://books.google.com/books?id=bvgtSypPpesC&pg=PA241&dq=%22JG+11%22+ Jagdgeschwader&lr=&as_brr=3&as_pt=ALLTYPES#PPA382,M1

[370] https://books.google.com/books?id=EYg47KqHv-EC&pg=PA411&dq=I./JG+1&lr=&sig= ACfU3U0Wl9OfCBit9Deud0oFMQaVeyCOfA#PPA448,M1

[371] Citino 2017.

[372] Ambrose 1997, p. 386.

[373] https://web.archive.org/web/20050306042820/http://efour4ever.com/44thdivision/nordwind.html

[374] //www.worldcat.org/oclc/211992045

[375] http://www.history.army.mil/brochures/ardennes/aral.htm

[376] http://www.100thww2.org/aid/geraid.html

Article Sources and Contributors

The sources listed for each article provide more detailed licensing information including the copyright status, the copyright owner, and the license conditions.

Battle of the Bulge *Source:* https://en.wikipedia.org/w/index.php?oldid=854129698 *License:* Creative Commons Attribution-Share Alike 3.0 *Contributors:* -glove-, A D Monroe III, Abce2, Adapad, Ammarpad, Anaruna, Antandrus, Arisen, Arjayay, Armymauser22, Atari001, Audaciter, BD2412, Benthenerd, Bermicourt, Binksternet, Bojo1498, BokicaK, BreakfastJr, Brucelee, CLCStudent, Carlotm, Choess, CityOfSilver, Clean Copy, ClueBot NG, Conrade99, Cpaligo, DMorpheus2, DePiep, Denisarona, Dennis&Daniel, Denniss, Drewmutt, Eastfarthingan, EdMcCorduck, Elassint, Excirial, EyeTruth, Fdewaele, Frietjes, Frogmann1, GeneralizationsAreBad, Gilliam, Griffineatgriffin, Gutmach, Hamiltondaniel, Hayman30, Helmut von Moltke, Historian932, Hohum, Hugo999, IAmCool2015Malaysia, INeedSupport, Ich1411, IdreamofJeanie, Illegitimate Barrister, Imthatdueha612, Iñaki Salazar, JJuran, Jackfork, Jeff G., Jim.henderson, Jmontouliu, John Cline, JohnAlbertRigali, Johnscribner, Johnstevenson1996, Julietdeltalima, KAP03, KGirlTrucker81, Kierzek, Kpgjhpjm, L293D, L3X1, Laurdecl, Loginnigol, Loopy30, MONGO, Malayedit, Malikin, MasonAsher, Materialscientist, MatiasGerlich, Mccapra, Melcous, Melvin Dole, Morphdog, Mr.TiNart, Mztourist, Name goes here, Naviguessor, Nechemia Iron, NewEnglandYankee, Niccbo1305, NiciVampireHeart, Nick-D, Nihiltres, Nihlus, Nihlus1, Non-dropframe, Notalibrarian, Operator873, Oshwah, Paul Siebert, Person who formerly started with "216", Philroc, Prinsipe Ybarro, Purplebackpack89, Quondum, Reb1981, Roberticus, Roches, Roddy the roadkill, Rogerd, Samee, Samf4u, Saturn star, SemiHypercube, Shaded0, Shellwood, Shock Brigade Harvester Boris, SimeonHovey, Sirswindon, Snickers2686, Souljivebrowhitey, Spug2bug, Starsmark, Surv1v4l1st, TAnthony, The PIPE, The Pittsburgher, TheGracefulSlick, TheModernJuan, Thefox0604, Theinstantmatrix, TiltuM, Tim!, Tirronan, Tom.Reding, Tombo7791, ToonLucas22, Traceyboba, TwinkleMore, TwoNyce, Weaseloid, Wesleyparker22, WikiPedant, Wikiuser100, Woody, Work permit, ZappaOMati, Zubin12, 151 anonymous edits 1

Battle of the Bulge order of battle *Source:* https://en.wikipedia.org/w/index.php?oldid=844524170 *License:* Creative Commons Attribution-Share Alike 3.0 *Contributors:* 7tharmddiv, Acsian88, Addihockey10, Airbornelawyer, Alois79VG, Andrew Gray, AntonyZ, Atani, Berserker276, Bigun6605, Bilhartz, Billinghurst, BrokenSphere, Btphelps, Bwmoll3, Caryl-280ecb, Chris the speller, Colonies Chris, CommonsDelinker, D6, Derfel73, DocYako, Dodgerblue777, Dormskirk, Einsatzgruppe C, Ejones4, Enterprisey, FDRMRZUSA, Fallschirmjäger, Fifehorse, Gavbadger, GraemeLeggett, Greenshed, Gtkelly, Hamish59, Hamleteer, Hammersoft, Hawkeye7, Ibericus Lusitanus, Illegitimate Barrister, Jim Sweeney, Karl Donitz, Knavesmire, Koavf, Kriegaffe, KylieTastic, Magioladitis, MisterBee1966, Mliu92, Monkeybait, Nobunaga24, Noclador, P. S. Burton, PRRfan, Patton123, Philg88, QuintBy, R'n'B, Rokfaith, SGT141, Signaleer, Snubcube, Tassedethe, Telecineguy, TheOldJacobite, Trfasulo, Vasyatka1, Vegaswikian, W. B. Wilson, Welsh, Wild Wolf, Zt692, 75 anonymous edits 57

Battle of Elsenborn Ridge *Source:* https://en.wikipedia.org/w/index.php?oldid=847680559 *License:* Creative Commons Attribution-Share Alike 3.0 *Contributors:* Adavidb, Anotherclown, Atani, BD2412, Bgwhite, Brigade Piron, Btphelps, Chris the speller, Clare., Clarityfiend, ClueBot NG, Davidcannon, Dbsseven, DissidentAggressor, DocYako, Don Brunett, Fnorp, Giraffedata, Grafen, Hohum, John of Reading, JohnAlbertRigali, Johnscribner086, Johnstevenson1996, Johnuniq, Jss199, JuanRiley, K.e.coffman, Kartane, Laughingyet, Lebob, Lightning Zapper, MagicMoose, MisterBee1966, Mr.TiNart, Mztourist, Naraht, Naviguessor, Niceguyedc, Nlovisa, Raoulduke47, Sentaro9678, Strongjam, The Quixotic Potato, Tim!, TitaniumCarbide, Tom.Reding, Tomseattle, TwinkleMore, WOSlinker, Wavelength, Wieralee, Witnessforpeace, Wwikix, 45 anonymous edits 91

Malmedy massacre *Source:* https://en.wikipedia.org/w/index.php?oldid=851076084 *License:* Creative Commons Attribution-Share Alike 3.0 *Contributors:* $1LENCE D00600D, ARTEST4ECHO, Abramius, AgentSniff, Ale jrb, AniMate, Aquamonkey, Arcandam, Arzel, Ashley Pomeroy, BD2412, Badgernet, Ben Ben, Berean Hunter, Bgwhite, BigJake54, Bigroger27509, Boneyard90, Brandmeister, Brigade Piron, Btphelps, COLONEL77, Capitalist Infidel, Capt Jim, Catsmoke, Charles T. Betz, Chenopodiaceous, Chris the speller, Clarityfiend, ClueBot NG, Cobra529, CommonsDelinker, Conung, CowboySpartan, Crispyinstilly, Cyberherbalist, D6, DVdm, David T Tokyo, DavidBailey, Davidcannon, Diannaa, DissidentAggressor, Dlabtot, Dodgerblue777, Dpschanen, Ed.capistrano, Edcolins, Enterprisey, Ericoides, Fdewaele, Ferroequus, Frania Wisniewska, Gabe1972, Gabriel HM, Germán E. Macías, Gillyweed, Halmstad, Hamish59, Hmains, Hohum, Howcheng, I am One of Many, Illegitimate Barrister, InterPersonalAutomaton, Jan1nad, Jaraalbe, Jdlh, Jeffmallory, Jeffrey Mall, John, John Decker NZ, Jojhutton, Jolly Stomper, JoshuaZ, Jrcrin001, Juliana Joye, Juno, K.e.coffman, Kbdank71, Keith D, Kendall-K1, Khazar2, Kierzek, Kingstowngalway, KylieTastic, Larrymcp, Laurinavicius, Lebob, Lilac Soul, Lotje, Lowesvisa, Lucky For You, Magioladitis, Mandruss, Marcocapelle, Miller17CU94, MisterBee1966, Mmccalpin, NathanBeach, Neun-x, Neutrality, Neverforgettheredholocaust, Nick-D, Nomdedefault, PacificBoy, Paradoctor, PaulVIF, Peterlewis, Pinfix, Plasticup, Polylerus, Potočnik, Preslethe, ProudIrishAspie, Rama, Rankefan, Reenem, Rexagu2, Rich Farmbrough, Rjensen, Rsquire3, Sadads, Satani, Satori Son, Sca, Sfan00 IMG, Shaliya waya, Shawn in Montreal, Slightsmile, SpanishSnake, Spellage, Stor stark7, Suerte007, TL36, Tabletop, Tchernobog, The Anomebot2, The Madras, Thesouthernhistorian45, Thewolfchild, Tim!, Treekids, Trfasulo, Ttogstlegrev, Twas Now, TzeSanningen, Ulric1313, Volker89, Volunteer Marek, WasslKitty, Wikid77, WilliamJE, Wolcott, Wped1962, Wwikix, Xyl 54, Zachwoo, ~riley, 150 anonymous edits 137

333rd Field Artillery Battalion (United States) *Source:* https://en.wikipedia.org/w/index.php?oldid=846479658 *License:* Creative Commons Attribution-Share Alike 3.0 *Contributors:* 82redleg, Andrew Gray, Anfieldman, AustralianRupert, Beyond My Ken, Bgwhite, Bobjuch, Brian in denver, Btphelps, Buckshot06, Chris the speller, ChrisGualtieri, DadaNeem, Dl2000, DocYako, Ed!, Einsatzgruppe C, Elagatis, Gigacephalus, High Contrast, Hohum, Hugo999, Iantheimp, Jansonmedia, Jodosma, Lebob, LilHelpa, LittleWink, Louis63, MileyDavidA, Moos Raaijmakers, Neun-x, Nick-D, Ohconfucius, Orangemike, Oreo Priest, Rattlers, Reedmalloy, Reyk, RobertLunaIII, Sadads, Soldierofchicago, Sundevilesq, The howling cow, ToddSweeney, TutterMouse, Vanquisher.UA, W. B. Wilson, Wan2tri, Xyl 54, 35 anonymous edits .... ??

Operation Stösser *Source:* https://en.wikipedia.org/w/index.php?oldid=788128469 *License:* Creative Commons Attribution-Share Alike 3.0 *Contributors:* Adamtwinbrooke, Berserker276, Btphelps, Doc Snafu, Gaius Octavius Princeps, Hmains, K.e.coffman, Mafritzha, Metal Gear Rex, Mztourist, Pahari Sahib, Seligne, The Anomebot2, TutterMouse, W. B. Wilson, WikHead, Wwikix, 9 anonymous edits 156

Chenogne massacre *Source:* https://en.wikipedia.org/w/index.php?oldid=852739223 *License:* Creative Commons Attribution-Share Alike 3.0 *Contributors:* Abramius, Angadar, BD2412, BFolkeSherman, Berean Hunter, Bigroger27509, Brad101AWB, Btphelps, Calair, Can't sleep, clown will eat me, DagosNavy, David Edgar, Dogface, Eugene-elgato, Fajne Farita, Fifelfoo, GraemeLeggett, GregorB, Hohum, Hugo999, Hux, Jaraalbe, Jdlh, Jmlk17, Jrcrin001, Jwy, K.e.coffman, Kinetik138, Kingstowngalway, Kolbasz, Lebob, Malcolm P., Markus Becker02, MorbidEntree, Nick-D, PBS, Professor Ninja, ProudIrishAspie, Revent, Rjwilmsi, RobNS, Rsloch, Rsrikanth05, Sadads, Schwedenzug11, Ser Amantio di Nicolao, Shaliya waya, Snoopdop, Stor stark7, Sysrpl, Tad Lincoln, The Anomebot2, Thisisbossi, Wachholder0, Wikiuser100, William Allen Simpson, WilliamJE, Wingman417, WookMuff, Yvelines-France, 51 anonymous edits 160

Battle of St. Vith *Source:* https://en.wikipedia.org/w/index.php?oldid=809864105 *License:* Creative Commons Attribution-Share Alike 3.0 *Contributors:* 30 SW, Atani, BD2412, Bellerophon5685, Bender235, Berserker276, Brigade Piron, Btphelps, Calendar5, Catsmoke, Chris the speller, Ciphers, CommonsDelinker, Crowish, Davidcannon, DocYako, Dodgerblue777, Eastfarthingan, Ehistory, Gavrant, Glevum, GraemeLeggett, GregorB, Hamish59, Hannibal21, Hmains, JackofOz, John of Reading, Khazar, Kiwifist, Lt.Pearson, Magus732, Mild Bill Hiccup, MisterBee1966, Moagim, Mogism, Muta112, Niceguyedc, Nigel Ish, One Salient Oversight, Parsecboy, Polylerus, Rankefan, Rich Farmbrough, Ruddah, Sadads, ShakespeareFan00, Sports fan 475, Stepheng3, SyriaWarLato, The Anomebot2, Tim!, TwinkleMore, Wwikix, Xyl 54, ~riley, 19 anonymous edits 163

Operation Greif *Source:* https://en.wikipedia.org/w/index.php?oldid=848434235 *License:* Creative Commons Attribution-Share Alike 3.0 *Contributors:* 1archie99, 2p0rk, Alcherin, Andy Dingley, Axeman89, Berean Hunter, Brigade Piron, Bry9000, Btphelps, CORNELIUSSEON, Chinstrap1, ChrisGualtieri, Citation bot 1, Clarityfiend, DMacks, DagosNavy, David Edgar, Dl2000, Dodgerblue777, Dodo19~enwiki, Download, DrFO.Jr.Tn~enwiki, EamonnPKeane, El bot de la dieta, Ezrimerchant, Faizhaider, Fletcher, Foofbun, FreeRangeFrog, GeneralPatton, Ghepeu, GrahamBould, H27kim, Hamish59, Hayttom, Hede2000, Hmains, Ingolfson, Jerseycam, Jim Sweeney, Jmg38, JohnZofSydney, Joshualouie711, Jsc1973, JustJust51, K.e.coffman, Klemen Kocjancic, Kostja, Laurifindil, Laurinavicius, Leandrod, Lebob, Liftarn, Like tears in rain, LindsayH, Longstreet1966, Lorenzarius, Maczkopeti, Maseratir, Mikaey, MisterBee1966, Mlibby, N328KF, NEMT, Nabokov, Newzild, Niceguyedc, Oberiko, OldakQuill, Oreo Priest, Oshwah, PBS, Patrick, PaulinSaudi, Prinsgezinde, R'n'B, Raul654, Roadrunner, Robert1947, Sabbatino, Sadads, Salmanazar, Scriberius, Semper-Fi 2006, Shem1805, Sjö, Srsghost, Sus scrofa, Syced, Tazmaniacs, Tec15, The Anomebot2, Themightyquill, Thib Phil, Timeshifter, Timwi, Tom.Reding, Tony1, TutterMouse, VanishedUser sdu9aya9fasdsopa, Wayward, Welham66, Wikiacc, Wingman417, WolfgangFaber, WolfmanSF, Wwikix, XXzoonamiXX, ZappaOMati, Zigger, ÄDA - DÄP, 90 anonymous edits 180

Siege of Bastogne *Source:* https://en.wikipedia.org/w/index.php?oldid=846830981 *License:* Creative Commons Attribution-Share Alike 3.0 *Contributors:* A D Monroe III, Acad Ronin, Acroterion, Andreasegde, Andrew Gray, AnonMoos, Anotherclown, Anthony Appleyard, Autocorrelation, B, Bastogne, Bchaosf, Be94ware, Bellerophon5685, Ben Ben, Bender235, Benea, Berean Hunter, Berserker276, BertMacklin69, Beruic, Bgwhite, Blue Tie, Brigade Piron, Bulls123, Caldwell7111, CapitalR, Captain Obvious and his crime-fighting dog, ChrisGualtieri, Chrissymad, Clarityfiend, ClueBot NG, Colonies Chris, Corusant, DAJF, DVdm, DadaNeem, Davidcannon, Dead Mary, DivineAlpha, DocWatson42, Docu, Dodgerblue777, Don Brunett, Donner60, DragonFury, Edward, Ehistory, El O'el Cooter, Endoftheo, Enterprisey, Ericorbit, Fabartus, Fdewaele, Francvs, Frietjes, Grandiose, Greatgray, HMSSolent, Hmains, Hohum, Howcheng, Hugo999, Ian Pitchford, Ironholds, Italia2006, JForget, Javanx3d, Jaysbro, Joedumlao, John Alexander Pape, JohnOwens, Johnscribner, Johnstevenson1996, Jss199, Just a guy from the KP, Killgore83, Kw0134, Laughingyet, Levienglish110-007, Lightmouse, LittleWink, Loopy30, Lux-hibou, MCTales, MagicMoose, Magus732, Mbednarick93, Midas02, MisterBee1966, Moosehadley, Mrg3105, Mzajac, Neun-x, Nirvana77, Noclador, NuclearWarfare, Nwbeeson, Nyttend, Owenlare, P. S. Burton, Palmisano007, Papercrab, Paul Barlow, Plastikspork, Preslav, RadiX, Rankefan, Reedmalloy, Reenem, Reidpau, Rich Farmbrough, Richardelainechambers, Robert.r.allen, Robertwekch, Rockypedia, Rogerd, Sadads, Ser Amantio di Nicolao, Serols, Shang2, Shearonink, Simishag, Sjö, Skinny87, Snow Blizzard, Stephcra, Sundayclose, T6558, Tabletop, TeriEmbrey, The

Anomebot2, The Madras, The PIPE, TheOldJacobite, Thumperward, Tim!, Tom.Reding, Trappist the monk, TwinkleMore, Ugen64, Unregistered.coward, Vieque, W. B. Wilson, Weedwhacker128, Werieth, Wildkatzen, Witchchester, Wolcott, WolfmanSF, Woohookitty, Wwikix, XLerate, Xanzzibar, ZappaO-Mati, Zehnra, Zppix, ~riley, ADA - DAP, 143 anonymous edits 191

Operation Bodenplatte *Source:* https://en.wikipedia.org/w/index.php?oldid=853180405 *License:* Creative Commons Attribution-Share Alike 3.0 Con-*tributors:* 30 SW, Angusmclellan, Anotherclown, Art LaPella, Azx2, BBuchbinder, BD2412, Bejnar, Bender235, Brian Crawford, Broccoli and Coffee, Buckshot06, Bwmoll3, Capt Jim, Catsmeat, ChrisGualtieri, CodeTalker, Colonialmarine9, CommonsDelinker, Dank, Dapi89, Davidcannon, Dead Mary, Delldot, Diannaa, Dl2000, Don Hollway, E-Kartoffel, Eastfarthingan, EkoGraf, Floquenbeam, Gavbadger, GeneralizationsAreBad, Grant65, Guthrum, Hmains, Hohum, Hugo999, Hydrargyrum, Indy beetle, Irondome, Jan olieslagers, Jim Sweeney, Josve05a, Jtle515, K.e.coffman, Kage Acheron, Klemen Kocjancic, Koavf, MLWatts, Magus732, Manormadman, MarkMLl, Minorhistorian, MisterBee1966, Mogism, Mrmicrowaveoven, Mveygman, Mztourist, Newzild, NicoScribe, Oneiros, Peacedance, PrimeHunter, RHodnett, Rcbutcher, Richard Keatinge, Scaledave, Sean Clark, Sentaro9678, Shock Brigade Harvester Boris, Srnec, StjJackson, Tabletop, The Anomebot2, The PIPE, TheFreeWorld, Tim!, Tom Pippens, Tom.Reding, TwinkleMore, TwoTwoHello, Uli Elch, Valoem, WOSlinker, Wally Tharg, Wolcott, WolfmanSF, Woohookitty, Work permit, Wwikix, ADA - DAP, شبه الجزيرة تعلب, 90 anonymous edits 207

Operation Nordwind *Source:* https://en.wikipedia.org/w/index.php?oldid=853361836 *License:* Creative Commons Attribution-Share Alike 3.0 Con-*tributors:* 14thArmored, Abel29a, Adamdaley, Andrein, Andrew Gray, Antisyntagmatarchos, Art LaPella, Attilios, Bossanoven, Boston Charles, Brian Crawford, Cannolis, Captain Obvious and his crime-fighting dog, Chwyatt, ClueBot NG, CommonsDelinker, DaWulf2013, Dapi89, Dead Mary, Dodgerblue777, DutchDevil, EITY10, Fdewaele, Frogmann1, Fryed-peach, Fuziion, Gabriel HM, Gdr, Gomm, GraemeLeggett, GregorB, Ground Zero, Hamish59, Howcheng, Hugo999, Ibericus Lusitanus, Italia2006, Ja 62, Jessicapierce, Jim1138, Jubei, K.e.coffman, Kendall-K1, Killgore83, Kirrages, Magus732, Mannentje van alles, Mfhulskemper, Miracle Pen, MisterBee1966, Mkpumphrey, MoRsE, Mr.TiNart, Mr.User200, Mztourist, N0TABENE, Nameless23, NeilN, Nick-D, Nihlus1, Oberiko, Oddharmonic, PBS, Papatt, Phillipsbourg, ProudIrishAspie, R9tgokunks, Red4tribe, Resigua, RetroCraft314, Rich Farmbrough, Roddy the roadkill, SNAAAAKE!!, Sadads, Sarge1965, Sentient Planet, Sfan00 IMG, Silverhorse, Soldat und Waffe, Sus scrofa, SyriaWar-Lato, TROPtastic, Tartarus, TeriEmbrey, The Anomebot2, TheCheeseManCan, Tim!, Timeshifter, Tom.Reding, Trident13, TwinkleMore, Victor falk, Volker89, Wikiuser100, WolfmanSF, Wwikix, Wwoods, 111 anonymous edits 233

Image Sources, Licenses and Contributors

The sources listed for each image provide more detailed licensing information including the copyright status, the copyright owner, and the license conditions.

Image *Source:* https://en.wikipedia.org/w/index.php?title=File:Padlock-silver-light.svg *Contributors:* User:AzaToth, User:Eleassar ... 1

Image *Source:* https://en.wikipedia.org/w/index.php?title=File:117th_Infantry_North_Carolina_NG_at_St._Vith_1945.jpg *License:* Public Domain *Contributors:* U.S. Army ... 1

Image *Source:* https://en.wikipedia.org/w/index.php?title=File:Flag_of_the_United_States_(1912-1959).svg *License:* Public Domain *Contributors:* Created by jacobolus using Adobe Illustrator. ... 1

Image *Source:* https://en.wikipedia.org/w/index.php?title=File:Flag_of_the_United_Kingdom_(WFB_2000).svg *License:* Public Domain *Contributors:* Illegitimate Barrister ... 1

Image *Source:* https://en.wikipedia.org/w/index.php?title=File:Flag_of_France_(1794–1815).svg *Contributors:* - ... 1

Image *Source:* https://en.wikipedia.org/w/index.php?title=File:Canadian_Red_Ensign_(1921–1957).svg *License:* Public Domain *Contributors:* User:Denelson83 ... 1

Image *Source:* https://en.wikipedia.org/w/index.php?title=File:Flag_of_Belgium_(civil).svg *License:* Public Domain *Contributors:* Allforrous, Andres gb.ldc, Bean49, Cathy Richards, David Descamps, Dbenbenn, Denelson83, Evanc0912, FreshCorp619, Fry1989, Gabriel trzy, Howcome, IvanOS, Jdx, Mimich, Ms2ger, Nightstallion, Oreo Priest, Pitke, Ricordisamoa, Rocket000, Rodejong, Sarang, SiBr4, Sir Iain, ThomasPusch, Warddr, Zscout370, יהלי־יושמר, 15 anonymous edits ... 1

Image *Source:* https://en.wikipedia.org/w/index.php?title=File:Flag_of_Luxembourg.svg *License:* Public Domain *Contributors:* User:SKopp ... 1

Image *Source:* https://en.wikipedia.org/w/index.php?title=File:Flag_of_German_Reich_(1935–1945).svg *Contributors:* - ... 1

Image *Source:* https://en.wikipedia.org/w/index.php?title=File:Flag_of_the_United_Kingdom.svg *License:* Public Domain *Contributors:* Anomie, Good Olfactory, Jo-Jo Eumerus, MSGJ, Mifter ... 2

Figure 1 *Source:* https://en.wikipedia.org/w/index.php?title=File:Wacht_am_Rhein_map_(Opaque).svg *License:* Creative Commons Attribution-Sharealike 3.0 *Contributors:* User:Grandiose, User:Matthewedwards, User:Yug ... 4

Image *Source:* https://en.wikipedia.org/w/index.php?title=File:Wikisource-logo.svg *License:* Creative Commons Attribution-Sharealike 3.0 *Contributors:* ChrisiPK, Guillom, INeverCry, Jarekt, JuTa, Leyo, Lokal Profil, MichaelMaggs, NielsF, Rei-artur, Rocket000, Romaine, Steinsplitter ... 10

Figure 2 *Source:* https://en.wikipedia.org/w/index.php?title=File:German_Wacht_Am_Rhein_Offensive_Plan.png *License:* Public Domain *Contributors:* AdamBMorgan, BotMultichill, BrokenSphere, CORNELIUSSEON, Jeanhousen, Väsk ... 11

Figure 3 *Source:* https://en.wikipedia.org/w/index.php?title=File:Western_Front_Ardennes_1944.jpg *License:* Public Domain *Contributors:* AdamBMorgan, CORNELIUSSEON, David Newton, Dove, Jeanhousen, Timeshifter, 1 anonymous edits ... 15

Figure 4 *Source:* https://en.wikipedia.org/w/index.php?title=File:Battle_of_the_Bulge_6th.jpg *License:* Public Domain *Contributors:* Amok82, Dove, Hohum, Jeanhousen, Martynas Patasius, Prüm, Roo72 ... 16

Figure 5 *Source:* https://en.wikipedia.org/w/index.php?title=File:GERMAN_TROOPS_ADVANCING_PAST_ABANDONED_AMERICAN_EQUIPMENT.jpg *License:* Public Domain *Contributors:* German military photo, unknown photographer, film captured by US Army ... 17

Figure 6 *Source:* https://en.wikipedia.org/w/index.php?title=File:Malmedy_Massacre.jpg *License:* Public Domain *Contributors:* Brigade Piron, High Contrast, Hohum, Jeanhousen, Monopoly31121993, PRODUCER, Roo72, Timeshifter, 2 anonymous edits ... 18

Figure 7 *Source:* https://en.wikipedia.org/w/index.php?title=File:Bundesarchiv_Bild_183-J28619,_Ardennenoffensive,_gefangene_Amerikaner.jpg *License:* Creative Commons Attribution-Sharealike 3.0 Germany *Contributors:* BotMultichill, Btphelps, Catsmeat, Hohum, Jeanhousen, Manxruler, Taterian, Themightyquill, Wutsje, 3 anonymous edits ... 20

Figure 8 *Source:* https://en.wikipedia.org/w/index.php?title=File:Captured_German_Panther_tank_crewman_1944.jpg *License:* Public Domain *Contributors:* Avron, Btphelps, Catsmeat, OgreBot 2 ... 21

Figure 9 *Source:* https://en.wikipedia.org/w/index.php?title=File:American_tank_destroyers.jpg *License:* Public Domain *Contributors:* User:W.wolny ... 22

Figure 10 *Source:* https://en.wikipedia.org/w/index.php?title=File:Stoumont_JPG02.jpg *License:* Creative Commons Attribution-Sharealike 2.5 *Contributors:* Jean-Pol GRANDMONT ... 23

Figure 11 *Source:* https://en.wikipedia.org/w/index.php?title=File:Battle_of_the_Bulge_5th.jpg *License:* Public Domain *Contributors:* Athaenara, Prüm, Roo72, TheVault～commonswiki, TommyBee ... 26

Figure 12 *Source:* https://en.wikipedia.org/w/index.php?title=File:British_Sherman_Firefly_Namur.jpg *License:* Public Domain *Contributors:* U.S. ARMY CENTER OF MILITARY HISTORY ... 27

Figure 13 *Source:* https://en.wikipedia.org/w/index.php?title=File:Battle_of_the_Bulge_7th.jpg *License:* Public Domain *Contributors:* Athaenara, Prüm, Roo72, TheVault～commonswiki, TommyBee ... 29

Figure 14 *Source:* https://en.wikipedia.org/w/index.php?title=File:DeadBelgiumcivilians1944.jpg *License:* Public Domain *Contributors:* Franklin D. Roosevelt Library Public Domain Photographs ... 30

Figure 15 *Source:* https://en.wikipedia.org/w/index.php?title=File:Bundesarchiv_Bild_183-J28589,_Kriegsgefangene_amerikanische_Soldaten.jpg *License:* Creative Commons Attribution-Sharealike 3.0 Germany *Contributors:* BotMultichill, Felix Stember, Kürschner, Manxruler, Taterian, Themightyquill, 1 anonymous edits ... 31

Figure 16 *Source:* https://en.wikipedia.org/w/index.php?title=File:McAuliffeBastogneChristmasLetter101Airborne.jpg *License:* Public domain *Contributors:* FastilyClone, OgreBot 2 ... 32

Figure 17 *Source:* https://en.wikipedia.org/w/index.php?title=File:German_soldier_Ardennes_1944.jpeg *License:* Public Domain *Contributors:* German military photo, captured by U.S. military ... 32

Figure 18 *Source:* https://en.wikipedia.org/w/index.php?title=File:Battle_of_the_Bulge_progress.svg *License:* Public Domain *Contributors:* derivative work: Hohum (talk) Battle_of_the_Bulge_progress.jpg: ... 34

Figure 19 *Source:* https://en.wikipedia.org/w/index.php?title=File:Y-34_Metz_Airfield_-_Destroyed_P-47s_Operation_Bodenplatte.jpg *License:* Public Domain *Contributors:* United States Army Air Force ... 36

Figure 20 *Source:* https://en.wikipedia.org/w/index.php?title=File:Infantry_near_Bastogne.png *License:* Public Domain *Contributors:* Berean Hunter, Bjung, Magog the Ogre, Moreau.henri, 1 anonymous edits ... 37

Figure 21 *Source:* https://en.wikipedia.org/w/index.php?title=File:P41(map).jpg *License:* Public Domain *Contributors:* Itu, Jeanhousen, Prüm, Roo72, TheVault～commonswiki, Timeshifter, TommyBee ... 37

Figure 22 *Source:* https//en.wikipedia.org *License:* Public Domain *Contributors:* Alexpl, Hohum ... 38

Figure 23 *Source:* https://en.wikipedia.org/w/index.php?title=File:6th_Armored_Division_in_Belgium_1945.jpg *License:* Public Domain *Contributors:* US gov ... 38

Figure 24 *Source:* https://en.wikipedia.org/w/index.php?title=File:Bundesarchiv_Bild_183-J28477,_Ardennenoffensive,_Lagebesprechnung.jpg *License:* Creative Commons Attribution-Sharealike 3.0 Germany *Contributors:* Alonso de Mendoza, BotMultichill, Brigade Piron, Mapmarks, Mtsmallwood ... 41

Figure 25 *Source:* https://en.wikipedia.org/w/index.php?title=File:Bernard_Law_Montgomery.jpg *License:* Public Domain *Contributors:* Docu, FSII, Get It, Hohum, Makthorpe, Mattes, Rottweiler, Sandpiper, SoLando, Uaauaa, 1 anonymous edits ... 42

Figure 26 *Source:* https://en.wikipedia.org/w/index.php?title=File:Dwight_D._Eisenhower_as_General_of_the_Army_crop.jpg *License:* Public Domain *Contributors:* Signal Corps ... 43

Figure 27 *Source:* https://en.wikipedia.org/w/index.php?title=File:General_Bradley.jpg *License:* Public Domain *Contributors:* US Army ... 43

Figure 28 *Source:* https://en.wikipedia.org/w/index.php?title=File:Mardasson_Memorial_Bastogne.JPG *License:* GNU Free Documentation License *Contributors:* Later versions were uploaded by Guinnog at en.wikipedia. ... 47

Figure 29 *Source:* https://en.wikipedia.org/w/index.php?title=File:Audie_Murphy_American_Cotton_Museum_July_2015_43_(Battle_of_the_Bulge_diorama).jpg *Contributors:* User:Michael Barera ... 49

Image *Source:* https://en.wikipedia.org/w/index.php?title=File:SHAEF_Schulterstück.jpg *License:* Public Domain *Contributors:* User:John N. ... 57

Image *Source:* https://en.wikipedia.org/w/index.php?title=File:12th_Army_Group.svg *License:* Creative Commons Attribution-ShareAlike 3.0 Unported *Contributors:* Beringar ... 57

Image *Source:* https://en.wikipedia.org/w/index.php?title=File:1st_Army.svg *License:* Public Domain *Contributors:* Aschroet, Beringar, BotMultichill, CORNELIUSSEON, Fred the Oyster, Joshbaumgartner, Nobunaga24, Rocket000, 1 anonymous edits ... 57

Image *Source:* https://en.wikipedia.org/w/index.php?title=File:V_Corps.svg *License:* Public Domain *Contributors:* Beringar ... 58

Image *Source:* https://en.wikipedia.org/w/index.php?title=File:United_States_Army_1st_Infantry_Division_CSIB.svg *Contributors:* - ... 58

Image *Source:* https://en.wikipedia.org/w/index.php?title=File:2_Infantry_Div_SSI.svg *Contributors:* - ... 58

Image *Source:* https://en.wikipedia.org/w/index.php?title=File:9th_Infantry_Division_patch.svg *License:* Public Domain *Contributors:* Steven Williamson, U.S. Army () ... 59

Image *Source:* https://en.wikipedia.org/w/index.php?title=File:78th_Infantry_Division_SSI.svg *License:* Public Domain *Contributors:* Avron, Cirt, File Upload Bot (Magnus Manske), Fvasconcellos, Illegitimate Barrister, Nobunaga24, Sarang ... 59
Image *Source:* https://en.wikipedia.org/w/index.php?title=File:5th_US_Armored_Division_SSI.svg *License:* Public Domain *Contributors:* 5th_US_Armored_Division_SSI.png: Noclador derivative work: Snubcube (talk) ... 59
Image *Source:* https://en.wikipedia.org/w/index.php?title=File:WWII_Ranger_Patch.svg *License:* Public Domain *Contributors:* Zayats ... 59
Image *Source:* https://en.wikipedia.org/w/index.php?title=File:US_99th_Infantry_Division.svg *License:* Public Domain *Contributors:* US_99th_Infantry_Division.png: Noclador derivative work: Snubcube (talk) ... 59
Image *Source:* https://en.wikipedia.org/w/index.php?title=File:US_VII_Corps_SSI.png *License:* Public Domain *Contributors:* Noclador ... 60
Image *Source:* https://en.wikipedia.org/w/index.php?title=File:United_States_Army_2nd_Armored_Division_CSIB.svg *License:* Public Domain *Contributors:* 2nd_US_Armored_Division_SSI.png: Noclador derivative work: Snubcube (talk) ... 60
Image *Source:* https://en.wikipedia.org/w/index.php?title=File:3rd_US_Armored_Division_SSI.svg *License:* Public Domain *Contributors:* 3rd_US_Armored_Division_SSI.png: Noclador derivative work: Snubcube (talk) ... 60
Image *Source:* https://en.wikipedia.org/w/index.php?title=File:83rd_Infantry_Division_SSI.svg *License:* Public Domain *Contributors:* Alexpl, File Upload Bot (Magnus Manske), Fvasconcellos, Illegitimate Barrister, Nobunaga24 ... 61
Image *Source:* https://en.wikipedia.org/w/index.php?title=File:US_84th_Infantry_Division.svg *License:* Public Domain *Contributors:* US_84th_Infantry_Division.png: Noclador derivative work: Snubcube (talk) ... 61
Image *Source:* https://en.wikipedia.org/w/index.php?title=File:18_ABC_SSI.svg *Contributors:* - ... 62
Image *Source:* https://en.wikipedia.org/w/index.php?title=File:7th_US_Armored_Division_SSI.svg *License:* Public Domain *Contributors:* 7th_US_Armored_Division_SSI.png: Noclador derivative work: Snubcube (talk) ... 62
Image *Source:* https://en.wikipedia.org/w/index.php?title=File:30th_Infantry_Division_SSI.svg *License:* Public Domain *Contributors:* File Upload Bot (Magnus Manske), Fred the Oyster, Illegitimate Barrister, Jcb, Kleon3, Leyo, Mike Peel, Nobunaga24, OgreBot 2, Sanandros ... 62
Image *Source:* https://en.wikipedia.org/w/index.php?title=File:US_75th_Infantry_Division.png *License:* Public Domain *Contributors:* User:Noclador ... 62
Image *Source:* https://en.wikipedia.org/w/index.php?title=File:82_ABD_SSI.svg *License:* Public Domain *Contributors:* Aschroet, CORNELIUSSEON, Florival fr, Fred the Oyster, Illegitimate Barrister, Legoktm, Nobunaga24, 1 anonymous edits ... 63
Image *Source:* https://en.wikipedia.org/w/index.php?title=File:106th_infantry_Division.jpg *License:* Public Domain *Contributors:* Avron, BotMultichill, File Upload Bot (Magnus Manske), Illegitimate Barrister, Lineagegeek, MGA73bot2, Monkeybait, OgreBot 2, One Salient Oversight, Sarang, 1 anonymous edits ... 63
Image *Source:* https://en.wikipedia.org/w/index.php?title=File:US_101st_Airborne_Division_patch.svg *License:* Public Domain *Contributors:* Darz Mol ... 63
Image *Source:* https://en.wikipedia.org/w/index.php?title=File:US3ASSI.svg *Contributors:* - ... 64
Image *Source:* https://en.wikipedia.org/w/index.php?title=File:3_Corps_Shoulder_Sleeve_Insignia.svg *License:* Public Domain *Contributors:* User:VanHelsing.16 ... 64
Image *Source:* https://en.wikipedia.org/w/index.php?title=File:4th_US_Armored_Division_SSI.svg *License:* Public Domain *Contributors:* 4th_US_Armored_Division_SSI.png: Noclador derivative work: Snubcube (talk) ... 64
Image *Source:* https://en.wikipedia.org/w/index.php?title=File:6th_US_Armored_Division_SSI.svg *License:* Public Domain *Contributors:* 6th_US_Armored_Division_SSI.png: Noclador derivative work: Snubcube (talk) ... 65
Image *Source:* https://en.wikipedia.org/w/index.php?title=File:Yankee_Division.svg *License:* Public Domain *Contributors:* Illegitimate Barrister, Nonno88, OgreBot 2 ... 65
Image *Source:* https://en.wikipedia.org/w/index.php?title=File:35th_Infantry_Division_SSI.svg *License:* Public Domain *Contributors:* – Steven Williamson (HiB2Bornot2B) talk 18:29, 6 August 2007 (UTC)] ... 65
Image *Source:* https://en.wikipedia.org/w/index.php?title=File:90th_Infantry_Division.patch.svg *License:* Public Domain *Contributors:* Basvb, DieBuche, File Upload Bot (Magnus Manske), Illegitimate Barrister, Jcb, King of Hearts, Nobunaga24, OgreBot 2 ... 65
Image *Source:* https://en.wikipedia.org/w/index.php?title=File:US_VIII_Corps_SSI.png *License:* Public Domain *Contributors:* Noclador ... 66
Image *Source:* https://en.wikipedia.org/w/index.php?title=File:9th_US_Armored_Division_SSI.svg *License:* Public Domain *Contributors:* 9th_US_Armored_Division_SSI.png: Noclador derivative work: Snubcube (talk) ... 66
Image *Source:* https://en.wikipedia.org/w/index.php?title=File:11th_US_Armored_Division_SSI.svg *License:* Public Domain *Contributors:* 11th_US_Armored_Division_SSI.png: Noclador derivative work: Snubcube (talk) ... 67
Image *Source:* https://en.wikipedia.org/w/index.php?title=File:USA_-_17_ABN_DIV.svg *License:* Public Domain *Contributors:* USA_-_17_ABN_DIV.png: United States Army derivative work: McSushtalk ... 67
Image *Source:* https://en.wikipedia.org/w/index.php?title=File:28th_Infantry_Division_CSIB.svg *Contributors:* - ... 67
Image *Source:* https://en.wikipedia.org/w/index.php?title=File:US_87th_Infantry_Division.svg *License:* Public Domain *Contributors:* US_87th_Infantry_Division.png: Noclador derivative work: Snubcube (talk) ... 67
Image *Source:* https://en.wikipedia.org/w/index.php?title=File:XII_CORPS_SSI.gif *License:* Public Domain *Contributors:* File Upload Bot (Magnus Manske), Illegitimate Barrister, Nobunaga24, OgreBot 2 ... 68
Image *Source:* https://en.wikipedia.org/w/index.php?title=File:4_Infantry_Division_SSI.svg *Contributors:* - ... 68
Image *Source:* https://en.wikipedia.org/w/index.php?title=File:US_5th_Infantry_Division.svg *License:* Public Domain *Contributors:* US_5th_Infantry_Division.png: Noclador derivative work: JovianEye (talk) ... 68
Image *Source:* https://en.wikipedia.org/w/index.php?title=File:10th_US_Armored_Division_SSI.svg *License:* Public Domain *Contributors:* 10th_US_Armored_Division_SSI.png: derivative work: Snubcube (talk) ... 69
Image *Source:* https://en.wikipedia.org/w/index.php?title=File:80th_Inf_Div_SSI_SVG.svg *License:* Public Domain *Contributors:* 1989, Asiela, Avron, Gbarta, Illegitimate Barrister, Kwasura ... 69
Image *Source:* https://en.wikipedia.org/w/index.php?title=File:21st_army_group_badge_large.png *License:* Public domain *Contributors:* Hawkeye7 (talk) ... 70
Image *Source:* https://en.wikipedia.org/w/index.php?title=File:XXX_Corps_1944-1945_shoulder_flash.jpg *License:* Public Domain *Contributors:* EnigmaMcmxc based on an original whose Crown Copyright has now expired ... 70
Image *Source:* https://en.wikipedia.org/w/index.php?title=File:British_Airborne_Units.png *License:* Public Domain *Contributors:* Ignasi ... 70
Image *Source:* https://en.wikipedia.org/w/index.php?title=File:51_inf_div_-vector.svg *License:* Public Domain *Contributors:* User:Mliu92 ... 71
Image *Source:* https://en.wikipedia.org/w/index.php?title=File:53_inf_div_-vector.svg *License:* Public Domain *Contributors:* User:Mliu92 ... 71
Image *Source:* https://en.wikipedia.org/w/index.php?title=File:British_Guards_Division_Insignia.png *License:* Public domain *Contributors:* Athaenara, Cathy Richards, Catsmeat, File Upload Bot (Magnus Manske), Henxter, OgreBot 2, Zaccarias ... 73
Image *Source:* https://en.wikipedia.org/w/index.php?title=File:43_inf_div_-vector.svg *License:* Public Domain *Contributors:* Mliu92, Sarang . 73
Image *Source:* https://en.wikipedia.org/w/index.php?title=File:50_inf_div_-vector.svg *License:* Public Domain *Contributors:* User:Mliu92 ... 74
Image *Source:* https://en.wikipedia.org/w/index.php?title=File:US_Army_Air_Corps_Hap_Arnold_Wings.svg *License:* Public Domain *Contributors:* United States Air Force ... 75
Image *Source:* https://en.wikipedia.org/w/index.php?title=File:United_States_Air_Forces_in_Europe.png *License:* Public Domain *Contributors:* United States Air Force ... 75
Image *Source:* https://en.wikipedia.org/w/index.php?title=File:Eighth_Air_Force_-_Emblem_(World_War_II).png *License:* Creative Commons Attribution-ShareAlike 3.0 Unported *Contributors:* User:Historicair ... 75
Image *Source:* https://en.wikipedia.org/w/index.php?title=File:Ninth_Air_Force_-_Emblem_(World_War_II).svg *License:* Public Domain *Contributors:* Wine Guy ... 76
Image *Source:* https://en.wikipedia.org/w/index.php?title=File:167th_Infanterie_Division_Logo.svg *License:* Public Domain *Contributors:* Vasyatka1 ... 77
Image *Source:* https://en.wikipedia.org/w/index.php?title=File:2nd_Panzer_Division_logo.svg *License:* Public Domain *Contributors:* Marco Kaiser 78
Image *Source:* https://en.wikipedia.org/w/index.php?title=File:9th_Panzer_Division_logo_3.svg *License:* Public Domain *Contributors:* Marco Kaiser ... 78
Image *Source:* https://en.wikipedia.org/w/index.php?title=File:SS_Pz_Lehr_divisional_insignia.svg *License:* Public Domain *Contributors:* OgreBot 2, Philg88 ... 78
Image *Source:* https://en.wikipedia.org/w/index.php?title=File:26._Infanterie-Division.jpg *License:* Public Domain *Contributors:* Seichelprinz . 79
Image *Source:* https://en.wikipedia.org/w/index.php?title=File:116th_Panzer-Division_logo.svg *License:* Public Domain *Contributors:* User:Marco Kaiser ... 80
Image *Source:* https://en.wikipedia.org/w/index.php?title=File:560th_Volks-Grenadier_Division_Logo.svg *License:* Public Domain *Contributors:* User:Vasyatka1 ... 80
Image *Source:* https://en.wikipedia.org/w/index.php?title=File:62nd_Infanterie-Division_Logo.svg *License:* Public Domain *Contributors:* User:Vasyatka1 ... 81
Image *Source:* https://en.wikipedia.org/w/index.php?title=File:S_SS-Pz_Abt_101.jpg *License:* Creative Commons Attribution-Sharealike 3.0 *Contributors:* Original uploader was GeneralPatton at en.wikipedia ... 82

Image *Source:* https://en.wikipedia.org/w/index.php?title=File:1._SS-Panzer-Division_Leibstandarte-SS_Adolf_Hitler.svg *License:* Public Domain *Contributors:* User:Willtron ... 82

Image *Source:* https://en.wikipedia.org/w/index.php?title=File:3rd_Fallschirmjäger_Division_(Wehrmacht_WW2).svg *License:* Creative Commons Attribution-Sharealike 3.0 *Contributors:* User:Joeyeti ... 82

Image *Source:* https://en.wikipedia.org/w/index.php?title=File:12th_SS_Division_Logo.svg *License:* Public Domain *Contributors:* Artem Karimov, Klemen Kocjancic, Sarang, Wolfmann ... 82

Image *Source:* https://en.wikipedia.org/w/index.php?title=File:12th_Infanterie_Division_Logo.svg *License:* Public Domain *Contributors:* Marco Kaiser ... 83

Image *Source:* https://en.wikipedia.org/w/index.php?title=File:277th_Infanterie-Division_Logo.svg *License:* Public Domain *Contributors:* User:Vasyatka1 ... 83

Image *Source:* https://en.wikipedia.org/w/index.php?title=File:Wolfsangel.svg *License:* Creative Commons Attribution-ShareAlike 3.0 Unported *Contributors:* MesserWoland ... 84

Image *Source:* https://en.wikipedia.org/w/index.php?title=File:9th_SS_Division_Logo.svg *License:* Public Domain *Contributors:* MK ... 84

Image *Source:* https://en.wikipedia.org/w/index.php?title=File:3.Infanterie-Division.jpg *License:* Public Domain *Contributors:* Seichelprinz ... 85

Image *Source:* https://en.wikipedia.org/w/index.php?title=File:Deut.7.Armee-Abzeichen1944.gif *License:* Public Domain *Contributors:* Küstenkind 86

Image *Source:* https://en.wikipedia.org/w/index.php?title=File:9th_Infanterie_Division_Logo.svg *License:* Public Domain *Contributors:* User:Vasyatka1 ... 87

Image *Source:* https://en.wikipedia.org/w/index.php?title=File:GDInsig.svg *License:* GNU Free Documentation License *Contributors:* en:User:Jecowa derivative work: Zedlander ... 87

Image *Source:* https://en.wikipedia.org/w/index.php?title=File:340th_Volks-Grenadier_Division_Logo.svg *License:* Public Domain *Contributors:* Vasyatka1 ... 88

Image *Source:* https://en.wikipedia.org/w/index.php?title=File:352nd_Infanterie-Division_logo.jpg *License:* Public Domain *Contributors:* User:Mit31 ... 89

Image *Source:* https://en.wikipedia.org/w/index.php?title=File:79th_Infanterie_Division_Logo.svg *License:* Public Domain *Contributors:* Vasyatka1 ... 89

Image *Source:* https://en.wikipedia.org/w/index.php?title=File:US_Gun_Position_on_Elsenborn_Ridge.jpg *License:* Public Domain *Contributors:* U.S. Signal Corps ... 91

Figure 30 *Source:* https://en.wikipedia.org/w/index.php?title=File:Bundesarchiv_Bild_146-1978-024-31,_Model,_v._Rundstedt_und_Krebs.jpg *License:* Creative Commons Attribution-Sharealike 3.0 Germany *Contributors:* BotMultichill, Drdoht, Felix Stember, GT1976, Ras67, Thgoiter, Ukas 95

Figure 31 *Source:* https://en.wikipedia.org/w/index.php?title=File:German_Wacht_Am_Rhein_Offensive_Plan.png *License:* Public Domain *Contributors:* AdamBMorgan, BotMultichill, BrokenSphere, CORNELIUSSEON, Jeanhousen, Väsk ... 96

Figure 32 *Source:* https://en.wikipedia.org/w/index.php?title=File:Battle_of_the_Bulge_6th.jpg *License:* Public Domain *Contributors:* Amok82, Dove, Hohum, Jeanhousen, Martynas Patasius, Prüm, Roo72 ... 96

Figure 33 *Source:* https://en.wikipedia.org/w/index.php?title=File:99th_Infantry_Division_Moving_Through_Wirtzfeld.jpg *License:* Public Domain *Contributors:* AdamBMorgan, Avron, Brigade Piron, Bukvoed, CORNELIUSSEON, Foroa, Mogelzahn, W. B. Wilson ... 99

Figure 34 *Source:* https://en.wikipedia.org/w/index.php?title=File:Camouflaged_Forest_Pillbox.jpg *License:* Public Domain *Contributors:* AdamBMorgan, BotMultichill, BrokenSphere, CORNELIUSSEON ... 101

Figure 35 *Source:* https://en.wikipedia.org/w/index.php?title=File:US_7th_Armored_Division,_Vielsalm,_Belgium_12.23.1944.jpg *License:* Public Domain *Contributors:* Andrew Gray, Billinghurst, Bukvoed, Cornellrockey04, Kleon3 ... 103

Figure 36 *Source:* https://en.wikipedia.org/w/index.php?title=File:German_soldier_Ardennes_1944.jpeg *License:* Public Domain *Contributors:* German military photo, captured by U.S. military ... 106

Figure 37 *Source:* https://en.wikipedia.org/w/index.php?title=File:Bundesarchiv_Bild_183-J28510,_Ardennenoffensive,_deutsche_Infanterie_geht_im_Wald_vor..jpg *License:* Creative Commons Attribution-Sharealike 3.0 Germany *Contributors:* Alonso de Mendoza, BotMultichill, Btphelps, Catsmeat, Diannaa, Hohum, Mtsmallwood ... 107

Figure 38 *Source:* https://en.wikipedia.org/w/index.php?title=File:First_Army_Ardennes_mortar_man_on_radio.jpg *License:* Public Domain *Contributors:* Alexpl, Avron, BotAdventures, Btphelps, Hohum ... 108

Figure 39 *Source:* https://en.wikipedia.org/w/index.php?title=File:Co_G_38IR_2ID_16_Dec_1944.jpg *License:* Public Domain *Contributors:* Avron, Btphelps, OgreBot 2, Pmau, Zeete ... 111

Figure 40 *Source:* https://en.wikipedia.org/w/index.php?title=File:Krinkelt_Belgium_17_December_1944.jpg *License:* Public Domain *Contributors:* Alexpl, Avron, BotAdventures, Btphelps, Hohum, OgreBot 2 ... 112

Figure 41 *Source:* https://en.wikipedia.org/w/index.php?title=File:AMERICAN_PRISONERS.jpg *License:* Public Domain *Contributors:* German military photo, film captured by US Army ... 113

Figure 42 *Source:* https://en.wikipedia.org/w/index.php?title=File:Co_F_3d_Batt_18th_IR_patrol_Belgian_woods.jpg *License:* Public Domain *Contributors:* Brigade Piron, Btphelps ... 115

Figure 43 *Source:* https://en.wikipedia.org/w/index.php?title=File:2nd_Division_Marching.jpg *License:* Public Domain *Contributors:* AdamBMorgan, Avron, Bapho~commonswiki, CORNELIUSSEON, PMG, Verdy p ... 116

Figure 44 *Source:* https://en.wikipedia.org/w/index.php?title=File:Captured_Soldiers_12th_SS_Panzer_Division_"Hitler_Jugend".jpg *License:* Public Domain *Contributors:* U.S. Army ... 117

Figure 45 *Source:* https://en.wikipedia.org/w/index.php?title=File:GERMAN_TROOPS_ADVANCING_PAST_ABANDONED_AMERICAN_EQUIPMENT.jpg *License:* Public Domain *Contributors:* German military photo, unknown photographer, film captured by US Army ... 118

Figure 46 *Source:* https://en.wikipedia.org/w/index.php?title=File:Losheimgraben_Crossroad_Bahnhof_Bullingen.jpg *License:* Public Domain *Contributors:* Frank (talk) 19:40, 15 October 2009 (UTC) ... 119

Figure 47 *Source:* https://en.wikipedia.org/w/index.php?title=File:Battle_Bulge_1944_HD-SN-99-02998.JPEG *License:* Public Domain *Contributors:* German military photo, film captured by U.S. Army ... 120

Figure 48 *Source:* https://en.wikipedia.org/w/index.php?title=File:Krinkelt_Snow_Scene.jpg *License:* Public Domain *Contributors:* AdamBMorgan, Avron, CORNELIUSSEON, Foroa, Hohum, LimoWreck ... 122

Figure 49 *Source:* https://en.wikipedia.org/w/index.php?title=File:1st_SS_Panzer_Division_Honsfield.jpg *License:* Public Domain *Contributors:* Btphelps ... 122

Figure 50 *Source:* https://en.wikipedia.org/w/index.php?title=File:26th_Infantry_Regiment_near_Butgenbach_Two.jpg *License:* Public Domain *Contributors:* AdamBMorgan, Ain92, Avron, Brigade Piron, Bukvoed, CORNELIUSSEON, Cycn, GeorgHH, Jeanhousen ... 124

Figure 51 *Source:* https://en.wikipedia.org/w/index.php?title=File:Company-a-612-tank-destroyer.jpg *License:* Public Domain *Contributors:* U.S. Army ... 124

Figure 52 *Source:* https://en.wikipedia.org/w/index.php?title=File:240mm_howitzer.jpg *License:* Public Domain *Contributors:* Avron, Benchill, Bukvoed, Interiot~commonswiki, Jim.henderson, Klemen Kocjancic, Lalupa, Lotje, Midnightcomm, Mogelzahn, PMG, Rcbutcher, W.wolny ... 125

Figure 53 *Source:* https://en.wikipedia.org/w/index.php?title=File:New_Years_Eve_99th_Inf_Div_Christian_service.jpg *License:* Public Domain *Contributors:* Btphelps, OgreBot 2 ... 126

Figure 54 *Source:* https://en.wikipedia.org/w/index.php?title=File:German_dead_Stavelot_Jan_1945.jpg *License:* Public Domain *Contributors:* Btphelps, Catsmeat ... 128

Figure 55 *Source:* https://en.wikipedia.org/w/index.php?title=File:26th_Infantry_Regiment_near_Butgenbach.jpg *License:* Public Domain *Contributors:* U.S. Army ... 131

Figure 56 *Source:* https://en.wikipedia.org/w/index.php?title=File:Bundesarchiv_Bild_183-J28519,_Ardennenoffensive,_Soldaten_in_Schützenpanzer.jpg *License:* Creative Commons Attribution-Sharealike 3.0 Germany *Contributors:* BotMultichill, Bukvoed, Denniss, Felix Stember, Pibwl, Ras67, SuperTank17, Thgoiter, Wieralee, 3 anonymous edits ... 132

Figure 57 *Source:* https://en.wikipedia.org/w/index.php?title=File:M7_Self-propelled_105mm.jpg *License:* Public Domain *Contributors:* Btphelps, Havang(nl) ... 133

Figure 58 *Source:* https://en.wikipedia.org/w/index.php?title=File:Mortar_4.2_Inch_Chemical_M2_1943.jpg *License:* Public Domain *Contributors:* Frank (talk) 17:16, 20 November 2009 (UTC) ... 134

Image *Source:* https://en.wikipedia.org/w/index.php?title=File:PD-icon.svg *License:* Public Domain *Contributors:* Alex.muller, Anomie, Anonymous Dissident, CBM, Jo-Jo Eumerus, MBisanz, PBS, Quadell, Rocket000, Strangerer, Timotheus Canens, 1 anonymous edits ... 136

Image *Source:* https//en.wikipedia.org *License:* Public Domain *Contributors:* Auntof6, Hohum, Kintetsubuffalo, Magnolia677, Maile66, Monopoly31121993, OgreBot 2, Ras67, 1 anonymous edits ... 137

Figure 59 *Source:* https://en.wikipedia.org/w/index.php?title=File:BaugnezCrossroads1.JPG *License:* Public Domain *Contributors:* Lebob, Rcbutcher, Tangopaso, Verdy p, Walké ... 139

Figure 60 *Source:* https://en.wikipedia.org/w/index.php?title=File:Bundesarchiv_Bild_183-R65485,_Joachim_Peiper.jpg *License:* Creative Commons Attribution-Sharealike 3.0 Germany *Contributors:* ABrocke, Florival fr, Gödeke, Hohum, Lechthaler, Lt.Specht~commonswiki, Mtsmallwood 140

251

License

Creative Commons Attribution-Share Alike 3.0
//creativecommons.org/licenses/by-sa/3.0/

Index

Hague Convention of 1907, 181
Haguenau, 235
Hampshire Regiment, 74
Handley Page H.P.54 Harrow, 226
Hans-Joachim Kahler, 87
Hanskurt Höcker, 77
Hans von Obstfelder, 233
Harald Freiherr von Elverfeldt, 78
Haren Airport, 213
Hargimont, 26
Harry Crerar, 44
Harry Hinsley, 239
Harry Kinnard, 33
Harts War, 188
Hasso von Manteuffel, 2, 11, 26, 35, 46, 77, 163, 166, 191, 193
Hawker Tempest, 213, 218
Hawker Typhoon, 213, 218
Headquarters, 215
Heckhuscheid, 186
Heesch (Netherlands), 213
Heinrich Bär, 227
Heinrich Freiherr von Lüttwitz, 26, 33, 78, 191, 193
Heinrich Himmler, 233, 234
Heinz Kokott, 79
Heinz Lammerding, 84
Henri-Chapelle, 187
Henri-Chapelle American Cemetery and Memorial, 154
Henry F. Warner, 123, 136
Herbert Ihlefeld, 215
Hermann Göring, 210, 214
Hermann Priess, 82, 116
Hermann Prieß, 22
High-explosive, 101
High Fens, 24, 99, 112, 156, 183
Highland Light Infantry, 72
History, 97
Hitler, 138
Hitler Youth, 98
Hopkins County, Texas, 154
Horace L. McBride, 69
Houffalize, 36
Howard Gutman, 202
Hoyt S. Vandenberg, 76
Hoyt Vandenberg, 207, 210
Hugh Joseph Gaffey, 64
Hugh M. Cole, 51, 136
Hugo Kraas, 82, 91, 116
Hürtgenwald, 217
Hut 3, 49
Huy, 138, 183

I Corps (France), 233
II Corps (France), 234

III Corps (United States), 64
II SS Panzer Corps, 84, 97
Illinois, 28
Indirect fire, 93, 132
Infiltration tactics, 168
International Standard Book Number, 51–54, 90, 136, 189, 205, 231, 232, 236, 237
Internet Archive, 178
Invasion of Normandy, 193
Irish Guards, 73
I SS Panzer Corps, 82, 116, 191
ISTAR, 17, 102, 140
Italian fascism, 186
IX Tactical Air Command, 76
IX Troop Carrier Command, 76

Jackson, Mississippi, 154
Jacob L. Devers, 233
Jagdgeschwader, 212
Jagdgeschwader 11, 222
Jagdgeschwader 1 (World War 2), 229
Jagdgeschwader 1 (World War II), 213, 215
Jagdgeschwader 2, 216
Jagdgeschwader 26, 224
Jagdgeschwader 27, 226
Jagdgeschwader 3, 227
Jagdgeschwader 300, 210
Jagdgeschwader 301, 210
Jagdgeschwader 4, 220
Jagdgeschwader 53, 220
Jagdgeschwader 54, 224
Jagdgeschwader 6, 217
Jagdgeschwader 77, 218
Jagdpanther, 118
Jagdtiger, 95
Jagdwaffe, 230
Jalhay, 156
James A. Van Fleet, 65
James H. Doolittle, 75
James M. Gavin, 21, 63, 177, 195
Jassy-Kishinev Offensive, 8
Jean de Lattre de Tassigny, 233
Jefferson County, Alabama, 154
Jet aircraft, 8
JG 11, 213, 228
JG 2, 213, 230
JG 26, 213, 229
JG 27, 213, 229
JG 3, 213, 229
JG 4, 213, 229, 230
JG 53, 213, 229
JG 54, 207, 213, 229
JG 6, 213, 229
JG 77, 213, 228
Jimmy Doolittle, 207
J. Lawton Collins, 60

259

Joachim Peiper, 16, 93, 98, 138, 140, 148
Johannes Blaskowitz, 233, 234
John C. Meyer, 222
John Eisenhower, 23, 127
John Millikin, 64
Johnnie Johnson (RAF officer), 225
John Toland (author), 54
John W. Leonard, 66
Josef Dietrich, 95, 140, 164
Jose M. Lopez, 119
José M. López, 135
Joseph Goebbels, 45
Joseph Schmid, 207
Joseph Stalin, 14
JSTOR, 54
Ju 52, 112, 157
Judgment at Nuremberg, 149
Junkers Ju 87, 211
Junkers Ju 88, 214

Kampfgeschwader, 211, 212
Kampfgeschwader 200, 182
Kampfgeschwader 51, 227
Kampfgeschwader 76, 227
Kampfgruppe, 13, 16, 93, 98, 138
Kampfgruppe Peiper, 195
Karl Decker, 77
Kenneth Strong, 13, 50
KG 51, 213, 229
Killed in action, 5
Kostrzyn nad Odra, 183
Kraft Suspense Theatre, 188
Kriegsmarine, 107, 168, 211
Kurt Bühligen, 216
Kurt Meyer (soldier), 40
Kurt Möhring, 88
Kurt Tank, 223
Kurt Vonnegut, 50

La Gleize, 20, 145
Landing Ship, Tank, 6
Laws of war, 28
Leibstandarte SS Adolf Hitler, 10
Leland S. Hobbs, 62
Leonard T. Gerow, 58, 102
Leutnant, 207
LHumanité, 149
Library of Congress Control Number, 51
Liège, 7, 23, 92, 94
Liège (city), 149
Lieutenant-general (United Kingdom), 70
Lieutenant general (United States), 6, 187
Ligneuville, 138, 184
Limburg an der Lahn, 14, 183
Lochem, 228
Longview, Texas, 154

Lorient, 183
Lorraine Campaign, 7
Lorraine (province), 233, 234
Losheimergraben, 138
Losheim Gap, 17, 95, 102, 164
Louis A. Craig, 59
Low cloud, 157
Low Countries, 35, 208
Ludwig Heilmann, 89
Luftflotte Reich, 210
Luftwaffe, 4, 8, 48, 107, 168, 200, 208, 235
Luftwaffenkommando West, 210
Lutrebois, 146
Luxembourg, 1, 3, 15, 192
LXIII Army Corps (Wehrmacht), 234
LXIV Army Corps (Wehrmacht), 234
LXVII Army Corps (Wehrmacht), 95
LXXXIX Army Corps (Wehrmacht), 233
Lyle Bouck, 102, 120

M10 tank destroyer, 110, 182, 183
M18 Hellcat, 133, 196
M1918 Browning Automatic Rifle, 110
M3, 22, 133
M36 Jackson, 133
M36 tank destroyer, 125
M3 Stuart, 1
M4 Sherman, 110, 179
M7 Priest, 94, 169
M8 Greyhound, 171
Machine gun, 171
Maginot Line, 235
Mainz, 195
Major General, 210
Major-general (United Kingdom), 70
Major general (United States), 177, 195
Maldegem, 213, 215
Malmedy, 13, 18, 99, 137, 138, 142, 144, 156,
    157, 177, 184, 210
Malmedy massacre, 18, **137**, 160
Malmedy massacre trial, 18, 138, 147
Manchester Regiment, 72
Manton S. Eddy, 68
Marche-en-Famenne, 26
Mardasson Memorial, 47
Mark Urban, 54
Marlene Dietrich, 149
Massacre, 138
Mass murder, 138, 160
Matthew Ridgway, 62, 177
Maurice Rose, 60
Maxwell D. Taylor, 63, 198
Medal of Honor, 123, 135
Medium bomber, 211
Meillerwagen, 228
Meinrad von Lauchert, 78

Melsbroek, 213
Melsbroek Air Base, 226
Messerschmitt Bf 109, 211
Messerschmitt Me 262, 227
Metz, 66, 213
Metz-Frescaty Air Base, 220
Meuse, 7, 177, 180, 183
Meuse (river), 105, 140, 167, 180
Meuse River, 9, 92, 138, 193
Mickey Mouse, 28
Middlesex Regiment, 71
Miklós Horthy, 180
Miklós Horthy, Jr., 180
Miles Dempsey, 44
Military campaign, 3
Military glider, 34
Military justice, 187
Military logistics, 5
Military Police Corps (United States), 28, 185, 188
Military reserve, 168
Military tactics, 230
Military tribunal, 28
Missing in action, 5
Moder River, 235
Monmouthshire Regiment, 72
Monschau, 10, 92, 138
Most decorated platoon of World War II, 17
Multiplayer, 188

Namur (city), 167, 193
National Socialism, 40
Naval mine, 6
Nazi Germany, 1, 91, 191, 207, 233, 234
Nebelwerfer, 118, 131
Neil Leslie Webster, 239
Netherlands, 195
Night-fighter, 211
Nijmegen, 193
Ninth Air Force, 208, 210
Ninth United States Army, 2, 64, 167, 187
No. 124 Wing RCAF, 229
No. 126 Wing RCAF, 217
No. 127 Squadron RAF, 218
No. 127 Wing RAF, 224, 229
No. 130 Squadron RAF, 230
No. 131 Wing RAF, 215, 229
No. 132 Wing RAF, 218, 230
No. 139 Wing RAF, 229
No. 140 Squadron RAF, 226
No. 143 Wing RCAF, 229
No. 145 Wing RAF, 228
No. 146 Wing RAF, 228
No. 147 Squadron RAF, 229
No. 16 Squadron RAF, 226
No. 271 Squadron RAF, 226, 229

No. 2 Group RAF, 76, 208
No. 322 Squadron RAF, 218
No. 331 Squadron RAF, 218
No. 332 Squadron RAF, 218
No. 349 Squadron RAF, 229
No. 34 Wing RAF, 229
No. 350 Squadron RAF, 230
No. 35 Recce Wing RAF, 229
No. 400 Squadron RCAF, 229
No. 401 Squadron RCAF, 229
No. 402 Squadron RCAF, 229
No. 411 Squadron RCAF, 229
No. 412 Squadron RCAF, 229
No. 414 Squadron RCAF, 229
No. 430 Squadron RCAF, 229
No. 442 Squadron RCAF, 229
No. 485 Squadron RNZAF, 229
No. 486 Squadron RNZAF, 230
No. 56 Squadron RAF, 230
No. 61 Squadron RAF, 230
No. 66 Squadron RAF, 218
No. 69 Squadron RAF, 226
No. 83 Expeditionary Air Group (United Kingdom), 76, 208
No. 84 Group RAF, 76
No. 85 Group RAF, 229
Non-commissioned officer, 98
No quarter, 139
Norman Cota, 67
Normandy, 150
Normandy landings, 168, 237
Norman Franks, 231
North American B-25 Mitchell, 213
North American P-51 Mustang, 213
Northern France, 151
Northumberland Hussars, 75
Noville-lez-Bastogne, 196

Oberbefehlshaber West, 76
Oberfähnrich, 186
Oberkommando der Luftwaffe, 212
Oberkommando der Wehrmacht, 7, 181, 209
Oberst, 24, 112, 156
Oberstgruppenführer, 140
Oberstleutnant, 215
Obersturmbannführer, 16, 116, 138
OB West, 2, 9, 181
OCLC, 236
Offensive (military), 3
Office of the Chief of Military History Department of the Army, 51, 136
Oklahoma, 151
Omar Bradley, 2, 6, 43, 46, 51, 57, 185, 195
Omar N. Bradley, 91
Operational history, 81
Operation Bagration, 7

www.ingramcontent.com/pod-product-compliance
Lightning Source LLC
Chambersburg PA
CBHW021502090426
42739CB00007B/423